T0330769

ROUTLEDGE LIBRARY EDITIONS:
DEVELOPMENT

THE GEOGRAPHY OF
UNDERDEVELOPMENT

THE GEOGRAPHY OF UNDERDEVELOPMENT
A Critical Survey

D. K. FORBES

Volume 68

Routledge
Taylor & Francis Group

LONDON AND NEW YORK

First published in 1984

This edition first published in 2011
by Routledge
2 Park Square, Milton Park, Abingdon, Oxon, OX14 4RN

Simultaneously published in the USA and Canada
by Routledge
711 Third Avenue, New York, NY 10017

Routledge is an imprint of the Taylor & Francis Group, an informa business

First issued in paperback 2013

© 1984 D. K. Forbes

All rights reserved. No part of this book may be reprinted or reproduced or
utilised in any form or by any electronic, mechanical, or other means, now
known or hereafter invented, including photocopying and recording, or in any
information storage or retrieval system, without permission in writing from the
publishers.

British Library Cataloguing in Publication Data
A catalogue record for this book is available from the British Library

ISBN 13: 978-0-415-58414-2 (Set)
eISBN 13: 978-0-203-84035-1 (Set)
ISBN 13: 978-0-415-59505-6 (hbk Volume 68)
ISBN 13: 978-0-415-85116-9 (pbk Volume 68)
eISBN 13: 978-0-203-83681-1 (Volume 68)

Publisher's Note
The publisher has gone to great lengths to ensure the quality of this reprint but
points out that some imperfections in the original copies may be apparent.

Disclaimer
The publisher has made every effort to trace copyright holders and welcomes
correspondence from those they have been unable to contact.

The Geography of Underdevelopment

A CRITICAL SURVEY

D.K. FORBES

CROOM HELM
London & Sydney

© 1984 D.K. Forbes
Croom Helm Ltd, Provident House, Burrell Row,
Beckenham, Kent BR3 1AT
Croom Helm Australia Pty Ltd, Suite 4, 6th Floor,
64-76 Kippax Street, Surry Hills, NSW 2010 Australia
New in paperback 1986

British Library Cataloguing in Publication Data

Forbes, D.K.
   The geography of underdevelopment. —
   (Croom Helm series in geography and
   environment)
   1. Developing countries — Economic
   conditions   2. Geography, Economic
   I. Title
   330.9172'4   HC59.7

   ISBN 0-7099-1012-6
   ISBN 0-7099-1095-9 Pbk

CONTENTS

TABLES

ACKNOWLEDGEMENTS

Writing is a solitary pursuit, but research, in general, is a highly social activity, or at least it is for me. Earlier versions of chapters in this book have been presented at seminars in the Development Studies Centre and Departments of Geography and Human Geography at the Australian National University, and at Flinders and Monash Universities, and have benefited from comments received in those institutions. In particular, my colleagues at the ANU have been instrumental in generating and sustaining, in uncertain times, an atmosphere conducive to writing and research. I am especially grateful to Nigel Thrift, Michael Taylor, Peter Rimmer, Doug Porter and Barbara Banks for their critical comments on aspects of the argument and good-natured general support. Pauline Falconer and Carol McKenzie typed and retyped the manuscript with tremendous skill and patience. Finally, my wife Janet Williams, as always, shared the anguish and hard work. Tessa, Faye, Megan and Sarah did their best to help me keep the book in perspective.

INTRODUCTION

The conquest of the earth, which mostly means taking it away from those who have a different complexion or slightly flatter noses than ourselves, is not a pretty thing when you look into it too much.

(Joseph Conrad)

Development and underdevelopment are passionate issues, and their significance for human welfare is undisputed. Yet this is not a book about geographic patterns of underdevelopment *per se*, but about the way geographers have seen and interpreted the processes associated with these patterns. Moreover, it is not intended as a comprehensive review of all the literature which geographers have written or drawn upon. It represents a personal viewpoint and is full of the idiosyncrasies of a personal interpretation. The book reflects my own faith in geography, despite the ignominious origins of geographers' interests in underdevelopment. It stresses the importance of space and place in interpretations of underdevelopment, and demonstrates the significance of contemporary debates in human geography to the constant and necessary reworking of explanation. Yet it has not been possible to consider the substantial geographic literature on development and the natural environment, as originally hoped, for the project would have become unmanageable. Further biases are born of a personal time-geography which has restricted and focused attention on an English-language literature, while the geographic locus of my interest has been the countries of the western rim of the Pacific Basin. In an attempt to overcome the latter, case studies from Africa and Latin America are discussed but, on the whole, my concerns have been restricted to the analysis of Third World capitalist countries, and not the 'socialist' Third World, despite its undoubted growing importance.

Broadly speaking, three interrelated arguments are interwoven through the book. The first stresses the importance of an understanding of the historical and social context of knowledge to a geography of underdevelopment. We need to understand and appreciate the evolution and social construction of knowledge, as much as to understand the knowledge itself, and we need to ask ourselves, and re-evaluate, what we really know. The best way to achieve this is through review and criticism, not of a destructive sort, but enlightened by an appreciation of the limits to knowledge at any one time. As many sociologists of knowledge would argue, these limits are, in a general sense, specified by the material environment. This does not imply a mechanistic determination of ideas by prevailing social and economic conditions, but the latter can be assumed to impose some sort of constraints on the former (this is most clearly illustrated in Chapter 2 in the discussion of geography between 1870 and 1930). Geographers must be aware of the way in which the geography of underdevelopment has been constructed, through both incremental additions to orthodox wisdom and sideways shifts in the basic building blocks upon which social science is based.

Second, I have adopted a radical approach to the geography of underdevelopment. Like many social scientists, geographers have too frequently accepted the view of the ruling elite as the view of the people and have been too prepared to assume that the only realistic options lie in a greater commitment to capitalism. When endless failures have become the norm and liberal consciences have been stirred, it has been too easy to withdraw from the Third World and to plead the impossibility of the task. Geographers have usually overlooked or underestimated the potential significance of radical political change. Such ways of attacking the problems are somehow beyond the pale: planners argue that political intervention is unacceptable when planning is itself political intervention on behalf of an elite; they argue the violence of revolution is excessive, but the major planning institutions go on working for the violent juntas in El Salvador and Chile while the world as a whole slides towards nuclear war; and they argue revolution is too disruptive in human terms when millions of children die each year of hunger. My purpose in this volume is to confront both the orthodox (Chapter 3) and political economy (Chapters 4 and 5) viewpoints on underdevelopment, and examine their arguments and criticisms. Both are found wanting, the orthodox theories for their shallowness of explanation, and the political economy viewpoint for its heavyhanded emphasis on functionalist and mechanistic theory.

The third theme, developed in the second half of the book, seeks to shift the focus of research on underdevelopment away from its close links with political economy. It would be absurd to argue that economic processes are still not central to 'economic development', but the humanist critique of political economy stresses the way in which economic problems are embedded in social relations which are far from well understood. To be more specific, a narrowly economistic viewpoint, with its characteristic focus on production, needs to be incorporated into and supplanted by an approach which emphasises social reproduction. Within the literature on development and underdevelopment the most important shifts away from political economy are evident in the growth of class analysis and the questioning, on the basis of principles derived from critical social theory, of the basis of theorising political economy (Chapter 5). However, it is argued here that the most important problems facing geographers are the need to satisfactorily resolve the two dichotomies of determination – structure/ agency and compositional/contextual (Chapter 6). The concept of structuration, as it has been modified through debate in theoretical human geography, is put forward as one way of resolving the nature of the determination in and through space, and is discussed in relation to two particular aspects of the geography of Third World countries in Chapters 7 and 8.

It would be presumptuous to claim too much can be achieved in a short theoretically-oriented review volume such as this. Hopefully, however, it will remind the reader of the long and complex struggle by geographers to conceptualise and theorise underdevelopment, and of the significance of Marxian political economy to this conceptualisation. Following on from this, serious doubts about the adequacy of the polarised orthodoxies in development studies point to a need to shift the focus of a geography of underdevelopment. Perhaps development geographers can be redirected towards the analysis of social relations and social reproduction, the formative role of human agency, and the significance of space (or more broadly conceptualised, the environment) as an active agent of social processes. Underdevelopment is much more than a question of relative levels of economic productivity and savings, or capital accumulation and means of extracting surplus labour. More important, yet relatively neglected, it is the social and spatial context in which these economic relations are nurtured, preserved and, ultimately, reproduced. These are the problems to which geographers increasingly should be turning their attention.

THE GEOGRAPHY OF UNDERDEVELOPMENT

PART ONE:
GEOGRAPHY AND DEVELOPMENT

The history of geography . . . is the history of geographical ideas.

(Wright 1966:11)

There must be *some* correspondence between the collective experience of a culture and the way in which this experience is generalized in thought.

(Lichtheim 1967:33)

The activity of discovering . . . truths, the practice of social science, is itself a social occurrence subject to historical conditions, and its present position is of such a kind that it is putative rather than an established, fully-fledged scientific discipline. In these circumstances, the inquirer must expand considerable effort in the formulation and clarification of issues, and more generally in establishing the *categories* or basic 'concepts' of the social field. In so doing he must also criticise confused views that prevail in the field, in particular mistaken beliefs or assumptions about what the social categories are. The social inquirer, therefore, in the course of making positive contributions, also has an important negative role.

(Baker 1979:4)

1 WORLD DEVELOPMENT IN A HISTORICAL CONTEXT

It is a cliché, though nevertheless true, that we live in an increasingly interdependent world. New communications and information equipment, of which the microprocessor is the latest in a series of dramatic technological advances, have facilitated the natural tendencies towards increased capital mobility, made necessary by the imperatives of continuous expanded capital accumulation. Not everyone has shared in the new technology; many isolated regions – the periphery of the periphery – have become increasingly marginal to the contemporary interdependent capitalist world while numerous others, even though they may have been altered by it, will not have benefited from the new technology at all. Most of us, however, will be affected by our increasing interdependence with others. One of the foremost characteristics of radical research is to try to view events in context, to see the picture as a whole. This involves two things: constantly searching out the temporal or historical context of the phenomenon of interest; and being aware of the spatial or geographic variations in the phenomenon. Chapter 1 begins with a brief history of the interdependent world since 1460, the process of European expansion, colonisation and imperialism, and the subsequent process of decolonisation. It then goes on to assess the plight of the 'Third World' today, the respective levels of social and economic development within these countries, and to consider whether a breakdown of the 'Third World' into smaller categories might be of some value.

The Origins of the Contemporary World

The last four decades of the fifteenth century were very important: they marked the beginnings of the Spanish and Portuguese empires and with them the start of an integrated world economy.[1] Up until the middle of the fifteenth century civilisations in Europe, India and China, though qualitatively different, were developing in parallel while Arab traders exerted considerable influence over the world's main trade routes. Then European developments in weaponry, shipbuilding and navigation facilitated a wave of Iberian exploration. Diaz rounded the

Cape of Good Hope in 1487, Columbus undertook his famous voyage across the Atlantic with Spanish backing in 1492, and in 1497 Vasco da Gama set off east from Lisbon. To underscore the new found confidence of explorers and their patrons, the Treaty of Tordesillas was signed in 1494 dividing the world between the Spanish and the Portuguese — the former taking the territory to the west of an imaginary line drawn west of Cape Verde on the African coast in present-day Senegal, the latter claiming all the territory to the east. By the beginning of the second decade of the sixteenth century the Portuguese had explored parts of the Netherlands East Indies. Approaching from the west they took the prize port of Malacca in 1511, and by the end of that decade Magellan had crossed the Pacific and reached the Philippines from the east. The two colonial empires joined in the island now known as Sulawesi in contemporary Indonesia.

Essentially, the Spanish empire was based on the mining of precious metals in Central America and the Andes, while both the mines and the agricultural estates which supplied them with food were worked by forced labour. By contrast, the Portuguese empire was based on a series of trading stations, designed principally to control traffic in spices, and later, slaves. In other words commercial capital secured products already produced in the conquered regions, but had only a limited effect on indigenous social structures and modes of production. Although capable of enormous destruction, the Portuguese occupied a similar niche in the Indian Ocean economy to that of their Arab trader forebears. As the sixteenth century wore on, however, Spanish settlements were increasingly raided by Britain and other European powers. These attacks heralded the beginning of a wave of European rivalry for colonies. The locus of power was to move from the Iberian Peninsula to North-west Europe, and first to emerge as a new power were the Dutch.

The period from late in the sixteenth century until the middle of the eighteenth century is often regarded as one of contraction and downturn after the flamboyant expansion of European powers in the preceding long sixteenth century (that is, 1460-1600). Yet, for the Dutch, it was an age of expansion.[2] They were a major force right through the period, and for about 50 years — into the middle of the seventeenth century — their dominance was so complete that it must have seemed to their rivals, notably Britain and France, that it would never end. The Dutch United Provinces were a loose coalition of seven states or provinces, each of which sent delegates to an Estates-General. Whereas this might seem a weak federal structure, in effect it provided a less turbulent government than those of her rival powers in Europe.

The roots of Dutch expansion were in the efficient organisation of agro-industrial production; the immediate incentive for Dutch overseas expansion came with the Spanish annexation of Portugal in 1580 and the threat this posed to Dutch spice imports, Lisbon being the port of entry into Europe for spices from the Indies. As a result the Dutch decided to bypass the Spanish colonies and trade directly with the Indies.

Thus began the first phase of Dutch colonisation. Cornelis de Houtman set sail for the Indies in 1592, in 1598 the first trading fleets departed, and in 1602 the Dutch East Indies Company (VOC) was formed. Though the Netherlands East Indies were to be the colonial jewel in the Dutch crown, other initiatives followed. After the Spanish-Dutch truce of 1609 Dutch traders moved into the Mediterranean establishing strong links with northern Italy and taking over the traditional Venetian role in the Levant. They also took control of a number of Portugal's colonies along the West African coast, particularly Elmina and Luanda, and established settlements along the Hudson River (1614), in Guyana (1609) and in northeast Brazil. In the Anglo-Dutch War (1652-4) the Dutch lost some of these possessions, notably Brazil, New Amsterdam and several of their West African forts. Nevertheless, they remained a power well into the following century.

The seventeenth century is often referred to as the 'age of mercantilism'. While there is much debate about the meaning and accuracy of this term, mercantilists undoubtedly embraced the importance of an economic nationalist viewpoint and an economy based upon the circulation of commodities. Yet, while the Dutch were the premier power of the age, state policies reflected a mixture of free trade and protectionism. On the one hand *Mare Liberum*, an influential book by Grotius published in 1609, espoused the State ideology of free trade; on the other hand critics, with some justification, argued that free trade was only applied to those areas under the control of other European powers. In places like the Netherlands East Indies potential rivals were simply prevented from having anything to do with the spice trade. The basis of Dutch power was efficient production. The United Provinces achieved 'hegemony' in the world economy, defined by Wallerstein (1980:38)

as a situation wherein the products of a given core state are produced so efficiently that they are by and large competitive even in other core states, and therefore the given core state will by the primary beneficiary of a maximally free world market.

The efficient agro-industrial complex evolved by the Dutch eventually helped develop (and was in turn developed by) an efficient transport, commercial and financial empire that embraced the world. Based on fish production, the Dutch economy expanded into industrial crops, and established efficient industries manufacturing textiles and building ships. The latter helped to reduce freight rates which, combined with competitively priced agro-industrial production, contributed significantly to Dutch commercial supremacy. In 1609 the Amsterdam stock exchange was founded and in due course became the centre of European deposits and exchange, developing a credit function in 1683 which greatly facilitated trading in distant places.

Control over the Dutch overseas empire was largely maintained through two trading companies, the Dutch East Indies Company (VOC) formed in 1602, and the West India Company, formed in 1621. The West India Company was far less successful than the VOC though it had the dubious distinction of having pioneered the notorious Atlantic triangular trade whereby slaves were shipped from West Africa to work the sugar plantations of the Caribbean and South America, sugar was exported to Europe, and manufactured goods and guns were exported to West Africa. In contrast, the VOC's main task was to appropriate the spices produced in those islands now known as Maluku (the Moluccas). This was achieved by various means. For instance, the communal mode of production of spices on Ambon and Halmahera, and the feudal mode of production of rice on Java, were left relatively unchanged by the Dutch insistence on forced deliveries. In other words a fixed proportion of output was stolen by the Dutch, backed up by threats of violence, but the way in which the crop was produced was left substantially unaltered. On Banda Island, however, nutmeg production was based on plantations and the use of slave labour. Spices being a luxury trade the potential market was quite small, even though profits were high. In order to ensure its continuing profitability Wallerstein (1980:47) believes the VOC had two options:

> Either one transformed the nature of the trade by incorporating the Indies as a peripheral zone of the capitalist world economy or one had to resort to 'administered' trade in the traditional fashion of the long-distance commerce between world empires.

Despite the desperate urgings of Governor-General Coen, the VOC directors opted for the latter; the profits of speculation triumphed over the profits of exploitation, and this view held until the middle of the eighteenth century.

The seventeenth and first half of the eighteenth centuries saw the consolidation of the world economy, dominated by European commerce.[3] The 'Atlantic triangle' was developed and agricultural products became the export staple but, in general, the goods exchanged were mainly luxuries (sugar, spices, tobacco), slaves and precious metals. As sugar production on the slave plantations in the Caribbean and South America became more important, so those places were totally transformed, though not in the same way as occurred in Africa and Asia. There the European impact operated differently. Neither the slave trade nor the system of forced crop deliveries changed the extant system of production, though that is not to say it did not have any effects (nor that it was any better or worse than the method of exploitation in the Americas). Finally, although the Dutch were the key actors for much of this period they were not alone and soon Britain and, to a lesser extent, France were to achieve greater prominence. In fact towards the end of the seventeenth century there were already visible signs of impending British commercial dominance, particularly in the growing links with the American continent.

The eighteenth century saw remarkable changes occur in the nature of colonial empires. On the one hand, it was a period of exploration and expansion in understanding of the earth's surface. Around 1750, 207 million sq. kilometres of ocean were known and in regular daily use by 180-200 ships. By the time of the French Revolution, the area had grown by 50 per cent and the number of ships had increased tenfold. On the other hand, it saw a qualitative change in the nature of colonial exploitation, referred to as the 'new colonialism', which was in the hands of a nascent class of 'proto-industrial capitalists'. It was

> not the merchant capitalism of the old colonialism in which goods were bought and sold at a profit, but the new colonialism in which slaves were set to work with the tools and weapons of a new technology as wider and wider areas of the world were incorporated into capitalist economic relations. (Barratt Brown 1974:78)

Where the Spanish, Portuguese and Dutch empires had failed to create industrial capitalism, the British merchants, who had a big impact on world commerce in the eighteenth century, did so 'by their sales of English manufactures as much as by their capture of Spanish gold and their monopoly of the slave trade' (Barratt Brown 1974:85). However, English manufacturing in the first two-thirds of the eighteenth century

was far weaker than after the Industrial Revolution. Much of the industry and manufacturing was based in rural areas, where village
artisans and smallholders worked in cottage industries, though it is
apparent there was an increasing tendency towards specialisation in
such items as cloth, hosiery and metal products.

The Industrial Revolution brought changes to Britain's position in
the world economy. The commodity which best exemplifies these
changes is cotton.[4] Imports of Indian calico in Britain had been banned
in 1700 to protect the local industry. Cheap, plentiful supplies of raw
cotton from the slave plantations in the West Indies and, later, towards
the end of the eighteenth century, from the southern regions of North
America combined with some simple but important technological innovations – the spinning jenny (1760s), 'water frame' (1768) and 'mule'
(1780s) – to produce the 'textile phase of British industrialisation'
(Hobsbawm 1969:109). Cheaply produced textiles were exported
initially to markets in the USA and Europe then, as those markets
closed, in the mid-nineteenth century to South America (for example,
Brazil) and later still to India and the rest of Asia. Between 1780 and
1815 Britain established its monopoly of industrialisation and moved
into an international trade vacuum, enforced by the British navy's control of the seas. Domestically produced exports assumed a larger and
larger share of national income, and the British economy was of
necessity dependent on international trade. Having few domestic raw
materials, no longer able to feed itself, and with a poor population
unable to provide an adequate market it 'relied . . . on exchanging its
own manufactures and other supplies and services of a developed economy (capital, shipping, banking, insurance, and so on) for foreign
primary products (raw materials and food)' (Hobsbawm 1969:135).

By the 1830s and 1840s 'textile industrialisation' was facing a crisis
and industrial capitalists were looking increasingly to coal, iron and
heavy industrial production. There were two reasons for this. First, the
growing industrialisation of Europe and North America meant they no
longer needed to import textiles, although they had built up a big
demand for capital goods to feed the industrial development. Second,
the success of Britain's industrial capitalists meant they had accumulated large amounts of capital which they were increasingly anxious to
invest. Consequently, there were massive investments in British production of iron and steel and a rise in the export of British capital abroad.
A large chunk of this capital went to the USA and Europe and was invested in government loans, railways and public utilities. With this
Britain moved into a phase of full industrialisation, no longer depen-

dent on the pioneer textile industries but focusing on broad capital goods production. By the middle of the century, however, the complementarity that existed between the 'workshop of the world' and the primary producing economies was beginning to become differentiated. Whereas exports to the 'advanced world' remained large, they tended to either stagnate or decline. In contrast, the underdeveloped world was edged into a permanent complementarity of economies, one industrial, the other based on primary products.

Achieving formal independence in the nineteenth century, many Latin American countries quickly became dependent on Britain. Brazil became the largest single market for British cotton in 1840 while, in the 1880s, Argentina was a prime focus for the export of British capital as were Chile and Uruguay. As far as the British were concerned, however, India was the key component of the Empire. It was a vital market for cotton goods, an essential link in trade with Asia, and also proved a source of capital flows back to Britain. India's surpluses were siphoned off through its trading deficit with Britain, through the charges Britain made for administering the colony, and through interest payments on India's public debt. Such was the significance of India that Saul (1960: 62) concludes that 'the key to Britain's whole payments pattern lay in India, financing as she did more than two fifths of Britain's total deficits'. The important point to note is that the British initiative promoted the integration of the world through capitalist relations of production, not just through capitalist market relations as in previous epochs. 'Britain's Colonial Empire established what was in effect an artificial world division of labour that has lasted down to our times' (Barratt Brown 1974:96). This international division of labour is at the root of one of the most important differences between neo-classical and Marxist theories of underdevelopment. The neo-classicists regard the world division of labour as a natural consequence of specialisation in production and free trade, and of benefit to all concerned. Conversely, Marxists stress that it was clearly of far greater benefit to the key industrial centres than it was to those regions reliant on the production of raw materials.[5]

Not all the colonial powers of the nineteenth century stressed free trade or encouraged the growth of capitalist relations of production in their colonies. The British East India Company briefly took control of Java in the Netherlands East Indies[6] between 1811 and 1816 and instituted a number of reforms in line with British colonial practice: forced delivery of crops was abolished, prices for produce were raised, a land tax was instituted and land was sold to Europeans. Yet when the Dutch returned they reinstated pre-industrial mercantilist and monopolistic practices. The most significant of these practices was the *Cultuurstelsel* or Culture System, introduced in 1830. Essentially, it was a system of forced deliveries of agricultural crops and forced labour. Such was the success of the system, as far as the Dutch were concerned, that between 1830 and 1850 it produced 19 per cent of Dutch state income, and between 1851 and 1860, 31 per cent (Dietz 1979:144). It has been said that the Culture System 'represented the apogee of quasi-Asiatic skimming of the surplus product within the framework of the social isolation and stagnation of the village community' (Tichelman 1980:113). Principally, it demonstrates that colonial practices did not develop evenly over space and time. While Britain industrialised, and in so doing came to realise the value of limited free trade and the possibilities inherent in capitalist relations of production, other colonial powers, like the Dutch, persisted with old practices designed to extract surplus product from their colonies by force.

The second half of the nineteenth century marked the beginning of another phase in world history. Britain entered the 'Great Depression' of 1873-96 as the premier world industrial power. It never recovered that position for the 1890s saw the emergence of the USA and Germany as major industrial powers, especially in steel production. The period is also referred to as the beginning of the 'age of imperialism'. Three critical, interrelated processes occurred which shaped the future of the world well into the present century. First, there was a rapid increase in the colonisation of the remaining independent territories by the major European powers: the 'scramble for Africa'; Britain and France added parts of the Pacific, Southeast Asia and Africa to their colonies; Russia acquired part of Persia: Germany, Italy and Belgium took over parts of Africa; Japan colonised Formosa; the USA secured Alaska, the Philippines and some Pacific Islands; and the Dutch greatly expanded the size of their possessions in the Netherlands East Indies. The precise reason for this increase in colonial possessions is the focus of much debate; some seeing it as a result of intense political rivalry, while Marxist interpretations tend to favour the explanation that it was brought about by the pressures of surplus capital in search of an investment.

The second trend during this period was a shift from competitive capital to monopoly capital. In mid-century, free trade had suited competitive capitalist enterprises and made colonialism somewhat unnecessary but, as Britain lost its productivity advantages and required secure sources of raw material supplies and guarantees of payments for exports, monopoly and colonialism became necessary again. The 1890s saw the emergence of companies like Lever Bros, the Salt Union and Coats Paton, while the number of cartels increased from 40 in 1897 to 100 in 1910 and 320 in 1931 (Mandel 1968:467).

Third, and closely related to this process, the second half of the nineteenth century saw a significant increase in European capital exports. The most rapid growth in foreign investment occurred in Britain in the 1860s, France in the 1870s, and in Germany and other European nations after 1900. Between 1874 and 1913 Britain's foreign investments grew by 266 per cent, while Europe's as a whole increased by 577 per cent in the same period (Barratt Brown 1974:121). In Britain it was not the monopoly concerns who provided the money for investment; it was usually small-scale investors – particularly the portfolio holdings of rentiers – who sought not large returns (for these were often lower than those available in domestic industry) but the security which government-guaranteed investments enjoyed. About half of the money was invested in loans to government and mixed public and private investments. Around 70 per cent ended up being invested in social overhead capital such as railways, public utilities and public works. The destinations for capital exports between 1870 and 1890 were by no means restricted to the new colonies. In fact, while the British Empire's share increased during this period, India's was reduced and the dominions' greatly expanded. Europe's share of British investment was also sharply cut, but Latin America's was extended.

These swings of direction of investment in the 1880s are quite marked and became stabilized thereafter until the sales of British-held United States stock in the First World War and its replacement by still further dominion and colonial investment by Britain in the 1930s. (Barratt Brown 1974:186)

Production in the colonies became focused increasingly on agriculture and raw materials – almost exclusively for export and not for sale on domestic markets. Foreign capital, on the whole, was not invested in manufacturing; nor in fact did the indigenous ruling classes invest domestic surplus in manufacturing but spent it instead on imports of luxury goods thereby ensuring that agriculture remained the dominant sector. The export of capital from Europe and North America cemented the international division of labour. The colonial powers monopolised the production of manufactured goods; Eastern Europe, the dominions (especially Canada and Australia) and Argentina came to specialise in the production of basic foodstuffs; and the rest of the world concentrated on the production of vegetable and mineral raw materials.

The Russian Revolution – 'the ten days that shook the world' – also made inroads into the the world division of labour. First the USSR, then nations in Eastern Europe and, later, China, Cuba, and a number of African (Angola, Mozambique) and Southeast Asian nations (principally Vietnam) partially disengaged from the world capitalist economic system. Yet, in the period after the First World War, it was the USA which came to dominate in the world economy.[7] Despite the much greater significance of domestic investment, production and marketing to the USA than to Britain, foreign economic activity grew more and more important to the American economy (Magdoff 1969). A central feature of this period was a gradual change in the nature of economic relationships between the chief capitalist countries and the colonies and former colonies. Most notable was the growth of private foreign investment in manufacturing industries and the relative decline of agricultural and mining investments. The bulk of American foreign investment was funnelled into Latin America where, in 1940, only 10 per cent of investment went into manufacturing compared to 25 per cent in 1964, while in the same period agricultural investments remained unchanged. Likewise in 1911, 75 per cent of British private direct investment in India went into extractive industries whereas, by 1956, 33 per cent went into manufacturing (O'Connor 1970:131-4). Essentially, the manufacturing industry which developed in the periphery was of two main types: either it was designed to avoid import tariffs into newly-independent nations or it concentrated on import-substitution. Few manufacturers tried to export from the periphery, perhaps due to the tariff walls erected around the main markets or because the multinational corporations had monopolies on distribution systems and market outlets and discriminated against peripheral production.

The Second World War intervened in this process and while it was a political watershed, it was not necessarily an economic one at least as far as the colonies and former colonies of the periphery were concerned. Nationalist forces which had clamoured for independence in the pre-war period received their just desserts in the wave of decolonisation which occurred in Africa and in South, East and Southeast Asia during the decade or two after the War. One after the other, the jewels of former colonial empires achieved independence – India (1947), Indonesia (1945), Nigeria (1960), Kenya (1963), Vietnam (1954). Despite the ending of the war and political independence, the countries of the periphery for the most part failed to achieve the elusive goals of economic independence and economic development. In contrast, the nations of the capitalist core in Western Europe and Japan faced the post-war world with optimism. Keynes's initiatives at Bretton Woods followed by the apparent success of the Marshall Plan in reviving war-ravaged economies (although not always returning them to their pre-war status) steered many away from their pre-war disenchantment with capitalism (Galbraith 1977). Meanwhile, the Korean War boom contributed to the belief that rapid growth in the western economies would persist and that recessions and depressions could be managed, if not eliminated altogether. Yet when Marshall Plan techniques were applied to the increasingly apparent underdeveloped economies in the newly independent colonies, they floundered.

Chief among the Marshall Plan prerequisites was an open economy receptive to large inflows of foreign capital. Large industrial and commercial firms (multinational corporations – MNCs) came to play a greater role in these financial transactions during this period. Throughout this century production has been increasingly concentrated in corporations: 'the one hundred largest manufacturing corporations in the U.S.A. controlled 59 per cent of the land, buildings and equipment used in manufacturing in 1962 compared with 44 per cent in 1929' (Barratt Brown 1974:203). The MNCs represented a new wave of capital export in their search for raw material sources and markets. Independence strengthened the hand of ruling classes in the periphery, allowing them to revoke special privileges for MNCs, refuse to negotiate patent controls, and adopt various other legislative measures to control foreign direct investment, but most continued to encourage foreign capital. The combination of pressure from local bourgeoisies to link with the MNCs, the dissipation of local sources of capital accumulation on luxury-good consumption, the need for foreign currencies and for distribution and marketing outlets maintained dependence on foreign capital and the particular post-war institution form – the MNC (O'Connor 1970).

The last decade and a half has seen a further major change occur in the structure of the world economy with the growth of 'internationalised production' (Palloix 1975) and a tendency towards a 'new international division of labour' (Fröbel, Heinrichs and Kreye 1980). Up until the mid-1960s the bulk of overseas production consisted, in large part, of the decentralised production of whole commodities. The new form of internationalised production, by contrast, consists of the selective relocation of highly standardised component-part production in the periphery, not for consumption there but for re-export either to markets in the core countries or to another location for assembly and consumption or export. Among the best known examples of inter-nationalised production is the 'world-car concept' − component parts are made in whichever country it is expedient to do so, and are then ex-ported to be assembled and marketed wherever the markets determine. This form of production has not supplanted trade in whole commodi-ties nor conventional international investment, but it is of growing importance relative to these more traditional forms of international interaction (Palloix 1977). Internationalised production has been brought about, firstly, by union wage and working conditions struggles, the exertion of state power and legislative control over the production process, and a shortage of raw materials; all of which have contributed to a declining value rate of profit for the MNCs. Secondly, it has been facilitated by the development of new labour processes and means of management of MNCs.

> By facilitating further divisions in the labour process and allowing the simultaneous concentration of control functions and the decen-tralization of manual execution this further incorporates the regions of the world not only into the world economy, but into specific international firms operating within that international framework, such that the industrial structure of any region can only be under-stood in the context of an understanding of the principles of organi-zation of the international firms themselves. (Perrons 1981:87)

The internationalisation of production is bringing about profound changes in the structure of the world economy. Old industrialised regions of the core − the north-east of the USA and Britain, for instance − are de-industrialising causing severe unemployment problems and regional underdevelopment. At the same time some so-called under-developed countries − Brazil, South Korea, Singapore − are now referred to as the 'new industrialising countries' (NICs), and the rapid turnabout in the economies of the richer OPEC countries since the oil-price rises barely a decade ago is legendary. The important questions which follow are these: does this make invalid a concern with the problem of underdevelopment? Can we any longer continue to talk of a 'developed' North and an 'underdeveloped' South, of a core and peri-phery, of a 'Third World'?

Towards a Multipolar World Economy

In the aftermath of the Second World War came decolonisation and political independence, and with it the emergence of socialist states in Asia, Latin America and Africa. The majority of newly liberated colonies remained in the capitalist world economy fold for numerous reasons,[8] while a number of charismatic leaders including Nkrumah, Sukaino, and more recently Nyerere toyed with theories of socialism which required balancing the demands of the capitalist and non-capitalist world. In the last decade the capitalist world system has been shaken by oil price increases and the so-called 'energy crisis', recession and inflation in the advanced industrial countries, and industrialisation and high rates of growth in some Third World countries, notably as a result of the internationalisation of production.[9] Such a mixture of processes has provided a real challenge to any conception of a homogeneous underdeveloped Third World, if such a simple classification ever were valid. Against the note of optimism which the industrialisation of parts of the Third World has promoted, three sets of observations should be borne in mind.

Economic Inequality

Despite high rates of growth in parts of the Third World there is growing inequality in the distribution of wealth. This can be illustrated in several ways. First, the economic distance between the rich industrial countries and the poor developing countries is widening. In the period 1960-70, per capita growth in GNP in industrial countries exceeded that of the developing countries; although the developing countries grew more rapidly than industrial countries in 1970-80 the margin was only 0.2 per cent and, in both cases, represented a decline on the previous decade (Table 1.1). The World Bank's projections for the current decade (1980-90) do not add much optimism: both the highest and lowest estimates of per capita growth rates give no indication of a catching up on behalf of the developing countries. As Griffin has shown, 'even if the two groups of countries expanded at the same rate, the absolute differences in *per capita* income would of course increase merely because the base to which the rates applied was so different' (Griffin 1981:221).

Second, as mentioned earlier, there is increasing economic inequality between the countries of the Third World. The 38 lowest income countries had an average per capita growth in GNP of only 1.8 per cent in 1960-70, 1.6 per cent in 1970-80, and a forecast growth rate of

Table 1.1: Growth and Growth Prospects

	1980 popula-tion	GNP per capita	Average annual growth of per capita GNP		projected low	projected high
			1960-70	1970-80	1980	1990
	(millions)	($US)	%	%	%	%
Industrial countries[a]	674	10,660	4.1	2.5	2.3	3.1
All developing countries	2,383	850	3.5	2.7	2.2	3.3
Low income developing countries[b]	1,307	250	1.8	1.6	1.5	2.6
Middle income developing countries[c]	1,075	1,580	3.9	2.8	2.2	3.4
Capital-surplus oil exporters[d]	27	7,390	–	4.2	2.1	2.8

Notes: a. Organisation for Economic Cooperation and Development Countries (OECD) except Greece, Portugal, Spain and Turkey.

b. Comprises those countries with a 1979 GNP per capita of $US370 and below.

c. Comprises those countries with a 1979 GNP per capita above $US370.

d. Iraq, Kuwait, the Libyan Arab Jamahiriya, Qatar, Saudi Arabia, and the United Arab Emirates.

Source: World Bank 1981: Table 1.

between 1.5 and 2.6 per cent in the present decade (Table 1.1). These low growth rates will not allow the bridging of the gap between the average per capita incomes of low-income countries ($US250), the middle-income countries ($US1,580) and capital-surplus oil exporters ($US7,390), *even if* the low-income countries perform at their best and achieve their full 2.6 per cent growth rate, while the other two categories of countries perform at their worst and achieve only growth rates of 2.2 and 2.1 per cent respectively. In fact, if such growth rates were achieved, by the end of the decade the gap between the per capita incomes in the respective sets of countries would have *increased* by $US311 and $US1,634. The geographically most notable feature of income distribution is the concentration of African and South Asian countries (for example, Bangladesh, Nepal, Burma, India) in the lowest-income category. By contrast, the newly industrialising countries of Asia (Hong Kong, Malaysia, Singapore, South Korea, Taiwan), Southern Europe (especially Spain, Yugoslavia, Greece and Portugal) and Latin America (Brazil, Mexico) all fall into the middle-income category.

Third, there is severe and growing inequality in the distribution of

Table 1.2: Household Income Distribution

Country	Year	Percentage share of household income[a]		
		Lowest 20%	Highest 20%	Highest 10%
Brazil	1972	2.0	66.6	50.6
Honduras	1967	2.3	67.8	50.0
Peru	1972	1.9	61.0	42.9
Mexico	1977	2.9	57.7	40.6
Malaysia	1970	3.3	56.6	39.6
Costa Rica	1971	3.3	54.8	39.5
Philippines	1970-1	3.7	53.9	–
India	1964-5	6.7	48.9	35.2
Chile	1968	4.4	51.4	34.8
Sri Lanka	1969-70	7.5	43.4	28.2
South Korea	1976	5.7	45.3	27.5

Note: a. Data on income distribution is not systematically organised and integrated into the official statistics of many countries. Most of this data has been acquired by surveys and should be treated with caution.
Source: World Bank 1980: Table 24.

income in Third World countries. Table 1.2 illustrates the percentage share of income among the poorest and richest groups in eleven Third World countries. It is remarkable that in Honduras and Brazil, 10 per cent of the population controls over half the total disposable household income, while the top 20 per cent of the population in the countries listed controlled between six (Sri Lanka) and thirty-three times (Brazil) the income of the bottom 20 per cent. Moreover, there is widespread evidence to suggest that even in those countries where average incomes may have risen, the standard of living of the poorest groups has been static or falling. For instance, 38 per cent of Filipinos lived below the poverty line in 1971, and 45 per cent in 1975 (*Far Eastern Economic Review*, 27 March 1981), while real wages in Sri Lanka's plantation sector 'fell continuously for 5 years between 1968 and 1972 [and] in Bangladesh, real wages in agriculture were lower in 1975 than they were in 1949' (Griffin 1981:222).[10] A parallel process is apparent in Africa and Latin America. It has been argued that in Mexico, despite a 2.7 per cent annual average growth rate in GNP per capita between 1960 and 1978, the material wellbeing of the poorest 40 per cent of Mexican families has remained virtually unchanged since 1910 (Griffin 1978:147).

Finally, the patterns of inequality are spatially differentiated. On the one hand, average incomes are usually much higher in urban areas than in rural areas. For instance, in the Central Region of Thailand the growth rate of average real incomes between 1968-9 and 1972-3 was higher in the urban areas than in the rural, while the proportion living below the subsistence line in the rural areas was double that of the urban areas (Douglass 1981:191).[11] On the other hand, there are rich and poor regions within the spatial economy of all Third World countries. In Brazil's northeast region, for instance, there is a much higher rate of underemployment than in other parts of the nation. Seventy-five per cent of employed workers in the northeast earned less than the legal minimum wage in 1972, compared to 8.9 per cent of workers in the Distrito Federal and 43.3 per cent of the workforce of Brazil as a whole (Haddad 1981:394-5). This regional pattern of income inequality cross-sects the class division of income: it is more than simply a pale reflection of the class structure. The characteristics of the region, like the characteristics of the nation-state − notably, but by no means exclusively, the class structure − provide a complex setting, both determining and being determined by the ultimate pattern of income distribution.[12]

Social Inequalities

There is no simple correlation between economic and social inequalities but clearly there is a complex relationship between the two. Looking at the low-income countries we find low adult literacy rates, low per capita consumption of energy (not that high energy consumption is necessarily desirable in itself), a life expectancy at birth of 24 years less than people in industrialised countries, enormous populations per physician, low rates of attendance at primary school and, perhaps most revealing of all, a daily calorie supply equivalent to only 91 per cent of that required to sustain a person at normal levels of activity and health (Table 1.3). We can quibble with the accuracy of the data, we can question the validity of some of the concepts and we can criticise the use of averages, but we cannot overlook the simple fact that the majority of the population in low-income countries is economically and socially deprived. There are indicators other than those mentioned above, and most are adversely related to the low and middle-income countries: the problems of political repression and the struggle for social justice in Argentina, Chile, Afghanistan and Malaysia (Amnesty International 1981; Gastil 1981), and the environmental decay of the once-forested areas in Nepal and Indonesia are among the more important.

Table 1.3: Social Indicators

	Adult literacy rate 1975 %	Energy consumption per capita 1978[a]	Life expectancy at birth 1978	Daily calorie supply as % of requirement 1977	Population per physician 1977	Number enrolled in primary school as % of age group 1977
Low-income countries[b]	38	161	50	91	9,900	77
Middle-income countries[b]	71 / 99	903	61	108	4,310	97
Industrialised countries[b]	99	7,060	74	131	3,377	98
Capital-surplus oil exporters[b]	50	1,620	53	115	2,963	94
Centrally planned economies[c]	–	2,117	70	114	2,752	119

Note: a. Kilograms of coal equivalent.
  b. See Table 1.1.
  c. China, North Korea, Albania, Cuba, Mongolia, Romania, Bulgaria, Hungary, Poland, USSR, Czechoslovakia, German Democratic Republic.
Source: World Bank 1980: various tables

Conclusion

The question 'Is there a Third World?', must, therefore, be answered, 'No, there is not.' The Third World has always been something of a residual category, defined chiefly by what it is not — not industrialised and not communist — rather than by what it is. The Group of 77 at the United Nations, a mouthpiece for Third World interests, is gradually losing what sense of cohesion and common purpose it once had. A.W. Clausen, the President of the World Bank, favours the idea of a 'multipolar world economy'. He has been quoted as saying that the dualistic North-South model of the world 'is no longer very helpful. It has become so static and vastly oversimplified and often so contentious and confrontational in its rhetoric that it tends to obscure reality rather than illuminate it'. Yet, while there is much to commend in Clausen's concept of a multipolar world economy and his criticism of the oversimplification embodied in the notion of the 'Third World' (or the 'South'), there are two further factors to consider.

> First, there are important political considerations. The growing inequality within the Third World is likely to undermine the solidarity of the poor countries. This solidarity never was great, but such commonality of interests as has existed is almost certain to diminish. In consequence, the bargaining position of poor countries *vis-a-vis* the rich is likely to become even weaker, dissension and criticism within the so-called Group of 77 is likely to increase, and attempts are bound to be made to separate some of the more prosperous underdeveloped countries . . . from the Group. (Griffin 1981:222)

Without posing a conspiracy theory, such a fragmentation of the Third World is likely to favour the West and major institutions like the World Bank, rather more than the Third World. Since the Bandung Conference in 1955, the sense of common purpose shared by many Third World nations has proved of considerable importance as a brake on the rapacious capitalist core countries at forums such as the United Nations, the World Bank, and the Law of the Sea Conference.

Second, questioning the value of the concept 'Third World' is not the same as questioning the validity of the process of underdevelopment. While different groups of countries may be characterised by different processes — the industrialisation of the middle-income countries and resource development in those exporting oil, for instance — they are all part of an integrated world economy. The status of particular regions is changing, and so too are the methods of exploitation, but will the particular form of Third World industrialisation or oil exploitation being experienced bring about sustained capitalist development and the creation of new cores in the capitalist world economy? While the rise of Japan is indicative of fluidity in the world hierarchy of nations, are the countries in the Third World entering upon a similar path, or are they locked into a temporary phase of growth, dependent upon a particular set of short-term needs in the capitalist countries, but with few prospects of sustained development? Capitalism is an inherently unstable mode of production, dependent on constantly increasing profits, and the only way these can be achieved is by frequent changes in the fundamental economic relationships between people. As the multinational firms at the cutting edge of capitalism reach crises in capital accumulation, they are forced into new and more ingenious ways of exploiting labour. The internationalisation of production is one such fundamental restructuring of capitalist relations of production underway at present, but how long can it last before a declining value rate of profit forces another major restructuring, before exploited peoples rise up in protest against their ruthless manipulation, before the ecological crisis overtakes us, or nuclear war brings its horrible final solution?

This book is not an exercise in futurology. Its purpose is to demonstrate that despite recent changes in the world economy – notably the high growth rates which some Third World countries have achieved – an analysis of underdevelopment is as valid a task as ever it has been. We cannot be sure these growth rates will continue, and, even if they did, a sizeable proportion of mankind would not benefit from them. The future under capitalism, its basis in exploitation and its need to lurch from crisis to crisis, make it necessary that we critically review and evaluate those techniques and explanations which have attempted to account for these processes: this is a book about theories of development and underdevelopment, not the processes themselves.

Notes

1. Because this is a highly simplified introduction I have cited only a few key references. For a perspective on the period which links in with discussions in Chapter 4 see Wallerstein (1974a; 1974b) and Frank (1978a). See also Boxer (1973) and Spate (1979; 1983).

2. Much of this section is based on Wallerstein (1980: Ch. 2). See also Boxer (1965).

3. Frank (1978a) and Wallerstein (1974a; 1974b; 1980) call this a capitalist

world system on the basis that it is a world system of production and exchange. They have been much criticised for this, the argument being that the world system during this period was not capitalist. In essence, a number of pre-capitalist societies were linked by exchange with an incipiently capitalist centre in Europe. This debate is considered in more detail in Chapter 4.

4. Much of the discussion of Britain in the nineteenth century is based on Hobsbawm (1969). See also Barratt Brown (1974).

5. See Chapters 4 and 5.

6. Populations in the colonial possessions of the European powers increased by 101 per cent between 1860 and 1876, 71 per cent between 1876 and 1900, and 11 per cent between 1900 and 1914 (Barratt Brown 1974:185).

7. For a good account of America's 'new imperialism' see Kiernan (1974; 1978).

8. For an account of the ups-and-downs of communist parties in Southeast Asia see van der Kroeff (1981).

9. There are a number of annual reports on world development published by major international agencies. They include the United Nations' *World Economic Survey*, the World Bank's *World Development Report*, the International Monetary Fund's *World Economic Outlook* and the United Nations Commission on Trade and Development's *Trade and Development Report*. With the exception of the last-mentioned, these reports are usually conservative and display a marked bias towards the major industrial nations, but all are useful sources of data. There are, in addition, numerous annual reports on the major underdeveloped regions of the world.

10. For a detailed account of rural poverty in India, Pakistan, Bangladesh, Sri Lanka, Malaysia, Indonesia and the Philippines see ILO (1977). See also Chapter 7.

11. See Chapter 7 for a discussion of migration as a means of equilibrating incomes in urban and rural areas, and Chapter 8 for a discussion of the city.

12. The significance of regions in an analysis of income distribution is a topic of great concern to geographers; some are said to have overplayed this significance and have been labelled 'spatial fetishists', others have downplayed it treating 'space as an epiphenomenon'. See Chapter 6.

GEOGRAPHY AND IMPERIALISM, 1870-1930

If we are to understand the way geographers think about and interpret the contemporary world then we must look both to the way they thought, wrote and acted in the past, as well as the relationships between their behaviour and the prevailing social, economic and cultural conditions of the time. Historians of geography have tended to take a narrow view of the development of their discipline, pursuing the 'exceptionalist' tradition by pointing to the roots of modern geography in the works of Kant, von Humboldt, Ritter, Richthofen and Hettner. By contrast, the influence of writers like Darwin, Marx and Freud upon geography have only recently come to be explored, while the viewpoint of the sociologists of sciences, and particularly the relationship between geography and social, economic and political conditions, have only been cursorily examined (Stoddart 1981:2-3). The following two chapters of this book focus on three key periods in the evolution of development geography. Chapter Two examines the institutionalisation and growth of geography during the last three decades of the nineteenth century and into the present century. It considers the relationship between the internal dynamics of geography, key thinkers of the time, especially Darwin, and the development of monopoly capitalism and imperialist expansion. Chapter Three concentrates on the emergence and expansion of development economics, the significance of Keynes to the process, the development of tropical geography and, later, modernisation theory and development geography. These trends, it is argued, were closely related to the recovery of the capitalist nations from the depression and decolonisation, and to their participation in the subsequent post-war long boom.

Geography and the Sociology of Knowledge

The sociology of knowledge is the study of the relationships between systems of thought, sciences and ideologies, and their socio-economic context. Although it is an increasingly important area of research in the social sciences, including geography, it occupies only a very small part of geographic research and, consequently, the ideas expressed in this and the following chapter are preliminary and await the development

of research on the 'sociology of geography'.[1] We begin with the preliminary assumption that 'there is a genuine science of society in the
sense both that there is a complex of truths concerning social occur-
rences or activities which (1) are the case, and (2) are open to discovery' (Baker 1979:4). In other words, there is an objective reality;
causality not randomness characterises the organisation of that reality,
and humans are able to grasp both form and process: that is, reality and
causation. The exercise is to look at the relationship between social
science (in this case geography) and bourgeois ideology, and its
function in social control or as 'a vehicle of bureaucratic utopianism,
scientific fantasy or social fear' (Samuel and Stedman Jones 1976:7).
This is best approached by critically evaluating the nature of the contribution made by geographers in the period of imperial expansion dating
from about 1870 in Britain, and a little later in Germany and North
America.

Essentially there are two, not necessarily conflicting, means of inter-
preting the development of an academic discipline. The 'absolutist' or
'endogenous' view argues that a discipline unfolds through the working-
out of an inner logic, whereas the 'relativist' or 'exogenous' view places
substantial emphasis on the historical environment. As Schumpeter explained with reference to economics:

> Since history is an important source − though not the only one − of
> the economists' material and since, moreover, the economist is him-
> self a product of his own *and all preceding time*, economic analysis
> and its results are certainly affected by historical relativity and the
> only question is how much. (Simpson 1976:635)

The contextual view of an academic discipline can, in turn, be
further subdivided as Berdoulay (1981:10-12) has done for geography.
He argued that there are three main views: the view that stresses the
world-vision of the scientist and 'the interdependence of a science with
the thought of the same epoch' (ibid.); the view that concentrates on
the human dimensions of science, especially the social and cognitive
nature of scientific research; and the sociology of knowledge viewpoint
which stresses 'the socio-economic conditions of an epoch in order to
explain the emergence of new scientific ideas' (ibid.).

The 'endogenous' viewpoint, which sees disciplines developing
through incremental explication of inner logic, is inappropriate for an
explanation of change over a long period of time. The 'exceptionalist'
tradition, which traces geography from the early Greeks through its

revival in the mid-eighteenth century under the influence of Kant and, later, von Humboldt and Ritter to its further revival at the turn of the present century under Vidal de la Blache and Ratzel, gives a false impression of continuous evolution. Geography's institutionalisation in Germany in the 1870s marked a major change in the meaning of the term 'geography'. Before this period 'it was regarded as a branch of knowledge dealing with exploration journeys and research travels' (Grano 1981:21). As it became an institutionalised academic discipline 'the first university geographers tried to create geographical tradition' (ibid.):

> reconstruction of developments before the discipline stage varied from writer to writer. It was made up not only of the teaching tradition of the old universities and schools but also of such widely differing fields as the achievements of cartographers, surveyors, merchants, explorers and adventurers. (Grano 1981:22)

This, of course, need not rule out 'endogenous' growth *within* a particular epoch, but clearly the most important factor to be taken into account is the *context* of the development of geography.

Modern geography — that is, geography produced in universities and research institutes — has been dependent for its theoretical innovation upon neo-classical economics and functionalist sociology (Gregory 1978:38). To be more specific, development economics has been the father of development geography, while sociological theory of social change has been the mother. Yet development economics as a discrete sub-discipline is commonly held to date from the 1930s. At this time there was political agitation by S.M. Bruce (Rimmer 1979) in the Health Organisation of the League of Nations, the beginnings of growth theory in the writings of Keynes, and the translation into English of the major works of J.S. Schumpeter. Prior to the 1930s, however, economists and geographers were actively engaged in work related to the colonies and it is on this work that the rest of the chapter focuses. As geography became institutionalised in the late nineteenth century it was, for the first time, able to systematically reproduce itself through the education system. Its expansion and consolidation as an academic discipline was closely related to servicing imperial expansion. Just as under merchant capitalism geography provided navigational and explorational aids, so regional-descriptive geography with its stress on exploration, resource inventories and the myriad problems of conquest was well-suited to the needs of the capitalist ruling classes in Europe and North America around the turn of the century. Yet, while this relationship has been mentioned frequently,[2] few studies have attempted to look at it in any depth (the exception is Hudson 1977).

Early Thoughts on Economic Development

> The necessity of the [geographic] knowledge has never been more apparent, than in the late wars; every body talk'd of them, and those that pretended to entertain company about them, without understanding Geography, often gave signal proofs of their neglecting so easy a science. How shameful is it for a Gentleman or Lady, otherwise well-educated, to ask whether *Holland* is not in the direct road from *Paris* to *Rome*! (Lenglet du Fresnoy 1737:v)

According to Hoselitz (1960:4), 'economic theories have been developed in the past in response to practical problems in the social and economic field which required a solution'. He argued that there were three periods when 'secular growth' was a key focus of intellectual thought: during the early industrialisation of Europe, in the period between about 1550 and 1750 when mercantilist economics held sway; between about 1775 and 1832 when the industrial revolution was in full swing and the classical economics of Malthus and Ricardo had come into being; and the period after 1875 when the industrialisation of Europe, particularly Germany, encouraged German theorists to discuss economic growth (Hoselitz 1960:5). The first period we can dismiss fairly quickly. Mercantilist writers were far from homogeneous, but their common primary focus was on an increase in the national wealth, which they thought could be achieved through state intervention in order to prohibit exports of bullion and so balance foreign trade. Geography at this time was encyclopaedic in its efforts to describe the earth's surface, as the quote from Lenglet du Fresnoy shows. It had little or no systematic or scientific framework with the result that between 1665 and 1848 only 77 of the 5,336 papers presented to the British Royal Society were on geography (Freeman 1965:50).

'Scientific geography' is sometimes said to have dated from about 1750, corresponding to 'the period when the prodigious mass of empirical knowledge, accumulated to a large extent under the guidance of the Scientific Academies, was organised on systematic lines (Tatham 1953: 38). In reality, this period is far less important than has been made out. It is true that Kant believed that both history and geography were essentially similar descriptive sciences, history being description in time and geography description in space (Capel 1981:39). This led to his claim that 'Commercial Geography . . . examines the reasons why certain countries have a superfluity of one commodity while others have a deficiency, a condition that gives rise to international trade' (Tatham 1953:41). Such a definition provided an intellectual challenge hardly more stimulating than the pre-scientific encyclopaedic goals of earlier 'geographers'. There followed an increasing tendency for work in this tradition to divide into a cognitive 'geography of nature' and an 'empirical natural science', and an attempt at the turn of the nineteenth century to establish geography as an independent discipline (Grano 1981:28-9). The giants of the early nineteenth century, Ritter and von Humboldt, marked the end of the old geography, and not the beginning of the new.

> von Humboldt represents the old exploration tradition of the learned societies of the age of enlightenment and Ritter the old university tradition according to which geography was but a propedeutic subject for studies of history and politics. (Grano 1981:29)

Yet their individually substantial contributions were insufficient to nourish a subject of study that had failed to achieve recognition in the major scientific institutions of the nineteenth century – the universities. Right throughout Europe in the first half of the nineteenth century geography lapsed into a state of profound crisis verging on disappearance, a situation that became more acute in the aftermath of von Humboldt's death in 1859. Paralleling its decline, new specialised branches of study emerged and seemed to be in much greater demand by the industrial sector (Capel 1981:40-6).

In the meantime, the classical economists – Smith, Ricardo, Malthus and Mill[3] – were beginning to make their mark. The acceleration of industrial development in the late eighteenth and early nineteenth centuries brought about sustained growth in the industrial centres of Europe and the achievement of peak rates of growth. The classical economists became very involved in the study of the conditions for economic progress, in contrast with their mercantilist predecessors' concern with national wealth (Higgins 1959: Ch. 3). It was also the age of liberalism:

> according to which each person was master of his own fate, and which considered not merely programs of public assistance, but, in

extreme cases, even programs of public education, as illegitimate interference with the freedom of the market. (Hoselitz 1960:9)

The role of the state was under attack: the 'invisible hand' of the free market under a policy of *laissez faire* was thought to provide a much more efficient way of allocating resources. The fundamental feature of economic growth, it was argued, was capital formation. Yet, according to Ricardo's model, accumulation was dependent on profits which, in turn, depended on wages, which depended on food prices, and these were ultimately determined by the availability of land and food imports. Thus classical economics earned the label of 'the dismal science' (Kindleberger 1965:42-4). Growth could occur, but only up to a point: the crisis caused by limits to the product extracted from the land at the margins meant that the long-run result would be diminishing returns to capital and labour. Combined with this was the classical economist's acceptance of Malthus's theory that population growth would of necessity outstrip the growth of production because of its dependence on the factor of production in limited supply – land. These theories have since been criticised repeatedly because they underestimated both the ability of technological change to halt declining returns to capital and labour and the inadequacy of the Malthusian view of population growth (Meier and Baldwin 1957:44-5).

Despite their interest in economic growth, none of the classical economists concerned themselves with the colonies. It seems their attitude was summed up by the view that 'colonial economies were simply an extension of metropolitan economies . . . one set of principles, one theory, should suffice for all' (Brookfield 1975:7). Adam Smith made occasional references to China and India (as did Marx), but, like Ricardo, his prime concern was England, Western Europe and North America. Then from the middle of the nineteenty century economic growth disappeared from the economics literature almost completely. Instead the majority of 'Western economists took growth for granted and worried about other aspects of economic welfare – allocative efficiency, distribution and stability' (Arndt 1972:14). Interestingly enough, the failure of classical economists to examine economic growth in the colonial and non-metropolitan economies is, in part, related to the emergence of geographical societies during the 1820s. As Adam Smith complained, a key difficulty of theorising economic growth in the colonies was the need to rely on accounts 'generally drawn up by weak and wondering travellers, frequently by stupid and lying missionaries' (from Arndt 1972:13). What better task could there have been for geographers than to provide this service, not just to economists, but far more importantly to the entrepreneurial class who were most involved in colonial exploitation?

Despite geography's lowly status — following its failure to become institutionalised at the beginning of the nineteenth century — and its survival crisis, the first geographical society (the Société Geographique de Paris) was formed in 1821, and was followed soon after by societies in Berlin (1828), London (1830), Mexico (1833) and Frankfurt (1836) (Freeman 1965:50). Yet the growth of societies was short-lived, for by 1865 there were only 16 in existence (Capel 1981:59). The Royal Geographical Society, which had begun under the title of the Geographical Society of London, by and large attracted travellers, soldiers and navigators to its membership, together with naturalists and geologists. The profile of its membership was to change substantially towards the end of the century, as we shall see later (Stoddart 1980). The impetus for the initial phase of society establishment came from a number of sources: historians of the geographical societies have mentioned the general growth in science during the period and improvements in technology, particularly in the fields of transport, communications and publication (Wright 1953:547), as well as the fact that the public pronouncements of the societies stressed their role in geographic education (Freeman 1965:12). Yet there seems a consensus that 'their main purpose was to encourage exploration and to gather up the fruits of enterprising penetration of the remoter areas of the world' (ibid). The peace that prevailed in the aftermath of the Battle of Waterloo permitted an increase in the amount of exploration, colonisation and settlement (Wright 1953:547), and the development of commerce, as well as more scientific enterprises such as 'the creation of meteorological stations, the making of astronomical observations, ethnographic studies, etc' (Capel 1981:58).

The geographical societies grew during a period when the needs of the merchant capitalist class were predominant. Commerce was the primary force in the world economy, and the systematic geographical promotion and examination of the results of exploration played a key role in its development. However, even the demand for greater trade needed to be wrapped in a blanket of ideologically acceptable justification; thus people spoke of the need to expand civilisation to the

more barbarous parts of the world . . . Geographical societies not only satisfied a natural curiosity on the more savage aspects of nature and society, but also cast a shrewd glance at the eventual possibilities of trade and colonial expansion. (Freeman 1965:51)[4]

The belief that exploration was a means of extending civilisation remained important well into the following century, though the socio-economic conditions within which it was embedded changed dramatically.

The Institutionalisation of Geography

The establishment of geography in the universities of western Europe occurred in earnest in the last quarter of the nineteenth century. The Prussian government started to create chairs in its universities in the 1870s, and was soon followed by the French and Swiss. The British lagged. Despite the initial appearance of a chair in geography at University College, London in 1833, the experiment was abandoned when the first appointee resigned to go overseas, and the next chair in Britain was not established until much later. Geography's position in the universities of western Europe, however, firmed later in the nineteenth century and 'the 1890's may be considered that of the coming of age of the scientific community of geographers' (Capel 1981:60). International Geographical Congresses had been held regularly since the first at Amberes in 1871, and by the fifth Congress in Bern in 1891, educators formed a clear majority (57.4 per cent) of the participants — unlike earlier meetings which had been dominated by the military, diplomats, merchants, engineers and scientists, and geographical society members (ibid.). The struggle to institutionalise geography had failed at the beginning of the nineteenth century but had succeeded at the end of it.

How do we account for this? Much credit must go to the efforts of both individuals and the geographical societies in getting geography accepted, but it is certain that conditions in western Europe at the end of the nineteenth century were very supportive. Prior to its establishment as a university 'discipline', geography had been considered as a branch of knowledge dealing with exploration journeys and research travels (Grano 1981:21). Thus, for instance, two travelling fellowships had been provided at Cambridge University for around 150 years, right from the beginning of the eighteenth century, to allow fellows to explore and report on what they observed. Yet the report of a Royal Commission of 1852 perhaps best summarises the changing view of 'geography as exploration'. It questioned the utility of such an exercise, noting in the process that there was 'no lack of travellers among our countrymen: no want of information from books on the state of foreign countries'. Instead it pointed out the need for a more systematic education for officers in the foreign service, part of whose requirements were 'an acquaintance with the History of Treaties, with Political Geography, with the Principles of International Law, the laws relating to aliens, to commerce and to shipping' (from Stoddart 1975:2). This seemed to indicate that in Britain at least there was a sense of dissatisfaction with the form of geography current at the time; its utility was fast disappearing as the needs of expanded commerce and colonial administration demanded a more refined set of skills.

The event that crystallised the new demands to be made on geography was the German victory in the Franco-Prussian War of 1870-1. Training in geography was seen by Germany to have been of considerable significance in her success and much emphasis was placed on geography training for military officers, not just as the science of war, but also as a means of generating a spirit of purpose and mission (Hudson 1977:13). France also partly attributed German success to a training in geography and, as a result, geographic education there took a great leap forward in the 1870s.[5] Similarly, the military played an important part in the establishment of geography in Britain, a relationship that was later reinforced by the key role geographers took in Intelligence in the First and Second World Wars, particularly through the publication of the British Admiralty Handbooks (Freeman 1965:44).[6] Yet the influence of the military waned. At the International Congress of Geography held in Paris in 1875, 34.5 per cent of participants were from the military or were diplomats and ministers, whereas by 1891 their participation had dropped to 19.3 per cent, and in 1964 was only 4.4 per cent (Capel 1981:61).

More important in sustaining the utility of geography was the expansion of colonial empires which occurred at about this time (see Chapter 1). This was not unrelated to military activity: in fact French expansion into Africa was in some ways a compensatory movement following their defeat by the Prussians. Geography grew in parallel with the growth of imperialism:

Africa, the New World, a partially known Asia, not to mention the polar seas, all attracted vast interest as nations in the surge of industrialization sought new economic, and sometimes political, conquests beyond their home territory. (Freeman 1965:48)

The literature of the period abounds with references to geography's usefulness in compiling inventories of countries' resources and advice on how best to use them. Geographers were encouraged to map the economic value of various parts of the world and to service the needs of the merchant class, reflecting the fact it was still seen by many 'as a practical rather than a purely academic subject' (Hudson 1977:15). Its practical value also extended to the domestic arena. The European bourgeoisie found it useful to encourage nationalist feeling in which 'the idea of "patria", or knowledge of the history and geography of one's own country, was an indispensible element' (Capel 1981:52). The colonies were included in this feeling for they were considered an integral part of the home country. Thus both the home country and the colonies were embraced within the 'universal descriptive geography' (Capel 1981:53). Yet this emphasis on the practical role of geography did not always square with the need to justify its institutionalisation through an emphasis on scientific contribution. Nor was the association between imperialism and geography always a successful one. In the United States a joint Columbia-Yale programme in geography established 'for the purpose of preparing students for consular or commercial purpose in the Far East, never did attract the numbers of students envisaged' and closed down in 1906 (Martin 1973:74).

How then did geographers[7] cope with the pressures calling for institutionalisation and scientific status on the one hand, and an extension of geography's practical role as a so-called 'tool of imperialism' on the other? The truthful answer is: not very well! The geographical societies played an important part in attracting those who were most vocal in their support of an imperialist role for geography, and in fact in 1882 it was suggested that a dualism of a sort existed: economic geography was an academic pursuit, commercial geography a practical pursuit (Freeman 1965:145). At the same time fledgeling university departments of geography persisted in promoting much the same sort of role for geography as did the societies. Courses at Cambridge in 1903 were meant 'to serve as training for those who wish to undertake exploration, or who while travelling or being stationed in foreign countries desire to contribute to our knowledge about them' (from Stoddart 1975:12). Similarly, when the geography tripos was established in 1918:

> the need was justified in terms very similar to those first used in 1871: it would be a suitable qualification for 'the future statesman, administrator, merchant or missionary', and it would be valuable for

the 'Home, Colonial and Indian Civil Services and for the Diplomatic and Consular Services'. (Stoddart 1975:21)

Despite the very practical reasons for geography's establishment, its ideological utility demanded of it a much grander justification of the role it began to play in society. The civilisation of the colonised world needed to be raised above the practical and given a more objective, 'scientific' purpose.

The two main stimuli to the growth of geography in the late nineteenth century were the force with which practitioners pushed it towards the 'natural sciences' (and hence it owes part of its success to the rapid growth of the sciences during this period) and its utility value as outlined above (Gregory 1978:17-18). It must be clear, however, that geography was not the only discipline that could be accused of serving the interests of the imperialist class. 'Orientalism' too could be accused (cf. Abdel-Malek 1981:74; see also Said 1978; Turner 1978):

Anthropology is [also] a child of Western imperialism. It has roots in the humanist vision of the Enlightenment, but as a university discipline and a modern science, it came into its own in the last decades of the 19th and early 20th centuries. This was the period in which the Western nations were making their final push to bring practically the whole pre-industrial non-Western world under their political and economic control. (Gough 1968:403)

However, neither the newly emergent discipline of anthropology nor the slightly older discipline of economics[8] had nearly as much influence on the scientific content of geography as did Darwinian theories of evolution and positivist method.

The task of making geography scientifically respectable involved taking a fairly clear route:

The identity of geography presupposed on the one hand a unified monastic discipline which, on the other, should have its own concrete object of study in the real world as befitted a science. . . [Moreover] attempts were made to eliminate the perceptual basis since it was subjective and instead the aim was to achieve a rational synthesis of the real environment instead of wholeness and immediacy of contact with nature. (Grano 1981:31)

The methodology of the 'new geography' was positivism and was based on five precepts: knowledge came from a direct experience of reality; there had to be a unity of method for all science; knowledge was concerned with means and not ends; science is the construction of testable theories; knowledge is unfinished and relative (Gregory 1978:26-8). By adopting a so-called 'scientific method', geography helped build up its claim to legitimacy as a science.

Human geography's 'object of study' became the man-environment relationship. Several themes emerged but none were more important to geography than the ideas of 'the region' and 'environmental determinism'. The regional concept (see also note 6) is most closely identified with French geography and particularly Vidal de la Blache (1926: 6-7) who said:

The dominant idea in all geographical progress is that of terrestrial unity . . . The phenomena of human geography are related to terrestrial unity by means of which alone can they be explained. They are everywhere related to the environment, itself the creature of a combination of physical conditions.

The early years of the present century saw many geographers attempt to make an orderly study of regional geography, based upon the accumulated data of explorers. It was the second phase in a sequence that began with primary exploration, was consolidated under the aegis of systematic regional geography and, in turn, could be followed up by detailed local study (Freeman 1965:38). The other key theme of the period — environmental determinism — is often linked with the prominent American geographer Ellsworth Huntington, though he was not the unbending 'determinist' that he is sometimes made out to be. In his work on Asia, Huntington was concerned with the influence of geographic environment on habit and character, arguing that fluctuations in the heat of the sun brought about climatic changes, and believing that elaboration of this insight could do for geography and history what evolution had done for biology and its allied disciplines (Martin 1973:58). Yet Huntington certainly did not think climate all-determining; his work, on balance, was concerned with climate, heredity and cultural causation, though he is usually remembered as an 'environmentalist'.

It has been said that 'the growth of science killed God in the nineteenth century: evolution became the new method of justifying the capitalist social order' (Rose and Rose 1979). Geography, straddling the natural and social sciences, absorbed some of the key principles of evolutionist thought,[9] in particular the notions of change through time, social struggle and selection.[10] The idea of development through time is implicit in work done on the geography of settlement by members of the Berkeley School; regional geography absorbed the Darwinian notion of 'the inter-relationships and connections between all living things and their environment'; and notions of selection and struggle nurtured work on environmentalism (Stoddart 1966:687-93). In 1896, Ratzel developed seven laws of growth from which he derived the concept of *lebensraum* (Fawcett 1953:418). His argument is summarised as follows:

> there was always a tendency for a state to expand or contract its political area according to the measure of its interests or capacities. Ratzel, as a biologist, thought of the anthropogeographic unit as an areal complex whose spatial connections were needed for the functioning and organization of a particular kind of human group, be it the village, town, or state. The concept of *lebensraum* deals with the relations between human society as a spatial (geographic) organiztion and its physical setting. Community area, trade area, milk-shed and labour-shed, historical province, commercial entity, the web of trade between neighbouring industrial areas across state boundaries – these are all subsequent variants of the concept of 'the living area'. (Dickinson 1969:71)

Though a scholarly concept, the biological analogy between the struggle for space in the plant and animal world and that of the economic or wartime expansion of territories was wide open to abuse, and it was taken advantage of by Nazi propagandists to justify their designs.

Yet, in many ways, Darwin's thought had an even greater influence on geography, around the turn of the century and after, than it is possible to demonstrate by selectively discussing particular concepts. It has been said of Huntington 'he reasoned Darwinly' (Martin 1973:243). The concepts made popular by Darwin and his acolytes were a fundamental part of the taken-for-granted world of geographers of the time. Particularly in North America – 'where Spencer's idea of the survival of the fittest and Darwin's of the struggle for life were used to justify *laissez faire* in politics and economics' (Stoddart 1966:694) – their importance to social thought should not be underestimated. The significance of this line of thought is that it closed the gap between the scholarly ambitions of geography practitioners, the need to develop the 'discipline' in order to successfully institutionalise, and its role as a 'tool of imperialism'.

The contribution of geographers to the welfare of peoples of the colonies was both paternalistic and naive. On the one hand, the value of the civilising mission of Europe was unquestioned. On the other hand, as one important book on commercial geography argued, the effect of trade 'when well established, is to smooth out these very inequalities to which it owed its first origin' (Newbigin 1924:18). Colonialism, imperialism and free trade eventually could be expected to bring about world development for, as Stamp argued, there was 'a tendency towards the equalization of economic development throughout the world in capital, in population density and in skill' (from Freeman 1965:149). This was not quite the simplistic notion it seems, for it was realised that the smoothing out of inequalities could never be complete, due to constraints such as local conditions, but quite clearly the question of whether a smoothing out would in fact occur did not arise.

Economists had turned away from differential growth rates as a focus of study towards the efficiency of domestic production and distribution. Geographers, coming from a direction that had more in common with Darwinism and natural science than economics, had likewise skated across the top of the economic growth issue — it was simply not a question to be addressed because it fell beyond the intellectual horizons of the scholars of the time. Its significance has only been apparent in retrospect.[11]

Geography in Schools and the Expansion of Geographical Societies

While the establishment of geography in the universities of Europe and North America led directly to the formation of the 'discipline', geographical ideas continued to have a substantial public airing through the significance of geography in schools and the rapid expansion of geographical societies in the 1870s. Curiously, the geographical societies played an important role in the institutionalisation process and, at the same time, were the main force perpetuating the 'pre-scientific' or 'public' geography which the establishment of geography in the universities was meant to transcend. The British Royal Geographical Society (est. 1830) appointed its Librarian, J.S. Keltie, to make a 'thorough inquiry. . . into the whole subject of geographical education in this country and abroad' (Keltie 1885:497). He reported that geography was reasonably satisfactory in the elementary schools, and its expansion during the nineteenth century had been rapid — in 1844 geography had been taught in one school in three, but by the 1880s it was taught in every elementary school. Yet Keltie was of the view that geography was in a very poor way in the 'middle-class' and 'higher-class' schools, being not taught in some, and poorly taught in others. He was particularly scathing about political geography which was 'little more than a long string of names and figures' to be memorised (Keltie 1885:500). Keltie was most severe though on the failure of English universities to teach geography; he was convinced that geography in the schools could only be improved by its establishment in universities:

> The universal testimony in Germany of geographers and teachers is that the present position of the subject in schools is mainly due to the establishment of Geographical Chairs in the Universities. . . There can be no doubt that if geography were recognised at our universities it would probably do more than anything else to raise the standard of the subject in our schools, and compel its solid recognition where now it is slighted (Keltie 1885:502).

The presence of geography in school syllabuses, combined with the persistent urgings of geographical society members and others, undoubtedly played a key role in eventually getting geography recognised as a discipline. Early in the nineteenth century the long debate about whether the 'inferior classes' should be educated was settled in their favour, and elementary education spread quickly as a result. As the century wore on, new pedagogic methods came to the fore: the growth of science, the influence of positivist method and many other forces created a climate where 'an active education, not a pedantic one' with plenty of contact with nature was deemed to be important (Capel 1981:50). Geography adapted quickly to these principles:

> [It] became active education, centred upon observation. And, as a science which taught basic notions about our planet, it was particularly to incorporate these new ideas and apply them to the study of the home territory of the child, as a first stage in the study of the earth as a whole. (Capel 1981:51)

The content of school geography was to reflect the same imperial requirements as university geography, as Keltie argued:

> there is no country that can less afford to dispense with geographi-

cal knowledge than England . . . . The interests of England are as wide as the world. Her colonies, her commerce, her emigrations, her wars, her missionaries, and her scientific explorers bring her into contact with all parts of the globe, and it is therefore a matter of imperial importance that no reasonable means should be neglected of training her youth in sound geographical knowledge. (from Stoddart 1975:4)

Yet while the RGS was actively supporting this process and, with the establishment of the *Geographical Journal*, had encouraged the growth of a 'geographical (that is, scientific) as opposed to merely "adventuring" flavour' (Mackinder 1895:367), the last decades of the nineteenth century witnessed a rapid growth in geographical societies and with it an increase in their complexity and significance.

In the half century following the formation of the first geographical society in 1821 some 20 others were formed; then in the years between 1870 and 1889 another 62 were established; a further growth spurt occurred during the decade beginning in 1920 when 30 new societies were formed. In all, by 1929, 143 geographical societies existed throughout the world (Capel 1981:56). There is a clear correlation between the growth of geographical societies and the expansion of European imperialism, especially in the period after 1870 (cf. Wright 1953:548), but the growth spurt in the early years of the present century was brought about by the establishment of professional associations (the Association of American Geographers, for instance, was established in 1904). Society membership in the late nineteenth century consisted largely of soldiers, naturalists, navigators, merchants, politicians and clergymen, while their goals 'included not only the organisation of exploration and the development of commerce, but also the creation of meteorological stations, the making of astronomical observations, ethnographic studies' and so on (Capel 1981:58).

Looking into the nature of particular societies, however, it becomes apparent that their purposes differed. The subtle shift of emphasis by the RGS has been mentioned (Stoddart 1975). In France, at the same time, the prestigious Société Geographique de Paris announced that 'it was no longer going to limit itself to scientific speculation' (McKay 1943:214). The response of the Société to France's defeat by Germany was to reaffirm the importance of geography. Although it argued that the superior map-making skill of the Germans, combined with their knowledge of local geography, had been critical to their success, for France's future it urged much greater attention be paid to overseas exploration and colonisation. Initially combining national honour, scientific interests, and commercial prosperity by way of justification, honour and commercial advantage gradually became relatively more important than science. Membership increased quickly, the Société attracted government support for its work and spawned new geographical societies. One fruitful liaison developed from the common interests of geographers and the members of the syndical chambers of commerce. The Society of Commercial Geography emerged from the marriage:

> [its] avowed aims were to include the development of French commercial enterprises all over the globe, the propagation of knowledge relative to commercial geography, the stimulation of voyages that might open outlets for French commerce and industry, the study of means of communication, the pointing out of natural riches and manufacturing processes useful to commerce and industry, and, finally, the investigation of all questions relative to colonization and emigration. (McKay 1943:217)

Similar, overtly commercial, geographical societies sprang up in other places. The Bulletin of the Marseilles Society eschewed scientific status. It claimed to be *an ouvrage de vulgarisation*, interested in the application of geography to 'realistic research' problems in shipping, industry and commerce. In Britain, the Edinburgh and Manchester branches of the RGS, both established in 1884, mainly concerned themselves with the promotion of commercial interests, focusing on shipping, ports and the problems of manufacturers, all of which the study of geography was said to assist (Freeman 1965:47-58).

Pre-scientific geography received its greatest impetus from the geographical societies established with that purpose in mind, just as others among the geographical societies pushed towards the establishment of geography in the universities. Yet, while the style of presentation of their respective urgings differed, it would be incorrect to overemphasise the differences in substance between the two. In both cases the ultimate justification of geography was its utilitarian value, whether this was manifest in blatant calls for commercial expansion or more subtly enveloped in the scientific study of regions. Similarly, in the schools, the low standard of geography teaching was thought to hinder geography's potential to ride the wave of imperial expansion. The distinction between scientific and pre-scientific geography needs to be very carefully drawn; at the turn of the century it was a distinction reflecting the people (academics as against businessmen) and institutions (universities as against companies) and their respective posturings, rather than the fundamental (albeit sometimes hidden) motivation behind the exercise.

Conclusion

The sociology of geography is an underdeveloped area of study, so the purpose of this chapter has been to indicate some of the possible relationships between the growth of geography in the late nineteenth century and imperial expansion. This is not a new argument. It has been foreshadowed in the writings of eminent historians of the discipline, such as Wright and Freeman, and has been mentioned in the writings of contemporary radical researchers. Neither geography nor social science as a whole evolves in a linear fashion, and it would be quite incorrect to argue that this is a stage (and especially a 'necessary' stage) in the emergence of contemporary development geography: it is not. Rather, it is an illustration of a particular aspect of the sociology of geography, and one which involved geographers and the relationship between the core and colonised periphery of the world economy. The geography of this period was much closer to natural science than to either anthropology/sociology or economics, even though, in retrospect, the emergence of anthropo-, economic and commercial geography had much more in common with them. The real beginnings of development geography did not occur until after the Second World War, and it is to this process we turn in the next chapter.

Notes

1. Some of the best analyses of contemporary geography are contained in the works of Mercer (1977), Gregory (1978) and the collection edited by Stoddart (1981).

2. See, for instance, Freeman (1965), Lacoste (1976), Gregory (1978), Blaut (1979), Peet (1979), Berdoulay (1981).

3. Marx is usually considered a classical economist, but his distinctive contribution is considered separately in Chapter 4.

4. To take this further, the American, John Quincy Adams, believed that China's reluctance to trade with the US was 'anti-commercial and therefore immoral' (Kiernan 1978:52). The failure to distinguish between morality and self-interest, it could be said, remains a characteristic of American foreign policy.

5. It was noted in 1885 that 'geography in its widest sense is the chief subject of education' in the two main French military colleges (Keltie 1885:501).

6. Fifty-two geographers were employed by the US government during the First World War. Ellsworth Huntington wrote in a letter to W.M. Davis 'As to the part taken by the geographers in the war it seems to me that one of the best things we can do is to assist in giving the officers and men of our army and navy a thorough understanding of those regions where there is chance of conflict . . . Therefore why not bend our efforts to getting together the best possible description of the geography of those regions? . . . it is highly probable that when peace is made our voice may be of particular weight in regard to the final disposal of parts of Turkey . . . Therefore we need concise, up-to-date and interesting descriptions of these regions with good maps' (Martin 1973:147).

7. Note that these people were not professional geographers in the contemporary sense until geography was institutionalised in the universities. Guillemard, the first geographer appointed to Cambridge, had a degree in medicine; Buchanan, the second, was a chemist and physicist (Stoddart 1975:8-9).

8. Both the natural and the social sciences expanded considerably towards the end of the nineteenth century. To give some examples from the USA, the American Historical Association (1884), the American Economic Association (1885), the American Anthropological Association (1902) and the American Sociological Society (1905) were all established in this period (James and Martin 1979:3).

9. Though it is important to note that Darwin was not simply concerned with evolution: his main interest was the 'mechanism whereby random variations in plants and animals could be selectively preserved, and by inheritance lead to changes at the species level'. In geography however, 'supposedly Darwinian ideas were applied in an eighteenth rather than a nineteenth century fasion' (Stoddart 1966:683-4).

10. Interestingly, Darwinian thought had a strong influence on geography, anthropology and sociology, but curiously not on economics (Stoddart 1981: 687-94).

11. Economic growth was not only a non-issue to 'bourgeois' scientists of the time. Marx and his followers had a poor conception of the difficulties associated with the 'transition to capitalism', as will be explained in Chapter 4.

3 GEOGRAPHY, AREA STUDIES AND DEVELOPMENT STUDIES

The world depression in the 1930s, followed by the Second World War, the post-war long boom and the severe recession in the 1970s and 1980s illustrate the cyclical nature of the world capitalist economy. It has been during this half century that the field of development studies, both in an interdisciplinary and a discipline-based form, has risen to importance. While it would be naive to assume a simple correlation between the two sets of events, clearly there are some relationships. Most colonial economies were appallingly hard hit by the depression, and this seemed to encourage and promote political interest in the colonies, particularly as many grew increasingly restless as the depression bit deeper. Then, after the war, the rise of Keynesian economics, post-war reconstruction policies and the Marshall Plan provided the right conditions for the emergence of growth theories and modernisation theories. With political independence (achieved, incidentally, with relatively little support from the academic community), former colonies turned their attention to domestic problems of national unification, but class and region-based social struggles were seldom easily resolved. Moreover economic development proved an elusive goal. Inheriting neglected administrations orientated mainly to the extraction of export crops and exportable natural resources, and faced with the smug intransigence of developed-country governments, the former colonies did not enter the exclusive club of industrial nations but became the 'Third World' or underdeveloped countries.

Initially, it was thought the extension of the Marshall Plan to the Third World would aid in correcting these imbalances within the world economy. As a result development was seen as the diffusion of economic growth to the poor countries, along with the diffusion of 'modern' values, such as increased newspaper readership, and various other attributes of western living. Yet it soon became apparent that this was not to be. Many of the countries of Africa, for instance, stagnated economically while those countries which exhibited signs of sustained economic growth (such as South Korea and Singapore) did so at the cost of basic human rights. This produced something of a crisis in the field of development studies. Growth and development increasingly came to be separated, the former being used to refer to an economic process, the latter to a series of normative changes associated with the improved well-being of the population as a whole. As a result there has emerged a new orthodoxy in development studies, one which is orientated to growth *and* redistribution, and is geared towards integrated rural planning and the delivery of basic needs. Yet it, in turn, is under attack from both the left (Chapters 3, 4, 5) and the right. The dependence of this form of development planning on bilateral aid from the OECD countries and multilateral aid from the World Bank and other supra-national sources is the weak link as far as the 'New Right' is concerned. Advocating small government and the free play of inter- and intra-national market forces, advocates of the New Right seem intent on reducing overseas development aid, thereby mounting a major challenge to current development planning practice (see Higgott 1984).

It is neither possible nor necessary to review these trends in development studies or development geography in detail. Over the last decade a number of books and journal articles have undertaken this task (see, for instance, de Souza and Porter 1974; Brookfield 1975; Slater 1973, 1977; Freeman 1979; Browett 1980a, 1980b, 1981; 1982; Rimmer and Forbes 1982). Instead, this chapter critically focuses on three important themes within the development geography literature: first, the emergence of colonial geography; second, the establishment of an explicit area studies focus; third, the impact of modernisation theory upon geography and the development of a post-modernisation grass-roots policy focus.

Colonial Geography

Around the turn of the century, the geography of the colonial world had been primarily concerned with instructions for travellers, basic exploration and mapping. However, in the first two decades of the century, and particularly in the period after the First World War, there were:

> various attempts to make regional geography a logical and comprehensible study of the world, using data from the widespread travels of explorers. Once the era of primary world exploration was over, so that for a large part of the world there was at least a reconnaissance survey, local study would follow — as many had urged for some time. (Freeman 1965:88)

The interests of geographers who ventured out to the colonies, particularly from Britain, were as diverse as geography itself, and included coastal geomorphology, settlement geography, economic geography and so on. Few geographers were very critical of the colonial impact though some, like Gilbert and Steel (1945), raised doubts about whether the social welfare of the colonised populations could be improved even if economic development did occur.

Robequain (1958) was one of only a small number of pre-Second World War geographers who tried to explain colonialism in terms of the imperatives of capitalist expansion (Lincoln 1979:102).[1] Yet even Robequain seemed divided about the net result of colonialism. Like most of his contemporaries he regarded colonisation as a material success, but was wary of subjectively evaluating the social impact on the colonised. He pointed out that 'the deep-seated anaemia which has occurred here and there among the native peoples of Australia and Oceania', and which was reflected in declining population growth rates had, on the whole, not occurred in the Malay world, and left the readership to draw their own conclusions (Robequain 1958:297-9). As if to underline the point, though, the final five chapters of the book sit beneath the major heading 'Colonial Achievement'.

On the whole, the overall size of colonial geography should not be overestimated. Only a few geographers working in Britain in the interwar period had experience in the colonies, for two reasons. First, geography was a minor discipline in the universities both in Britain and in the colonies. Second, the 1930s were a period of tight finances in the universities so the amount of research funding for overseas work was restricted. The work of British-based geographers was supplemented by British geographers who moved overseas to work in universities, schools and colonial survey departments (Farmer 1983). Many of the geographers who worked in the colonies remain well known. Gourou's (1945, 1955) books on Indochina, Robequain's (1944, 1964) works, Geddes's (1937, 1941) contributions on India, and Forde's (1934) *Habitat, Economy and Society: A Geographical Introduction to Ethnology*, come to mind. Perhaps the most well known contribution was that by Stamp (1929).

Stamp's main book was called *Asia: A Regional and Economic Geography*. The study, with its affectionate dedication to his wife 'in memory of bullock-cart days and Irrawaddy nights', is an encyclopaedic account of Asia. Beginning with a series of overview chapters in which the macro-regions of Asia are a core component, the volume then goes on to a chapter by chapter account of the main countries and regions. The list of subheadings in the chapter on China illustrates the descriptive content: physiography (in which 'natural regions' were important), geology and minerals, soils, climate, natural vegetation, agricultural production, fishing, manufactures and industrialisation, distribution of population, history, communications and foreign trade, followed by systematic descriptions of the micro-regions. The concept of the region, associated with Vidal de la Blache, emerges as a strong theme, though there is no explicit reference to any conceptual material on regions.

The difficulties of compiling such a volume were quite substantial. By comparison with today there was little published research available upon which to base an argument, and travel through the region was slow (though not always hard). These were by no means the only limitations to the study. In a chapter on 'The European Exploration of Asia', Stamp documents interaction between Europe and Asia up to about the end of the eighteenth century before noting that to include anything after this period would have been 'too long and complicated a narrative for this volume' (Stamp 1929:65). The follow-up chapter on 'Asia's Position in the World' is a very short summary of the main products of the region. Whereas geography around the turn of the century aided in the promotion of exploration and the dissemination of these geographical 'facts', in the inter-war period geographers both launched some original research and were concerned with the synthesis of this information (which contained a significant input of physical geography) and its display in encyclopaedic volumes of the sort produced by Stamp. The material presented was highly descriptive and inventory-like. Processes and relationships between the imperial power and the colony were reduced to a summary of trade links, and not considered of particular significance.

The history of development economics parallels in some important ways the history of geography. In the inter-war years there was no explicit sub-discipline of development economics, and the leading economists (including Fisher, Taussig, Marshall, Pigou, Schumpeter and Keynes) all but ignored the underdeveloped world. Nevertheless, issues pertinent to development and underdevelopment were discussed. These issues were of two kinds. First, a number of theories and arguments were developed by economists during those years which formed a set of tools for later application to the Third World. The main ones include Schumpeter's (1934) ideas about innovation and the role of the private entrepreneur Keynes's (1936) notions of the role of government intervention in the promotion of full employment; Hansen's (1938, 1941) explanation of the causes of 'secular stagnation'; Harrod's (1939, 1948) emphasis on the importance of savings and capital accumulation in economic growth; and Clark's (1940) pioneering work on national income estimates, which opened the way to comparative analyses of living standards and development. Though not directed specifically to poor countries, many of these ideas proved of great importance in the post-war evolution of development economics.

A second group of economists were interested specifically in the problems of poor countries (Arndt 1972). They can be divided into those who were concerned with aspects of the international economy, such as trade and commodity issues, international migration, and world-wide patterns of industrialisation, and those with some interest in colonial economics and the economies of the independent under-developed countries, such as China. However, this type of work seemed to have little impact on the economics profession. The more important works comprised Boeke's (1942) study of social dualism in the Nether-lands East Indies, Furnivall's (1939) discussions of economic develop-ment in Burma and the Netherlands East Indies, and Tawney's (1932) work on China. In addition, there was a large body of work being pro-duced by economists from the underdeveloped countries, but it had little impact on the discipline of economics – with the possible excep-tion of Soviet economists, such as Bukharin, Preobrazhenski, Bazarov and Rykov who 'produced what is without question the most realistic and profound discussion of the main issues of development strategy before 1945' (Arndt 1972:22).

It was also during the inter-war period that development and under-development were first conceptualised by politicians on the interna-tional stage (Rimmer 1979; 1981). During the mid-1930s great progress was made in nutrition research, and the relationship between diet and health became startlingly clear. It prompted the beginnings of what later was to be called the international food movement. A report pre-pared in 1935 for the Health Organisation of the League of Nations considered the world food situation and concluded that a key problem was the gap between the dietic needs of many of the world's people and the standard of diet they were able to achieve under prevailing economic conditions. The problem needed to be tackled by integrating economic and public health development. Another report, this time by the Director of the International Labour Office, advanced the argument by pointing out that the nutrition question could well benefit those developed countries who had an agricultural surplus:

It is evident that a higher and more variegated standard of food consumption would go far to solve the problem of agricultural over-
production . . . The best hope of finding a way out of the present
troubles is to raise the standards of the millions who are now under-
fed, underclothed and underequipped. (Rimmer 1981:218)

The representatives of the food-exporting countries, including New
Zealand, the United States, Canada, Argentina and Romania supported
a similarly worded resolution when it was put to the nineteenth session
of the International Labour Conference in June 1935.

The international food movement's chief success in the inter-war
years was in making the world nutrition conscious, but there was also a
series of spin-offs. It encouraged the measurement of poverty and
patterns of consumption, and though this was primarily for intra-
national comparison rather than international comparison (as became
important after the War), it provided a benchmark by which to specify
'minimal or optimal conditions for a healthy or full or normal human
life [and] the scientifically established birthrights of all men' (Rimmer
1981:233). Moreover, it awoke a number of the wealthy countries to
their international obligations *vis-à-vis* the poor countries. Finally, the
debate which the international food movement generated was essentially 'distributionist' in orientation, that is, it concerned itself with the
distribution of food and income, rather than focusing on production or
growth in production. It was assumed that world agricultural production could more than adequately feed the world's population if only
appropriate policies were adopted. This is in marked contrast to the
kinds of growth and modernisation theories of development which
emerged after the War, and much closer, it has been argued, to the
recent distributionist approaches to development like the 'basic needs'
approach (Rimmer 1981).

In an earlier chapter the close relationship between geography and
imperialism was portrayed in a manner touching on functionalism. With
the institutionalisation of geography in the early years of this century
and the growth of academic geography, this relationship became more
subtle and diffused. Scholarly inquiry of the sort pursued by, for
instance, coastal geomorphologists could be much less clearly linked
directly to colonialism, though this is not to say that with a fuller
analysis some connection could not be shown. The descriptive regional
volumes of the type produced by Stamp, and the shift of interest by
international agencies towards questions of economic development, in
contrast, are a more tantalising object for a sociology of knowledge

analysis. The self-interest of the imperial powers would be served just as well by a detailed assessment of the resources of foreign parts, as they would by the economic development of the poor countries and the increased consumption of surplus agricultural product. However, it is too early to consider these points in any depth because both lines of inquiry have persisted through the post-war period.

Regional Geography and Area Studies

The modern growth of geography commenced in the post-war period, but its focus on 'areal differentiation' had strong pre-war roots. It drew on the methodology of nineteenth-century geographers like Carl Ritter and Elisee Reclus and the contributions, around the turn of the century, by Vidal de la Blache and Ratzel. Hartshorne (1959:21) was a leading advocate of the focus on areal differentiation, proclaiming geography to be 'concerned to provide accurate, orderly, and rational description and interpretation of the variable character of the earth surface' (in italics in the original). The question of at what scale a region should be defined and of what criteria were relevant to specify the limits of a region, proved to be the focus of much discussion within geography (see Minshull 1967; Dickinson 1976). Vidal de la Blache had used the French *pays*, Ratzel thought the nation-state the most appropriate, while Stamp and many economic geographers, like Chisholm, often concerned themselves with even larger regions. Yet whatever the differences of detail, the consensus view was put by Fisher (1970: 374-5):

> At least since the time of classical Greece, the recognition that different ways of life flourished in different parts of the world, and the assumption that these two sets of differences were probably in some way interrelated, have provided the *raison d'être* of geography as it has developed within the Western tradition.

During the quarter century after 1945 numerous bulky, regional geographies of the non-western world were published. A forerunner was the Geographical Handbooks Series published by the Naval Intelligence Division in Britain, under the general editorship of H.C. Darby. Not only was the information on which these volumes were based of immense military value during the war, but proved subsequently to be a major research tool.[2] There were other outstanding examples, such as

Spate's (1954) volume on India and Pakistan which has often been acclaimed for its style and perceptiveness. Southeast Asia proved to be a focus for research and was studied in a number of important regional geographies including Broek (1942), Pelzer (1948), East, Spate and Fisher (1950), Dobby (1950), Spencer (1954), Fisher (1964) and Fryer (1970). The establishment of new universities in former colonies after the war was associated with this expansion of research interest. As Steel (1956:7) noted, the research that had hitherto been organised and directed from institutions in Britain was increasingly being undertaken by institutions in the tropics themselves, though often by expatriate staff. Yet although more information was available for post-war 'regional geography' its structure yielded little proof of any methodological or theoretical progress.

The shift within geography during the late 1960s, and through the 1970s, towards spatial theory and the application of quantitative techniques hastened the demise of this form of regional geography. A rearguard action was quickly mounted in its defence, but many of the traditionalists seemed to discover a deterioration in standards within regional geography (though few, if any, confessed *mea culpa*). Fisher (1970:376) detected a withering away of interest, as did Mead (1980: 294) who commented that 'the dinosauric age of European textbooks − country by country or region by region − has virtually passed'. Farmer (1973:10) suggested one of the chief causes was the lack of commitment by geographers to the regions about which they wrote. Without an intimate personal knowledge of place he believed accounts of regions often were characterised by an 'unsatisfying unreality', and this was compounded by these volumes' 'deadening stylization and factual aridity'. Hart (1982:17), while lamenting the lack of regional monographs produced within the USA, and American geographers' poor understanding of foreign parts, thought most regional geography simply 'dreary'.

Paradoxically, at the same time as regional geography was on its downhill slide, 'area studies' became more important within the social sciences. As a result of military and government service overseas during the war, Americans came into contact with foreign peoples and places at an unprecedented rate. During these years the demand for regional expertise in Intelligence, training programmes, and general information to facilitate military programmes helped create a whole new batch of 'area experts', who, after the war, settled into civilian life. The area studies focus, therefore, originated in the USA, in the language and area study programmes during and immediately after the Second World War

(Singer 1964:31). Although 'area studies' programmes have faced great difficulties in becoming established in the universities – due to the inflexible division of labour within and between disciplines – many now have carved out important niches. Geography does not seem to have played as big a role in area studies programmes as might have been expected. Geography's historical devotion to regionalism and its claims to an overview perspective would seem to have equipped the discipline to play a leading role in contemporary area studies programmes. Yet, on the whole, geographers have not been able to draw up the agenda for area studies research programmes, and past contributions by geographers to area research and to the concept of region are totally ignored in the contemporary literature.[3]

Some geographers, however, have been able to capitalise on extensive experience in regional research and have headed various area studies schools and centres.[4] Although they have had a perceptible influence on directions in teaching and research, this does not invalidate the point that the impact of geography has been fairly small. With the growth of area studies programmes regional geography of the sort practised up until around 1970 seems to have been displaced by a literature which combines both thematic and regional orientations. However, area studies and development studies are not synonymous. In fact, advocates of area studies programmes feel they bring a different perspective to problems, and strenuously resist any attempts to integrate the two. They point to the important contribution made by historians and historical geographers to the understanding of people and place in the Third World; a contribution considered relatively unimportant in the development studies field (Farmer 1973:6). Nevertheless, with the re-emergence of a stronger 'themes and issues' approach to specific underdeveloped regions (evident in, for instance, Brookfield with Hart 1971; Missen 1972; Odell and Preston 1973; Gilbert 1974; Bromley and Bromley 1982; Forbes *et al.* 1984; Rimmer 1984) there appears to be among geographers some convergence between area and development studies. However this form of literature does not seem to have placated many regional geographers who persist with their calls for a reconstituted regional geography.[5]

These calls centre on two general points. First, it is argued that 'good' regional geography is part of the humanities and, therefore, should highlight those aspects of people and place that are different or unique. According to Hart (1982), geography must be practised as an art because the significance of place cannot be reduced to a formal set of relations. The practice of geography in its highest form is 'producing good regional geography – evocative descriptions that facilitate an understanding and an appreciation of places, areas, and regions' (Hart 1982:2). Regions themselves are not pre-given but are shaped by the geographer in the pursuit of his or her art, and thus there are no formal rules for recognising, defining, delimiting or describing the region (Hart 1982:22). It also involves a commitment to place what is believed by some to be absent from the more recent thematic/regional geography. Farmer (1973:11) calls for the re-establishment of the 'dedicated specialization by area' which, he argues, once characterised regional geography. One could, unkindly perhaps, call this the vacuum cleaner approach:

> By 'dedicated specialization by area' I mean the willingness to devote a lifetime, or the best part of a lifetime, to a specific area, so that one becomes thoroughly familiar with its physical geography and natural resources, its civilization and culture, and its history . . . ; and also with the sources, nature and reliability of the relevant data and with the not unimportant matter of relations with official bodies able to help or to hinder research. (Farmer 1973:11)

Second, geography is seen as analogous to history. Whereas history might be considered the study of what people of one time thought significant about the people of another time, geography might be considered the study of what people in one place found significant about people in another place (Fisher 1970:377). It has been pointed out that the greatest achievements by geographers early in this century were a direct product of the breadth of vision which they brought to the topic in hand. Characteristically, this work had the 'capacity – in Vidal's words – for not dividing what nature has brought together, and its recognition that a world which . . . had become a closed system, must be viewed as a totality and not as a mere assemblage of isolated parts' (Fisher 1970:385-6). The importance of contextual and integrative analysis to history and geography has been reaffirmed recently by Hart (1982). He recognises the significance and uniqueness of geography's integrative approach which seeks to bring back together in space, and synthesise, the different phenomena which social science disciplines had separated for the purpose of closer scrutiny. Yet, for Hart, adopting this course requires that geographers abandon their search for causal determination:

The acid test seems to be that geographers are concerned with context and meaning rather than with cause. Scholars in cognate disciplines study phenomena as specific instances of general laws or theories, whereas geographers examine their relationships with other phenomena. Their context gives them geographical meaning. Geographers are interested primarily in the results of processes, rather than in the processes themselves, and they are interested primarily in those results that relate to and affect the distribution of other features of areas. (Hart 1982:14)

Such calls for the rejuvenation of regional geography have not been directed exclusively at the underdeveloped world but are usually directed to the mainstream of geography. Moreover, they are usually not expressed dogmatically. In many ways they represent a plea for a pluralist approach to geography, one that recognises the value of both regional and systematic geography and the advantages which accrue from their combination:

The regional side of geography is concerned with patterns, associations, and synthesis; the systematic side is concerned with analysis of the processes that help us to understand and explain these patterns and associations; and they are two sides of the same coin, geography. (Hart 1982:14)

Although such calls do not yet seem to have had much impact on research within the discipline, some aspects of them are important and worth questioning.

What has this reconstituted regional geography to offer that is new? What guarantee is there that it will not simply lead to another set of 'dreary' descriptions of place? What differentiates this sort of exercise from 'superior journalism'? Hart (1982: 23-4) offers three key themes: good regional geography 'must be informed by a sense of time, or becomingness'; the region should be conceived at various different scales determined by the theme of the analysis; the physical environment is an important part of the region. Yet how can we be sure that such guidelines, desirable though they may be, can actually bring about a lively and perceptive regional geography. A number of doubts spring to mind.

First, Hart's (1982:14) agenda stresses that geographers are primarily interested in the *results of processes* rather than processes themselves. This is an extraordinary claim yet it recognises a real limitation of this particular conception of regional geography (along the lines of the maxim that the decision to cook meat is not made in the kitchen). Second, the proposition to refurbish regional geography is essentially atheoretical. It is backward-looking in its idealised references to the work of Vidal de la Blache, and, aside from vague appeals to the methodology of history and the humanities in general, there is no attempt to elaborate a theoretical context. The relationships between society and space are assumed to be obvious and non-problematic, if only researchers were to devote sufficient time and pay enough attention to their field area. Methodology is essentially intuitive. Third, there is no attempt to make regional geography interactive. Firsthand fieldwork and 'talking to people' are important to regional geography, but no mention is made of local or indigenous scholars' perception of their region and the relationships within it, nor is the regional geography envisaged necessarily addressed to a regional audience. It might be said that the absence of theory increases the possibility of interactive communication, but this can be disputed. Assumptions underpin all geographic research. It is not obfuscatory to express these assumptions openly: quite the reverse, for obfuscation is more likely when assumptions are hidden or left unarticulated.

Abdel-Malek's (1981:73-96) examination of the emergence of 'neo-orientalism' in Western Europe is instructive for geography. In the post-war world traditional Orientalism has given way to a form of modern Orientalist research based on the North American model which places much greater emphasis on social science research and contemporary problems. Yet there are elements of this which concern Abdel-Malek:

> It is the structuralist philosophy that will mediate between the socio-political demand for these typologies [of people in the Orient] and modernism; and that philosophy, as we know, sees its task as examining the sectors of reality as such, as 'structures', and not, or no longer, as the product, the sum or the meeting-point of historical evolution. Thus conceived, structuralism in the human sciences appears as the most acceptable, the most 'objectified' expression of phenomenology, the dominant form of irrationalist philosophy in our times. (Abdel-Malek 1981:85-6)

The rigidities of this form of scholarly practice are compounded by the tendency to deprecate the work of scholars in Oriental countries and to perpetuate a division of labour which allocates to them relatively unexciting tasks, such as the organisation of local archives and documentary materials. Furthermore, it inevitably emphasises the uneven geographic patterns among the scholarly community and centralises research activity:

> The Western powers, and notably the United States, aspire to add to their already existing stocks new centres of accumulation of cultural wealth and materials. Their means are disproportionately greater than anything that the Orient, its scholarly institutions and its researchers have at their disposal. (Abdel-Malek 1982:86-7)

One branch of traditional Orientalism was closely associated with nineteenth-century imperialism. This disparate group of academics, colonial functionaries, military men, businessmen, missionaries and adventurers had as their prime objective to 'reconnoitre the ground they were to occupy, and to penetrate the consciousness of the peoples, the better to ensure their subjection by the European powers' (Abdel-Malek 1981:76). The post-war revival of Orientalism, area studies, and regional geography could be ascribed to a similar self-serving motive. 'Dialogue, and the interests of state, should be ensured by extending and bringing up to date such work as has been done and by improving the qualification of researchers' (Abdel-Malek 1981:85). The appeal to self-interest in the post-war period could be better dressed in rhetoric in the wake of the flood of countries which achieved political independence. Essentially, however, the material skeleton of government and university supported interest regularly penetrates the veneer of scholarly and academic motivation.

Regional geography should not be abandoned, however. Taylor (1976:129-42) has observed that during the so-called quantitative revolution the 'revolutionaries' found it necessary to assimilate aspects of the old tradition, refurbishing old ideas and giving them new names. Geography is currently shifting ground again, its mainstream questioning positivist methodology and tilting towards social theory. Geography and history are the *only* contextual social sciences, and this provides them with a great deal of potential power of explanation *vis-à-vis* the compositional social sciences, such as economics and sociology. Place and space are very important to the structure of people's lives, shaping and constraining patterns of behaviour (and vice versa), and mediating the effects of outside forces. Regional geography, therefore, should focus on the spatial context, of human behaviour. However, a new theoretical context, within which regional geography can be fitted, needs to be built. We need to theorise the significance of place and space and, hence, build up a framework to interpret contextual relations, rather than relying on description and superficial associations. This argument is further explored in Chapter 6.

Development Geography

By general accord, development studies only became an important focus for teaching and research in the post-war world (and retrospective examinations of the field have only appeared in number during the last decade).[6] There were several reasons for this, the most important were embedded in the changing material conditions of the world after 1945. As Myrdal has noted:

> For social scientists it is a sobering and useful exercise in self-understanding to attempt to see clearly how the direction of our scientific exertions, particularly in economics, is conditioned by the society in which we live, and most directly by the political climate (which, in turn, is related to all other changes in society). Rarely, if ever, has the development of economics by its own force blazed the way to new perspectives. (Streeten 1980:23)

First, decolonisation highlighted problems that had been hidden behind colonial patronage in many countries who now regarded development planning as an early priority after political independence. Second, the growth of East-West rivalry was extended to new nations and one of the many battlegrounds to emerge concerned development assistance. Third, declining mortality rates in Third World countries, combined with the persistence of fairly high birth rates, led to high overall population growth. The ensuing 'population explosion' exacerbated the plight of the poor, opened up new problems of unemployment, and intensified pressure on scarce resources. Development issues assumed a new urgency as a result. Finally, better communications and transportation technology, combined with increased use of propaganda between East and West, raised world consciousness of disparities in standards of living (Streeten 1980).

The development economics that emerged in the 1950s and 1960s basically concentrated on the need to shift countries from a low productivity agricultural base to a high productivity industrial base. Various theories seeking to bring about this shift were propounded. Generally, they were 'single-barrier' theories which attributed the failure to achieve economic growth to a single factor, such as low labour product-

ivity or capital shortages. The corollary was that development programmes should promote external capital inputs or encourage the redistribution of labour surpluses from the rural areas to the towns and
cities. Most proponents of these approaches assumed that the chief
obstacles to development were internal, rooted in some historical
inability in the indigenous population to adapt to the modern world
(Livingstone 1981). Overall, the majority of work was directed towards
achieving economic growth, and assumed a linear progression. According to Rostow (1958), a key theorist of this period, countries travel
along a path through various 'stages of growth'. The developed countries achieved 'take-off' some time ago. It is now the turn of the underdeveloped countries if only they could be freed of such constraints to
advancement as the lack of capital.

A more important influence on post-war development geography
was modernisation theory. It overlapped with growth theory in economics, but its origins appeared in sociology. Modernisation theory was
also based on the assumption of a linear transition from a 'primitive,
undifferentiated and pre-rational society entity (*Gemeinschaft*) to a
modern, differentiated and bureaucratically rational social entity
(*Gesellschaft*)' (Rimmer and Forbes 1982:199). The Parsonian 'pattern
variables' can be made more explicit:

> the evaluation of actions in a modern society is based on the prin-
> ciple of universalism rather than particularism; the scope of one's
> sympathies are specific rather than diffuse; a person is judged by his
> performance rather than by qualities ascribed to him at birth; a
> person learns to develop an attitude of lukewarmness (affective
> neutrality) rather than emotional responses (affectivity) toward
> societal objects in general; and finally the goals of collective society
> take precedence over personal gratification. (Varma 1980:37)

In essence, modernisation theory was underpinned by an assumption
that societies achieved this transition as a result of the diffusion of
Western capital and technology, as well as Western political and cultural
values.

Modernisation theory was only one of several diffusionist streams of
thought pursued by development geographers in the 1950s and 1960s.[1]
Yet it was, in retrospect, probably the most important. The argument
being put forward has been summarised as follows:

> economic growth and development in less developed areas will

eventually be achieved through the transmission of growth impulses
. . . from the more developed areas via aid programmes, financial
institutions, trade and multinational corporations. Hence, increasing
interaction and integration between less and more developed areas
will, at some stage, lead to the onset of development in the former
areas. (Browett 1980a:61)

Among the more prominent examples of diffusionist modernisation
theory were Friedmann's (1969) core-periphery model, the polarisation
and spread effect concepts of Perroux (1950), and the geography of
modernisation school led by Soja (1968), Gould (1970), Riddell (1970)
and Berry (1972).

Modernisation theory effectively aimed to provide a 'gradual, non-
revolutionary model of development based on a belief in progress,
rationality and mechanization or industrialization' (Rimmer and Forbes
1982:200). This body of thought, it was felt, was distilled from the
American and Western experience of economic growth, and could be
applied with comparative ease to the experience of the underdeveloped
world. More importantly,

spawned during the Cold War it was shaped by bureaucrats to be
congruent with American foreign policy in providing a democratic
counter-revolutionary model to that proffered by Communist insur-
gents in Asia and a counter-ideology to radicalism in general and
marxism in particular. (Rimmer and Forbes 1982:200)

Yet it failed in its objectives. It was criticised for its Euro-centrism and
for its simplistic assumptions (modernisation = westernation = progress) but, most importantly, it failed in practice. In abstracting historical experience out of context it totally ignored the causes of the
complex patterns of world uneven regional economic development and
completely misunderstood the dimensions of effective intervention in
problems of underdevelopment.

At the same time as modernisation theory flourished in the theoretical wilderness of pre-quantification geography, other approaches to
underdevelopment persisted, notable among them the work on man-
environmental relations.[8] On the whole, however, many of the contributions to development geography in this period lacked any clear
theoretical purpose, nor did they fit into any definable school of
thought. There was a tendency to ignore the major theoretical under-
currents and to concentrate on broad questions traditionally defined.

Population growth and the environment, economic geography defined as areal differentiation according to product, and the geography of resource distribution were the sorts of foci of the major volumes of the period. Geography was seen as a broad synthesising subject and used description as its basic technique (Stamp 1960; Fryer 1965; Hodder 1968). There was no substantial, explicit discussion of theory until the early 1970s, which saw volumes by de Souza and Porter (1974) and Brookfield (1975), but, by then, there had been a notable shift in the nature of development studies and, simultaneously, in development geography.

It can be argued that there were four major shifts in the perception of the development process around this time (Streeten 1980:25-35). First, the popular explanation of the causes of underdevelopment came under serious attack from a coalition of 'dependency' theorists, of whom the most prominent was A.G. Frank (see Chapter 4). Growth and modernisation theories had always been questioned and criticised for such things as their excessive concentration on physical capital, their equating of development and westernisation, and the overall simplistic nature of their explanations. The main aspect that differentiated the dependency critics from their predecessors, apart from the vigour of their attack, was that they had a coherent and powerful alternative explanation. Moreover, it was an explanation that shifted a good part of the responsibility for underdevelopment from the Third World back to the former colonial and new industrial powers, a fact quickly seized upon and promoted by many embattled Third World leaders. Underdevelopment was no longer viewed as an original condition: it was a result of the incorporation of colonies and newly independent nations into a world economic system weighted heavily in favour of the rich countries.

Second, there was a marked shift in notions of the meaning of development. Economic growth had been considered the principal criterion of development on the understanding that it was necessary to establish a productive base through accumulation first, and only when that had been achieved was it necessary to confront problems of redistribution. The trickle-down effect was thought to ensure redistribution, and corrective government action could always be invoked to speed up the process. However, it became apparent that the trickle-down process was small and slow, governments were reluctant to redistribute, and increasing evidence questioned the need to concentrate on growth to the exclusion of equity considerations. Development was gradually redefined as a more complex entity. Non-material quality of life objectives, for example, self-determination, self-reliance, political freedom and participatory decision-making came to be seen as more important and, in the material sphere, 'basic needs' assumed a new importance. All people needed to be assured of access to an income in order to purchase the necessities of life: food, clothing and housing. The provision of public services such as education, health and safe water needed to be improved to provide an appropriate living environment. Employment policies assumed a new importance, the 'informal sector' became a serious focus of research and policy, and there was a shift from concern with macro-indicators of change (for example, GNP) to disaggregated measures of poverty and inequality.

Third, the particular problems of individual Third World countries became increasingly subsumed by the world context and shared problems of scarcity. Third World countries were no longer anomalies and special cases but part of an interdependent world sharing common environmental problems and constraints, such as energy and resource limitations, pollution and environmental degradation. The emergence of multinational corporations disrespectful of national boundaries, and increasing shifts of capital and labour on a world scale, helped to break down set views of rich and poor regions in the world economy. One result of the emergence of the so-called multi-polar world economy is a heightened realisation that there are great differences between the countries of the Third World; the distinction between the oil-exporters of the Organisation of Petroleum Exporting Countries and the rest being perhaps the main example. Moreover, as the world economy attains levels of unparalleled complexity, there is simultaneous growth of conflict between countries, and an emphasis on zero-sum balances. Despite the proliferation of international regulatory organisations and forums for debate, world politics – as acted through the commodity associations and the protectionist interests – have become more conflict-orientated. The shift to a global perspective emphasising interdependence has been accompanied by increased expectations of conflict, not less.

Fourth, and finally, the consistent failure of development programmes to induce a substantial improvement in the well-being of the world's poorest has brought about a profound shift from optimism to a deep pessimism concerning the prospects for world development. The challenge was initially taken up with great enthusiasm, particularly during the period when the world worked its way through the post-war long boom, and the answer seemed as uncomplicated as a transfer of capital, skills and technology from rich to poor countries. With the subsequent slump in the world economy, the growth of unemployment in industrialised countries and mounting evidence of social protest in cities, attention has been diverted away from the problems of under-development and towards the consequences of depression. Some still argue that the high growth rates in the 'new industrialising countries' are a cause for optimism, but others point out the impossibility of duplicating this experience and ask whether countries such as India and Indonesia could possibly have similar prospects. Likewise, those who once held up Tanzania as a shining example of socialist development are now much more conscious of the intractability of its problems. On the whole, debate in development studies is much more cautious about future prospects than it was in the 1950s and 1960s.

There can be no doubt that the major shifts in development studies which occurred through the late 1960s and 1970s had a profound impact on geography. The growth of radicalism (though, initially, not Marxism) enabled the birth of *Antipode: A Radical Journal of Geography* in 1969 (Peet 1977); while, more specifically, notions of dependency were applied to questions of regional uneven development in Europe and elsewhere (Carney, Hudson, Ive and Lewis 1975). Within development geography the growth of work on the urban informal sector, the increased study of rural problems (as a response to a concern about 'urban bias' in development policy), and a concern about decentralisation and 'bottom-up' planning for regional development were representative of the new foci of geographic research. Characteristically, this sort of research, in its search for relevance, had a strong orientation towards policy and planning. It was an interventionist strategy with a common focus on small groups and communities and with local solutions to local problems. The basic needs approach remains the current orthodoxy both in geography and development studies as a whole. The assumptions upon which it rests have been seriously challenged by work emanating from a Marxist and neo-Marxist perspective but recently the gap, which at one time seemed unbridgeable, is beginning to narrow. In a sense, the two sets of approaches have been trying to achieve different things. The strength of the basic needs strategy is that it is a form of practice (for example, through policy-making) whereas the Marxist and neo-Marxist perspective is primarily a form of theoretical practice. It is not possible to paper over the fundamental differences which separate the two, but it is possible to conclude, for the moment, that theory cannot and should not be separated from practice (this argument is taken up again in Chapter 6).

Conclusion

Almost invariably, a review of evolutionary and revolutionary change within a body of thought imposes a false sense of orderly consensus and progression. The reviewer determines which ideas predominate, places them in an order he or she presumes to be chronological, and decides on the period during which these ideas are supposed to have held sway. It is a very arbitrary process, which reveals much about the values of the reviewer. We never see accounts that read like a Tom Sharpe novel, where chaos and contingency predominate, and the human control of his or her surroundings is only ever partial and incomplete.[9] Yet these conditions much more closely resemble the reality of scholarly research than does ordered rational discourse. Although it has been argued here that the basic needs approach — together with its innumerable variants — predominates at present, at the same time there are many competing views on the question of development and underdevelopment. Some of these seem to hark back to a period when the uneven distribution of the earth's resources was thought to fundamentally constrain the prospects of world development. Others appear to dispute the fundamental shifts in thought about underdevelopment which have occurred in the last few years (see Cole 1981; Chisholm 1982). Yet for want of time and space and because they have been overtaken by theory and events, it is necessary to ignore these contributions. Instead, the next section of the book goes on to look at the entry of Marxist and neo-Marxist theories into the debate on underdevelopment. Following that, the final section of the book looks at the conflict between the prevailing 'basic needs' approach and the neo-Marxist approaches through the examination of a number of substantive issues in the examination of the geography of underdevelopment.

Notes

1. The French edition of this book first appeared in 1946. Robequain, incidentally, was Professor of Colonial Geography at the Sorbonne.
2. See, for instance, the volume on 'Indo-China' (Darby 1943). It is, even today, a valuable source of information on the region.
3. This is an arguable proposition and one that is difficult to prove (or disprove). However, like urban studies and environmental studies, area studies were historically fairly central to geography's problematic, yet now seem to be genuinely inter-disciplinary areas retaining only tenuous and often idiosyncratic links with geography.
4. Two of the five Directors of the Research School of Pacific Studies, Institute of Advanced Studies, Australian National University, have been geo-

graphers: O.H.K. Spate (1967-73) and R.G. Ward (since 1980).

5. A disproportionately large number of Presidential Addresses at annual conferences have called for a revival of regional geography.

6. For general reviews of development economics see Todaro (1977), Seers (1979), Arndt (1980), Livingstone (1981); the sociology of development see Oxaal, Barnett and Booth (1975), Hoogvelt (1976), van Nieuwenhuijze (1982), Alavi and Shanin (1982); political development theory see Higgott (1983); history and development see Blussé, Wesseling and Winius (1980); and development studies see Sunkel (1977), Lehmann (1979), Streeten (1980), Varma (1980) and Kitching (1982). Reviews of development geography were mentioned earlier in the chapter. Recent volumes on development geography include Mabogunje (1980), Vogeler and de Souza (1980), Cole (1981), Riddell (1981), Chisholm (1982).

7. Browett (1980a) also talks of the 'spatial differentiationists' who were interested in comparative patterns of development (for example, Ginsburg 1961) and the single region stage models (for example, Taaffe, Morrill and Gould 1963; Friedmann 1966). See the discussion of regionalism in Chapter 6.

8. There is a brief summary of the contributions of key figures, such as Gourou, Pelzer, Boserup and Brookfield, to this area of geography in de Souza and Porter (1974:70-4). See also Porter (1970). A major statement of the application of the man-environment theme to rural research in the island Pacific is contained in Brookfield (1973). For a recent attempt to bring together time-geography and man-environment relations see Carlstein (1982).

9. Even Tom Wolfe's (1982) account of the development of modern architecture reads a little too straightforwardly, and this from a writer of immense skill and control.

PART TWO:
THE POLITICAL ECONOMY OF UNDERDEVELOPMENT

This recrudescence [of Marxist analysis] has a real basis in developments during the sixties: the collapse of consensus politics; the decomposition of the affluent society and the failure of the Americans to win a decisive victory in Vietnam. It also has ideological roots, for as the world has moved on academic social science has stood still.

(Kay 1975:ix)

Most social theory is not reflexive. It does not consider its own origin in the theoretical and practical thought of a period, as this is determined by the prevailing social and economic conditions. Thus it does not consider what there is to be thought and, in particular, what material is present that can provide the simple metaphorical equivalence on which human 'language-thought' is based . . . Yet no social theorist can, other than very partially, escape thinking in terms of the society she is socialised into.

(Thrift 1983:25)

4 THEORIES OF IMPERIALISM AND UNDERDEVELOPMENT

Having dwelt on the inadequacies of 'development research' in earlier chapters, it may be expected that this section will offer a polished, alternative set of theories, but, in truth, one does not exist. Instead it will be argued that contained in the long, disjointed literature of Marxism, in the relatively recent debates among Marxist and neo-Marxist underdevelopment theorists, and in the even more recent explorations of geographers taking a critical theoretical approach to underdevelopment, are the makings of a set of theories of underdevelopment. However, there is much to be done before such a goal can be achieved. Not only is there a good deal of confusion and disagreement between proponents of the various materialist approaches to underdevelopment, but there is also a dearth of empirical research challenging or sustaining the theoretical work. These theories are reviewed in two stages. This chapter provides a general overview of the contributions of many of the key writers working on theories of imperialism and underdevelopment from within a Marxist framework, as well as locating the contributions of geographers within this general literature. The following chapter focuses on two distinct but related sets of theorists of underdevelopment, namely those working on the articulation of modes of production and those using a class-analysis framework. It is impossible within the space of two chapters to adequately review and critically evaluate all these contributions, which spread over more than 130 years. The reader is referred to the original literature referenced in the text, or the reviews of Marxist theories of underdevelopment contained in Brewer (1980), Peet (1980) and Mommsen (1981), or the excellent review papers by Palma (1978) on dependency theories, and Foster-Carter (1978) on modes of production.

This chapter is structured chronologically. It begins with a brief summary of Marx, Lenin and Luxemburg's contributions to the imperialism literature, goes on to look at the dependency and world systems theorists and their critics, and concludes with a section concerning the theories of capitalist crisis and world industrial restructuring. While the structure is chronological, it is not meant to imply an evolution of ideas. Dependency, world systems, restructuring and crisis theories all acknowledge debts to Marxist analysis, but the societies they analyse are very different from the ones Marx knew, and our theories and techniques are located within a more complex scientific division of labour. As a result the following chapters place a much greater stress on contemporary trends in underdevelopment theory than they do on the original work of Marx or the 'classical' and other pre-war theorists. Among the most important characteristics of recent research are the use of a world-scale analysis and an emphasis on changes within the global division of labour. It is this particular viewpoint which is highlighted here.

Capitalism and Imperialism

Marxist or, more accurately, neo-Marxist theories of underdevelopment, like those under the 'dependency' and 'world-systems' umbrellas, have emerged in little more than the last two decades. Their antecedents were the classical theories of imperialism. Marx and Engels were primarily concerned with the laws of motion of the capitalist mode of production and could afford to spend little time on pre-capitalist formations. What time they did spend seemed largely devoted to India and China, and the concept of the Asiatic mode of production. Marx believed implicitly that capitalism would incorporate all these backward regions and 'the dynamism and capacity for expansion of the youthful capitalism of his period would be reproduced in any society which it penetrated' (Palma 1978:888). The prime reason for capitalist expansion, Marx argued, was to counter the declining rate of profit in capitalist countries; whilst the process would of necessity create havoc and hardship within those backward countries it touched, it was a necessary part of the transition to socialism.[1]

The imperialist imperative was elaborated by Lenin and Luxemburg.[2] The emphasis of their analyses once again was the driving force of capital rather than the details of change in the backward nations. In essence, they recognized that the transition to capitalism in the backward countries would be long and drawn out during the colonial period, but argued that the inevitable breaking of colonial bonds would unleash the incipient national bourgeoisie and allow them to lead the nation on to industrialisation. The central problem of present-day underdevelopment theorists — the protracted transition to capitalism for some, for others the apparent terminal underdevelopment of the capitalist periphery — was not considered in any detail. It was not until the 6th Congress of the Communist International in 1928 that theorists began to ask whether capitalist development really was inevitable. The change was brought on by the recognition that a significant section of the elite in backward nations — namely the traditionally dominant feudal class — would actually resist capitalist development. Thus the transition to capitalism, still regarded as inevitable and necessary, would be constrained by the 'feudal-imperialist' alliance. It was the historical task of the national bourgeoisie and the local state to overthrow this alliance (Barratt Brown 1974:71-2).

One more major change occurred in the thinking of Marxists between their development of a coherent view of the non-capitalist world and the beginnings of the dependency writings in the 1960s. In the aftermath of the Cuban Revolution of 1959, it was argued forcefully that the bourgeoisie would not bring about the necessary transition to capitalism. Like the old feudal classes, the bourgeoisie's dominant interests lay with imperialism and not with structural change. The point was driven home: do not expect bourgeois revolution — the only revolution is socialist revolution (Palma 1978:897-8).

Theories of Dependency

The modern dependency school came into existence in the mid-1960s, the first major publication being a book by Frank in 1967 entitled *Capitalism and Underdevelopment in Latin America*. Since then the influence of the dependency school has been widespread and, not surprisingly, it has come to incorporate a number of different lines of argument.[3] Perhaps the most popular has been associated with Frank's search for a theory of underdevelopment. The argument is well known: the world is dominated by a single economy such that all peoples are integrated into the sphere of capitalist production. They are linked by a series of metropolis-satellite chains which draw towards the centre the surplus which is produced at each stage of production. The result is that the periphery — the satellites — is impoverished, whilst the centres accumulate and grow. Wallerstein's work on 'world systems' analysis is often linked with Frank's work. Though it differs in emphasis, being concerned with the structure and growth of a world economy in its rich historical detail, in essence, the causal explanation of underdevelopment is similar.

> The trade-induced world division of labour . . . gives rise to an international structure of unequally powerful nation states: a

structure which through maintaining and consolidating the world division of labour, determines an accelerated process of accumulation in certain regions (the core), while enforcing a cycle of backwardness in others (the periphery). (Brenner 1977:30)

Buchanan was among the first geographers to recognise the power of the earliest dependency writings. In an essay first published in 1964 in a Hong Kong periodical called *Eastern Horizon*, and reprinted in a volume of his collected essays (Buchanan 1968:77-94), he elaborated upon the insights which he had gained from Frank's work. Underdevelopment, he pointed out, was not simply the product of differential resource endowments.

The 'chasm between the level of prosperity in different countries' was created by an economic process in which the development of one sector of the globe — 'the white north' — resulted in the stagnation or actual retrogression of dependent areas such as Southeast Asia. . . Capitalist development simultaneously generated development and underdevelopment, *not* as separate processes but *as related facets of one single process.* (Buchanan 1968:81-3)

The capitalist powers systematically reduced colonies to economic appendages: indigenous production was diverted to the home market, and new 'semi-societies' were created, dependent on the export of minerals and tropical raw materials, while any indigenous industry potentially competitive with home industry was destroyed. The gap in incomes between countries like India and the United States steadily increased. Whereas 'average' incomes in Northwest Europe were probably not much different from 'average' incomes in Southeast Asia prior to the period of capitalist domination; by the 1930s 'the income of the average American was about fifteen times that of the average Indian and by the late 1950s the ratio of 15:1 had risen to a ratio of 35:1' (Buchanan 1968:85).

Misshapen economies increasingly came to characterise the colonised regions such as Southeast Asia. The agricultural sector remained large and split between export crops and the inefficient production of food for local consumption, while imports of foodstuffs steadily grew. Old industries declined and no new ones emerged to take their place, although the tertiary sector quickly expanded, prompting Buchanan (1968:87) to point out that the 'ratio of some 250 workers or more in the tertiary sector to every hundred workers in secondary industry [is] roughly twice as high as in the developed economies of Northwest Europe'.

Fundamental changes in the social structure were an integral part of the 'development of underdevelopment'. The decline of peasant handicraft industries aided in the 'agrarianisation of rural life' and an undermining of the peasant economy. This brought about increased migration to the cities, but there was little or no employment for the displaced peasantry who were forced instead to turn, for example, to petty trading leading to the formation of a large 'proto-proletariat' but a very small indigenous proletariat. At the other end of the class spectrum a 'colonial bourgeoisie' was created. Buchanan was particularly critical of the role this class played in colonial and post colonial societies. Unlike the 'industrial bourgeoisie' in Western Europe at the same time, it was virtually unconcerned with industrialisation and economic growth.

[It] was a largely parasitic group, preoccupied with grabbing such administrative crumbs as were dropped to it from the white man's table or with the high profits to be gained from trade or from money-lending. Its values and aspirations were modelled largely on those of the West and its sedulous cultivation by colonial governments served a double purpose; it alienated from the indigenous society those who should have been its natural leaders and it created a medium through which, after decolonization, the economic, social and political influences of the metropolitan country could be prolonged. Such *elite* goups today constitute one of the heaviest millstones around the necks of some of the emerging Southeast Asian peoples. (Buchanan 1968:84)

The arguments of Frank, Buchanan and their dependency theory contemporaries were well received because they were presented at a time of mounting dissatisfaction with the conventional theories of development, and offered plausible suggestions as to why, in the light of the post-war economic expansion, the great majority of poor, newly independent nations were not sharing in economic development. Moreover, they did not need to rely on the tired old explanations forwarded by dualist theorists who focused the blame on the masses with vague descriptions of inappropriate 'mystical behaviour' or excessive 'peasantness'. On the contrary, the dependency theorists' argument was located in the historical dynamics of the expanding capitalist mode of production. They pointed out that the integration of the world economy led to both development at the centre and underdevelopment in the periphery. It was not the inevitable process of capitalist expansion that Marx and Engels in the *Communist Manifesto*, and many contemporary bourgeois theorists of the left and right, had imagined. Significantly also, they were posing a structural theory of underdevelopment which shifted the focus of inquiry away from detailed but isolated case studies towards macro-studies of world economic integration and the relationships which were the essence of this integration. Thus it is correctly pointed out by Palma (1978) that these branches of underdevelopment theory, which must be seen as derivations from the theories of imperialism initiated by Marx and Engels, are attempts to stress the unity of the economic relations of production and distribution, and the social-political dimensions of the modern state.

Critics of Dependency Theories

Despite the popular success of this generation of underdevelopment theories (or perhaps because of it), a critique spreading across a wide front emerged in the middle years of the last decade. Coverage of it is restricted to four interrelated points which have emerged from the Marxist-orientated literature.[4] The starting point of the critique focuses upon its parentage. Although it has been correctly seen as a part of a long tradition of Marxist studies of imperialism, dependency theory — as expressed by Frank at least — was presented first and foremost as a critique of dualism and its separation of the 'modern' from the 'traditional', the capitalist from the non-capitalist. On the one hand, this has come to represent Frank's most important and enduring contribution to the literature of underdevelopment. On the other hand, critics have conceded the value of his critique of conventional diffusionist economic development theory, but argue that, in general, his work has failed to transcend these origins and has ended up being confined by the mirror-image limitations of the diffusionist problematic. As a result many of the main assumptions of dependency and diffusionist theory cover the same ground albeit in mirror-image form. Thus, for instance, one considers the spread of development, the other the spread of underdevelopment, one the need for greater world interdependence, the other the need for greater self-reliant development (Browett 1980b:8-11). This has been labelled a form of radical structuralism which conforms more to an ideology than a scientific method of analysis (Leys 1977:96-7).

The most serious weakness, according to Brenner, is that dependency theory assumes the operation of the same forces, originating in the market, which are at the core of Adam Smith's conception of capitalist development; only, in the case of Frank and Wallerstein's theories, their impact is reversed. Whereas Smith saw market forces bringing about increased specialisation and, hence capitalist economic development, dependency theorists have argued that specialisation through the increasing international division of labour only brings about development at the core, and underdevelopment in the periphery (Brenner 1977:33-41; Palma 1978:900). The critique of diffusionist theory was directed towards an attempt to explain the unity of development and underdevelopment within a capitalist world system. It failed because it did not tackle the core issue of the significance of market forces. By accepting the Smithian proposition its subsequent development was doomed to lie largely within the same problematic as its predecessor.

The result, and the second point to be focused upon, was that dependency theories were not able to explain adequately the causes of underdevelopment. The essence of their explanation was that the integration of the world system led to a transfer of economic surplus from the colonised and, later, underdeveloped regions to the coloniser or core regions and nation-states. Moreover it was argued that this transfer of surplus was a necessary part of capitalist economic development at the core. Thus the two processes – development and underdevelopment – were two necessarily integrated sides of the one coin. In other words, this theory implied a 'zero-sum' process whereby the advances of one nation were, and could only be, made at the expense of another. The exchange relations which linked countries – analysed in terms of both 'primitive accumulation' and 'unequal exchange' – in Frank's analysis dominated the relations of production (see Frank 1978b: 13-14). This part of the argument has been attacked from several directions. For instance, it was implicit in this notion that dependent social formations were, to a certain extent, 'passive victims' of their place in the world capitalist economy which was the single main determinant of their internal economic and class structure. This failure to recognise the significance of autonomous Third World histories, especially the process of class formation, or to highlight the resistance to colonialism, represents a venture into a Euro-centrism that utterly fails to understand the two-way nature of the relationships between social formations.

The transformations wrought within societies by their insertion in the world market must be seen as an on-going reciprocal relationship: between the forces and relations of production within a social formation and those that operate through the world market. (Petras and Trachte 1979:126)

Moreover, the mechanical underdevelopment of nations as a result of their place in the world system has never satisfactorily been able to explain why colonialism, and the creation of a dependent economy based on the export of primary products, underdeveloped some countries (Indonesia) but developed others (Australia). Wallerstein's conception of the 'semi-peripheral' countries is of limited use; it lumps Australia and Indonesia together in the semi-periphery (Wallerstein 1976). Another line of criticism has been developed by Brenner who argues that capitalist economic development does not simply result from the accumulation of economic surplus transferred across space. The origins of capitalism cannot be assumed to follow from specialisation and trade, nor can development and underdevelopment simply follow from the expansion of that system. His point is that capitalist economic development is a qualitative process and not a crudely quantitative one. For Brenner the qualitative essence of capitalism is the expansion of relative surplus labour. This, Brenner stresses, is necessarily a question of class, both in the sense of the creation of a bourgeoisie and a proletariat, and in the structure of economic and noneconomic forces which determine the relationships between classes. Thus he demonstrates the importance of, for example, innovation in core capitalist countries which has allowed the capitalist class to systematically increase its surplus through increases in labour productivity (hence higher rates of exploitation), resulting in cheaper goods and greater output. Wallerstein, being dependent on quantitative changes (the expansion of the world system, specialisation and the transfer of surplus) is unable to either confront or explain these qualitative changes (Brenner 1977; Taylor 1974). In sum, Brenner argues that Wallerstein begs the main question – why did not the transfer of surplus from the core to the periphery 'result merely in the creation of cathedrals in the core and starvation in the periphery?' (Brenner 1977:67).

Unlike dependency theorists, Brenner locates the origins of capitalist development in the historic conjuncture of class conflicts, namely, the freeing of the peasantry, the securing of land by the landlords, and economic forces – specifically, the changing requirements for the extraction of surplus and the development of the productive forces. Similarly, in the modern epoch, the process of economic development or underdevelopment is not determined simply by the demands of a world economy but, ultimately, by the productivity of labour, which, in turn, is the result of class structure and conflict and the means of extraction of the surplus. It was these forces, Brenner argues, that determined there would be little investment in home areas, and what there was would be concentrated in the metropolis and devoted largely to luxury good production. Thus:

> . . . the development of underdevelopment was rooted in the class struggle of production based on the extension of absolute surplus labour, which determined a sharp *disjuncture* between the requirements of the development of the productive forces (productivity of labour) and the structure of profitability of the economy as a whole. (Brenner 1977:85)

This brings me to the third criticism which is the corollary of the one above. The failure of dependency theories to properly consider class formation is more than a mere omission. It is a result of their inability adequately to explain different levels of development and underdevelopment – or more appropriately, levels of exploitation – between nations, a reflection, according to Leys, of the excessively economistic and mechanistic nature of dependency theories. It is economistic because the prime socio-economic features of Third World social formations – social classes, the state, politics, ideology and social reproduction – are superficially treated, where they are considered at all, and are assumed to be the products of narrow economic processes, specifically, the influence of the world market on surplus-generation and the development of production. Furthermore, the processes which dependency theories deal with are mechanistic because they inevitably produce underdevelopment and offer no escape from it. Leys (1977:95) calls it ' . . . a system of vicious circles reinforcing each other'. The result is that nations are considered to be locked into the world system, and each structural adjustment (for example, industrialisation) doomed to failure. Once again there is a reluctance to appreciate the ability of social movements, especially class struggle, to change the path of socio-economic developments.

Wallerstein has been accused of reductionism in the matter of class structure, which he sees primarily as a result of exchange relations and not as relations of production. Mortimer argues that no class in the periphery is simply the result of the interests of world capital; furthermore, the dominant class, whether core bourgeoisie or comprador bourgeoisie, is not able to impose its interests, willy-nilly, upon the social formation. His plea is for a realistic, dynamic study of class which 'must aspire to capture the agony and ecstasy of the age if it is to be more than a static portrayal of stratification' (Mortimer 1979:4-9). The point at issue, as far as Mortimer is concerned, is the inadequacy of a sweeping world scale analysis for properly understanding the evolution of a class formation (he also quibbles with Wallerstein's categories such as the semi-proletariat/proletariat distinction, and his apparent over-looking of peasants). Also, more importantly, the failure of this approach to appreciate the complexity of the contradictions and con-flicts which result from it, not all of which can be understood through the impact of external forces. Not only is this criticism well directed at the nations of the periphery, it is also relevant to the heterogeneous nations of the core. The focus of dependency theories on the structure of external relations:

> . . . leads to an incapacity to differentiate the different moments of capital development, the specific configuration of types of capitals, the particular class relationships and conflicts engendered between capital and labour. . . But not only is the core constantly changing in its internal organization of capital – shifts from merchant to industrial to financial – but the relationships of capitals within the core are in unstable competition; moreover, the social relations of production themselves are changing, creating new sets of demands and crises. (Petras and Trachte 1979:126)

It is important to note that implicit in the critique is the concept of scale. Dependency theories were dependent on the contemporary and historical analysis of the world economic system. This very important point had naturally been central to Marxist theories of imperialism but had been forgotten by the contemporary proponents of development theory. Once it was reaffirmed, it was perhaps inevitable that the forces of critical examination would dwell on the inability of explanations conceived at this scale to explain the stage of development or under-development of any particular social formation.

Finally, a number of writers have pointed to the limitations of dependency theory as a guide to action. Its central argument was that underdevelopment was a product of the loss of economic surplus as a result of exchange relations. This led to the conclusion that the severing of these relations between geographic regions – 'selective regional closure', or nationally, policies of self-reliant development – could be expected to bring about domestic accumulation and development. In this form it was quickly co-opted by both scholars and planners who, nevertheless, remained essentially committed to reformism. Even the former President of the World Bank has allowed many of the main ideas of dependency theory to creep into his speeches, 'though naturally in skilfully deradicalised versions' (Leys 1977: fn.11). Dependency theories were able to be co-opted for precisely the same reason that they provided a poor theoretical framework for the transition to socialism which Frank so strongly proclaimed. By locating the argument in exchange relations and not in class formation and class struggle, dependency theory on the one hand made itself ripe for co-optation by the reformists who would have baulked at a theory in which class conflict and exploitation are central, and on the other hand provided little or no guide to those anxious to understand the potential for class struggle (Leys 1977:98).

Perhaps this best explains why the practical implications of dependency theories have been relatively ignored. One logical outcome of this type of thinking is a vision of socialist self-reliant development. This myopic view has been strongly criticised. What is the long-term future of the world if we are to move into a period of 'semi-autarkic socialist development?' (Brenner 1977:92). At a more practical level we can seriously question the viability of any attempt to manipulate national boundaries in an endeavour to cultivate self-reliance, especially in a long drawn-out archipelago like Indonesia, where the physical barriers to isolation are insurmountable.

In summing up it would be wrong to imply that the mounting criticism referred to above spells out the end of the 'dependency' and 'world systems' contributions to underdevelopment theory. Frank has two books recently published in English (Frank 1978a, 1978b), whilst Wallerstein presides over a virtual growth industry of world systems analyses.[5] Nor should the current wave of criticism be allowed to hide the real and important contribution which these schools made and continue to make to the development of underdevelopment theory. Most important in this regard have been the critique of modernisation and dualism, and the enormous popularity which these schools enjoyed which has, in turn, stimulated further developments in underdevelopment theory. Whether or not the rapid growth of output of material on imperialism[6] and underdevelopment[7] during the last two decades is a product of the lively debate generated by dependency theories, or the result of fundamental social changes related to changes in the world economy, is not easily resolved. Nevertheless, it is beyond dispute that their impact on theories of underdevelopment has been profound.

A number of others are often included under the umbrella of dependency theorists, but their distinctive contributions stand them apart. Emmanuel's (1972) theory of 'unequal exchange' proposes that there is a tendency for the terms of trade to favour increasingly the place with the more advanced productive forces. In other words, exchange between places with high and low wages, given certain assumptions about the mobility of capital and the tendency for rates of profit to equalise internationally, will result in a transfer of value from the low to the high wage place. This process effectively inverts the Ricardian concept of comparative advantage by proposing that trade, far from maximising the returns to each place, effectively drains value from the poor to the rich regions. It is telling that Emmanuel subtitled his work 'A Study in the Imperialism of Trade'. The theory of unequal exchange is in substantial part a geographical theory about value transfer, and has been applied at a variety of spatial scales including the regional (Chapter 6) and the urban (Chapters 5 and 8), as well as at the world scale by theorists like Amin.[8] It has also come in for much criticism, not least because it implies that labour exploits labour (and its corollary, space exploits space), rather than capital exploiting labour (Becker 1977).[9]

Yet, despite their significant heuristic value, there is clearly much dissatisfaction abroad with the world histories and world systems theories which have been the hallmark of Frank and Wallerstein. In general the criticisms reflect dissatisfaction at two different levels. Many are concerned with the problem of scale, arguing that explanations conceived solely at the macro-level over-simplify underdevelopment. Specifically, it is the crude use of terms which this brings about, the excessive abstract theorisation that it encourages, and the underlying impression it gives that capitalism inscribed its pattern on a *tabula rasa*. To a certain extent these criticisms have been countered by the growing literature which has emerged around the concept of articulation of modes of production. There is also the criticism that dependency theories have not fully explained the cause of underdevelopment, nor have they adopted a consistent theoretical and practical standpoint. The reason for this is that they have failed to devote enough effort to the history and dynamics of the class formation, to the various forms of appropriating surplus within peripheral social formations, and to the class struggles which have characterised and continue to characterise these places. By unwittingly straying into economic determinism their explanations have become mechanistic and the practical value of the theories limited. Such an argument may prove unduly harsh. Seen as a contemporary attempt to transform conceptions of imperialism into a theory of underdevelopment, it becomes apparent that the key problem of the dependency and world systems schools is that they are only partial explanations of socio-economic change in peripheral capitalist social formations.

Theories of Capitalist Crisis and the Industrialisation of the Periphery

A cornerstone of the type of underdevelopment theory discussed above was the proposition that the transition to capitalism in the periphery was blocked. In other words, because peripheral-capitalist relations of production persisted and countries were unable to withdraw from the world economy, underdevelopment had become a terminal condition of the periphery. This proposition had been questioned in the early 1970s by Warren (1973; 1980) who had taken a more orthodox Marxist line. He argued that capitalist development was occurring in the periphery and that imperialism – defined as domination – was declining. Moreover, he was strongly of the view that capitalist development had to go ahead in order to develop the productive forces in society. The 'neo-colonialism' argument, according to Warren, was little more than a petty bourgeois ideology which exaggerated the significance of the external forces in determining the directions in which a society could develop. In the years after Mao Tse-tung's successful revolution in China, many Marxist groups worked on the assumption that the peasantry represented the most potent revolutionary force, but Warren argued against this, reasserting the point that the extant working class remained the key to revolutionary struggle. Others have taken up the point argued by Warren about the transition to capitalism in the periphery. Schiffer (1981) has assembled macro-statistics in support of a critique of the notion of blocked capitalism. He argues four points:

(1) the less developed countries in the post-war period have achieved impressive growth rates in Gross Domestic Product, basic needs provision, and domestic saving and investment;
(2) manufacturing production, both for the export and domestic market increased during this period;
(3) heavy industry, in particular, demonstrated substantial growth;
(4) employment in manufacturing increased more rapidly than population growth rates, while there was some evidence of a shift of employment from light to heavy industry (Schiffer 1981:518-32).

Clearly, there is a growing body of literature which sheds doubt on the proposition that the transition to capitalism in the periphery is blocked. Also, there is a great deal of discussion about 'economic miracles' such as South Korea, and the emergence of the NICs (the 'new industrialising countries') in Asia and Latin America (Higgott 1984).[10] Yet the industrialisation of the periphery is a relatively recent process, and does not necessarily prove the argument that the transition to capitalism is going ahead in a similar way to that of the West. In fact if we look at theories of capitalist crisis we are led to the view that the periphery may be industrialising, but it is a form of industrialisation which is indicative of some far-reaching changes in the nature of capitalism itself, and can only be understood in that broader context.

Crisis, according to Marx, represented 'the real concentration and forcible adjustment of all the contradictions of bourgeois economy' (Alcaly 1978:16). Economic crises are an integral part of capitalist development, not an anomaly which can be avoided by clever management of, say, effective demand, as the Keynesians had supposed.[11] It is no coincidence that there was a marked revival of interest in crisis theories in the 1970s. Suddenly jolted out of a neo-Keynesian induced sense of security by the deepening recession and the twin evils of rapid inflation and high unemployment, one of the key responses was to blame exogenous forces – particularly oil-price rises – but this was never a very convincing thesis. Much has been written about the cyclical character of the world economy, both from Marxist and bourgeois perspectives, and various empirical regularities have been isolated, including Kitchin cycles (3-4 years), Juglar cycles (9-11 years), Kondratieff cycles (40-60 years), Simiand's A (rising) and B (falling) phases and the 'logistic' or *trend seculaire* (200 years) (Barr 1979). Few explanations, apart from those offered by Kondratieff and Schumpeter, have tried to account for long cycles over 40 years in terms of the contradictions of the accumulation process. Kondratieff 'explains cyclical movements by reference to the introduction of technological innovations, the expansion of the world market and increases in the money supply', whereas innovations form the basis of Schumpeter's analysis of business cycles which entail 'the coalescence of new investment, technology, markets, and enterprises in a particular economic sector' (Research Working Group 1979:491).

With the end of the boom Marxist theories of the economy reasserted their importance but many radical theorists, unlike their predecessors, were wary of predicting the imminent demise of capitalism. Recognising the resilience of capitalism (in the short term, at least), it became clear that one response to crisis was restructuring. A number of theoretical approaches were developed to account for this pheno-menon, including work on 'long waves' (Research Working Group 1979; Mandel 1980), and a new set of works on stage theories of capitalism which incorporated an explicit notion of 'levels of abstraction'. This enabled Uno (1980) to develop a concept of 'stages', Gordon (1980) an 'intermediate level' and Gibson and Horvath (1981, 1983) 'sub-modes' of production, all of which are theoretical constructs which exist at a lower level of abstraction than capitalism, and at a greater level of abstraction than concrete history. Underpinning these concepts is a common concern for the periodic needs of capitalists to offset declin-ing rates of accumulation by a fundamental reorganisation of produc-tion, for instance, the labour process, and hence bring into being a new stage, sub-mode and so on. Much of this work is still in its formative stage and is largely theoretical (Forbes and Rimmer 1983). Another set of stage theories has taken the growth of multinational corporations as its starting point for a theory of capitalism and imperialism. Briefly stated, the argument runs like this:

> the classical international division of labor − on the basis of which a small number of industrialized countries and a much greater number of underdeveloped countries (integrated into the world economy essentially as suppliers of raw materials and occasionally of cheap labor) stood ranged against each other − is being replaced by a *new* international division of labor. For the first time in centuries the underdeveloped countries are becoming sites for manufacturing industry on a vast and growing scale. Concomitantly, the new inter-national division of labor entails a growing fragmentation of the production process into a variety of partial operations performed worldwide at different production locations. (Fröbel, Heinrichs and Kreye 1978:23)

The motivation for a new division of labour lies in the fundamental requirements of 'capital expansion and accumulation and its deter-minants, i.e. its exigencies, opportunities, and obstacles' (Fröbel, Hein-richs and Kreye 1977:73). The mode of capital expansion and accumu-lation within capitalism is constrained by the need both to maximise accumulation and ensure the conditions for the expanded reproduction of the system of capital accumulation. This has taken different his-torical forms:

(1) a period essentially of free trade and colonialism up to 1914 ('Pax Britannica');

(2) a crisis-ridden period of national protectionism, import substitution, mass unemployment, world economic crisis, Fascism, major inter-imperialist wars, decline of Britain, rise of USA and USSR, etc., between 1914 and 1945;

(3) . . . the reappearance of the market on a higher level between 1945 and 1965 . . . ;

(4) the emergence of a new crisis period which may well bring about major new adaptations within the capitalist world system resulting, for example, in authoritarian state rule also in the centre, the rise of some semiperipheral 'subimperialist' powers, and even possibly new inter-imperialist wars. (Fröbel, Heinrichs and Kreye 1977:79)

The history of the last 100 years can be schematised as the progressive internationalisation of the major forms of capital (Palloix 1975, 1977). The emergence of a genuine world trade system and with it a colonial policy that vacillated between free trade and protection represented the first phase in the scheme – the internationalisation of the circuit of commodity capital. It brought about a fundamental realignment of the world economy and created a specific international division of labour. Merchant capital was used to purchase raw materials and consumption goods from throughout the world.

> Production, organized differently by each social formation, gave rise to commodities whose international value resulted from the confrontation of different national values and the setting of an average value (price of production). In this case unequal exchange allowed a transferral of surplus value internationally via the sphere of circulation. (Gibson 1980:171)

The advent of imperialism in the late nineteenth century represents the phase of internationalisation of money capital. With it the internal policies of the major economic powers became geared to external policies, witnessing the beginning of the interpenetration of productive processes. During this phase money capital was invested in production in the periphery, and the profits derived from the sale of the materials produced (either raw materials or goods for import substitution) were repatriated to the home base. Both these circuits of social capital persist into the present – indeed Palloix (1977:7) puts a book value of $US300 billion on world trade and $US 165 billion on international investment in 1971-2 — but they are increasingly overshadowed by the most recent phase of internationalisation of production, the value of which he estimates at $US330 billion. The multinational firm is the key figure in this phase, organising:

> the production process at localities scattered across the globe. Commodity production has been dissected into component operations each of which is located in the region which will most benefit capital accumulation in general. Value production itself, that is the capitalist labour process, operates on an internationally organized and co-ordinated basis. (Gibson 1980:171)

Surplus value is extracted not through the sphere of circulation as in previous periods, but directly through the exploitation of labour at the point of production.

The need to maintain rates of capital accumulation and reproduce the structure of exploitation are, in the most abstract sense, the determinants of the new international division of labour. Put more simply, multinational corporations are involved in a competitive struggle for profits (Fagan 1980:1976) and need to act to maintain the 'marketable quality' of their 'commodities for mass consumption' (Palloix 1975:63). The significance of capital-capital rivalry is sometimes overlooked in the rush to examine the capital-labour struggle. In the current phase the exploitation of world supplies of labour is the chief means of maintaining commodity marketability, corporate profitability and rates of capital accumulation. The creation of a world-wide reserve army focused on the Third World has many benefits for the multinational corporation: labour has a cheaper reproduction cost than in traditional locations; the working week is longer; the productivity of labour is usually higher; the labour force can be attracted and repelled more easily; labour unions are usually weak; and repressive state apparatus helps maintain the supply of labour, as well as creating generally favourable conditions, by generous policies towards corporate profits, subsidies, and the formation of free production and contract processing zones. These new conditions, emerging in the 1960s, saw an initial relocation of mainly labour-intensive manufacturing production to countries close to the economic powers (for instance, north American manufacturers moved into Mexico). More commonly, in Europe, labour was imported to service domestic industry (the guestworker schemes). Increasingly, investment has moved farther afield to Asia and Latin America, while 'raw material, energy, and pollution-intensive production is transferred to places with cheap labour if these places also provide otherwise favourable conditions' (Fröbel, Heinrichs and Kreye 1977:84). In other words, the new international division of labour is being supplemented by a new international division of resources (Forbes 1982).

A series of technological innovations have aided multinational corporations' decentralisation of production. New technologies have allowed complex production processes to be decomposed so that they are appropriate for semi and unskilled labour; transport innovations (for example, containerisation and the development of air cargo) have helped reduce the friction of distance; developments in telecommunications and data processing systems have facilitated the decentralisation of organisations; while the expansion of the international capital market and the emergence of a superstructure of international regulatory organisations (for example, the International Monetary Fund) has aided the world-wide operations of the large corporations. These technological and organisational developments have been a necessary complement to the drive to extract surplus value directly from the labour force of the Third World.

Hymer (1975) saw a close relationship between the changing structure of capital accumulation and the organisational framework and labour process within the multinational corporation. Single function firms existed in the USA in the 1870s, generally controlled by a single entrepreneur or family group. In the early years of the present century many of these firms were consolidated into national corporations managed through an administrative pyramid, and, gradually, new departments were added to the firm. Then, after the First World War, the multidivisional structure developed, initially with a national geographic base but, increasingly internationally. In fits and starts these corporations would invest in foreign customers, suppliers and creditors but, in the 1960s, a new administrative and spatial firm structure began to develop, corresponding with the internationalisation of production. It had three tiers: tier one comprised the top managers in the firm. Their role was, basically, the determination of goals and long-term planning and they, of necessity, remained located in the world financial centres. The middle-level managers slotted into tier two, their role being to manage the head offices of the corporation's subsidiaries, and in particular to co-ordinate the field managers. Usually they were located in the capital cities of the countries where the corporation was operating. The third tier consisted of the day-to-day managers of the branch plants, and they were, of course, located wherever the supply of manpower, markets or raw materials determined.

Hymer tried to relate this pattern to the law of uneven development, arguing that 'the new international division of labour through the transnational corporations created hierarchical superior/subordinate relationships between centres and peripheries' (Fagan 1980:176). The expansion of corporations into the periphery may bring a certain amount of export-orientated industrialisation, but it is not the form of 'development' that planners seek, in that it is not consciously or primarily intended to improve the welfare of the populations and regions affected by it; it results merely from the fact that bigger profits are to be made in the periphery and therefore it 'perpetuates the historical process of dependent development' (Fröbel, Heinrichs and Kreye 1978:26). Advocates of this form of industrialisation have been known to argue that it is a significant contributor to employment, that it aids in the transfer of technology to the periphery, and is a source of significant inflows of foreign exchange. Yet each of these can be questioned. While internationalised production generates some employment it is a very small unbalanced sample of the workforce as a whole; corporations seek out those segments of the labour force — predominantly young women — offering 'the lowest wage cost and highest performance and productivity, using unskilled and semiskilled labor' (Fröbel, Heinrichs and Kreye 1978:25). Moreover, this means there is little need for training the workforce, nor is there much transfer of technology, for the research and development segments of the corporation remain in the advanced countries. Finally, there are doubts about the foreign-exchange inflow due to the fact that corporations repatriate profits and use transfer pricing to minimise tax and maximise their share of revenue, while the foreign-exchange earnings of exports are offset against the cost of raw-material inputs and the infrastructure of industrialisation which is often paid for in foreign loans.

There are many consequences of this world-wide relocation of industry, among them distinctive and pronounced geographical patterns. The emergence of a new international division of labour has meant that many of the old industrial centres are de-industrialising, bringing high rates of unemployment, while the other side of the coin is the development of new export-orientated manufacturing zones in the so-called 'new industrialising countries'. At a lower level of spatial disaggregation we find the status of regions changing *vis-à-vis* other regions as the new structure of production reverberates through the space economy (Chapter 6). Yet it is also true to say that we know relatively little about the actual consequences of this phase of industrialisation in particular countries, and what we do know is biased towards de-industrialisation rather than industrialisation. In other words, we know proportionately more about capitalist development and restructuring than about underdevelopment, for the theories discussed above were not meant to be theories of underdevelopment, but contributions to the literature of capitalism-in-crisis. However, it seems that these theories have laid the groundwork for a revised view of imperialism and underdevelopment.

It is in the recent literature associated with industrial geography that these sorts of issues are being raised by geographers, particularly in the works of Massey (1978), Massey and Meegan (1979), Taylor and Thrift (1981, 1982, 1984), Walker and Storper (1981) and Storper and Walker (1983). Yet, for the purposes of this account, much of this literature is of marginal relevance, for though it looks at world processes it focuses on the problems of the core industrial nations and is more concerned with sub-national than supra-national regional development. There is no shortage of analysis of Third World industrial development,[12] but relatively little using the framework outlined earlier.[13] However, it is useful to look at the implications of the internationalisation of production in three different situations: the impact on the so-called 'semiperiphery' (Ireland); the relationship between semiperiphery and periphery (for example, in southern Africa); and the direct impact of core capital on the periphery (Brazil).

Ireland (that is, Eire, but Northern Ireland has many parallels) is one of those countries that are neither core capitalist, nor periphery, but located economically somewhere between the two. Consistent with the development of a new international division of labour, Ireland has experienced a marked increase in inflow of investment over the last few years. It has been dominated largely by the establishment of foreign-owned branch plants, which tend to concentrate on engineering and machinery, textiles and clothing, and electrical and electronic goods. Characteristically, the commodities and semi-finished products are for export (Perrons 1981:82). There are a number of reasons for this influx:

> The low level of development of native industry, the existence of a surplus of relatively low-cost, inexperienced industrial workers, the existence of coastal sites and land for development, relatively lax laws on pollution and working conditions, an abundance of relatively small towns but with access to the labour supply in the surrounding rural regions, an improving infrastructure and finally the

existence of a highly stable political system in which both of the major parties are fully committed to attracting foreign capital. (Perrons 1981:93)

On top of the abundant supply of labour, and despite 'the merging of Irish and UK wage levels', it seems that labour costs and labour pliability have proved quite significant in industrial relocation. The Industrial Development Authority (IDA) has had an important but by no means key role in attracting industry to Ireland. By contrast, it has been 'the very peripheral characteristics of the country which have proved to be attractive to the foreign branch plants' (Perrons 1981:94).

Yet the impact of this form of industrial development has been mixed. While Ireland's growth rate in output, exports and imports has been impressive, there has been much criticism of the broader impact of economic growth:

These criticisms focus on the low level of value added created in Ireland, the lack of linkages with local firms, the lack of research and development activities and the lack of development of new products in Ireland, meaning that the economy becomes dependent on imported technology with few skills being developed within Ireland. Further criticisms relate to the effects of the strategy on the balance of payments for when payments for royalties, licences and imports are taken into account together with the expatriation of profits and interest payments on funds initially borrowed by the state, then the overall effect can be negative. Further problems have arisen more recently in relation to the overall level of the state expenditure... as the level of state expenditure rises while the numbers employed remains stationary or even declines and an increasing burden of taxation falls on a decreasing tax-paying population. (Perrons 1981:95)

Even more importantly, perhaps, industrial development has seemed to have little overall impact on unemployment, which runs at about 9 per cent of the workforce, and, in fact, new industry seems unable to generate an equivalent number of jobs to those being lost in the established industries. The response of the Industrial Development Authority has been to try and promote high-technology firms and also develop domestic industries and small firms. However, these strategies are unlikely to be successful, given the world competition for high-technology firms and the difficulties of establishing domestic industry at a time when international firms seem to be developing a stranglehold on production. Increasingly, the type of industry that is locating in Ireland, is on the whole, not labour-intensive and, because it is export-orientated, requires low wages to maintain its international competitiveness. Finally, the decision-making part of the firm is located elsewhere and, therefore, is unlikely to adopt a strategy attuned to Irish needs. It will rationalise its operations according to its international operations, not those conditions existing in any one country (Perrons 1981).

Semiperipheral − or sub-imperial −countries, of which South Africa is a good example, are also important as staging posts for capital transfers. Existing 'as "centres" within the world "periphery", they exercise a regional hegemony akin to the global dominance of an imperial power but at a localized scale' (Rogerson 1981:406). In the past, British capital dominated foreign investment in South Africa. The South African state provided strong support for investment; the mineral wealth (gold and diamonds to name but two) in this part of Africa was legendary, and migratory labour was a significant factor in keeping wage-costs down. During the 1960s the changing investment climate on a world scale led to a boost in capital investment in South Africa:

Transnationals from the leading industrial nations − especially the United States and the Federal Republic of Germany poured capital into South Africa in competition with the British whose colonial roots gave them a head start. By the mid '70s, transnational corporations owned forty percent of South Africa's manufacturing industry, almost two thirds of its bank assets, and about ninety percent of its oil refining capacity. Seidman and O'Keefe 1980:2)

For our purposes, the changing circumstances of the neighbouring independent African states of Botswana, Swaziland and Lesotho during this period is more significant than the impact of transnationals within South Africa. Joined in a customs union with South Africa since 1910, they became economic appendages to the sub-imperial power, exporting labour, food and raw materials to South Africa and importing manufactures and investment goods. With independence in the 1960s, an essentially similar strategy was maintained; the new governing classes 'were committed to a path of dependent capitalist development which involves a more intensive participation as peripheral producers in the world economy' (Rogerson 1981:408). The customs union was renegotiated in 1969 to allow Botswana, Lesotho and Swaziland to protect infant industries, while all three countries set up state-sponsored industrial development corporations and offered generous incentives to investors – including assurances against expropriation, few restrictions against profit repatriation, tax incentives, monopoly rights and abundant assistance from local development banks and corporations. Yet, despite their wish to industrialise, the bulk of multinational capital has been invested in primary resources. In Swaziland, most investment has been in agri-business (sugar, pineapples, forest products); in Botswana, capital has flowed into copper, nickel and diamonds; while in Lesotho, diamonds are the chief investibles. Tourism has grown in significance for all three states. However, the impact of these types of investment has been relatively small:

> The pattern is typically one of 'export enclave development' with associated manufacturing, if present at all, confined to simple raw material processing. No substantive backward or forward linkages are present within the host peripheral economies of Southern Africa. (Rogerson 1982:198)

On the whole, though, industry in southern Africa remains strongly concentrated in South Africa, on whom Botswana, Lesotho and Swaziland are still dependent for industrial goods. There has been some development of import-substitution manufacturing in Swaziland, and a little export-orientated industry but, in general, industrial policy has met with little success. Clearly, strong state support, a cheap disciplined labour force and all the other attractions of the three southern African states have provided insufficient inducement to the multinational manufacturers.

Part of the explanation for this lies in the relationships with South Africa.

> South Africa's burgeoning manufacturing industries sold their mass produced goods throughout the region, undermining pre-existing handicrafts and small-scale industries, and further destroying precapitalist modes of production . . . South African based transnationals and South African mining finance houses, have expanded capital-intensive mining and agri-business projects in neighbouring countries to feed South African factories or to ship raw materials overseas to earn profits and foreign exchange to finance South African growth . . . Together, the transnational corporations and mining finance houses annually extract as much as a third of the neighbouring countries' gross domestic production in profits, interest, dividends, and high salaries of their managerial personnel.

(Seidman and O'Keefe 1980:4)

South African multinational corporations – such as the Anglo-American Group which in 1976 controlled at least 140 different companies in southern Africa – play a substantial role in investment in nearby countries, with the result that the division of labour within the region complements South Africa's specialisation. The South African state has played a key role in trying to prevent any reorganisation of the division of labour which would see South Africa's major industries relocating in nearby countries or becoming industrial powers in their own right. One action prohibits a protected 'infant industry' from neighbouring states selling on the South African market (Rogerson 1981:407-8). Moreover, 'opposition from Pretoria prevented Honda from initiating a motor assembly plant in Lesotho in 1971 and, more recently, thwarted proposals for the establishment of television assembly operations in both Swaziland and Lesotho' (Rogerson 1982: 199). The southern African states have two major potential export markets not available to South Africa – Black Africa and, as a result of the Lomé Convention, the European Economic Community – yet it is still questionable whether they will struggle free of South African economic domination and, if they do, whether these potential trade links will produce any benefits. It has been said of the Lomé Convention that it 'perpetuates inequalities and inherited Euro-African linkages, and generally rationalises rather than challenges the inequities inherent in the established international division of labour' (Rogerson 1981:411). Underdeveloped southern Africa, it seems, is unlikely to play a key role in the new international division of labour for the time being.

In marked contrast, Brazil is one of the 'new industrialising countries' and faces problems more akin to Ireland than southern Africa. Newfarmer and Topik (1982) examined Brazil's electrical industry in order to test the consequences of multinational-led industrialisation. Dependency theory was used to generate three hypotheses about the sort of changes that could be expected: first, that the benefits of corporate investment, due to a transfer of investible surplus, would accrue in favour of the corporations rather than the host countries; second, corporations would undermine the domestic economy by suppressing local enterprise, introducing inappropriate technology, emphasising inequities in income distribution, and inducing new consumer tastes; and thirdly, foreign investors might be expected to 'pervert or subvert host country political processes' (Newfarmer and Topik 1982:33). Their empirical research generally affirmed the first two hypotheses, and they rejected the third. Multinational corporations in the electrical industry received an unfair share of gains because they secured an international oligopoly and raised prices well above marginal costs.

> The distributional consequence of these concerted actions of the MNCs was to increase returns to the owners of capital and techno- logy located in the advanced countries and their managers at the expense of consumers in the developing countries . . . In other words, the concentrated structure of international production and the restrictive practices it facilitated served to shift investible surplus from the developing periphery to the industrial centre. (Newfarmer and Topik 1982:52)

Moreover, the multinational corporation's market power produced 'a symbiotic structural tie between the domestic and international industry that favoured foreign corporations by leaving them in "control" of the industry, contrary to what occurred in the indus- trialised countries' (Newfarmer and Topik 1982:52). Yet the study found no 'perversion' or 'subversion' of politics: instead it found that political influence grew out of the steady emergence of an alliance between foreign and domestic 'groups'.

Conclusion

This chapter has attempted to sketch in some of the main issues raised in the literature on imperialism, capitalist restructuring and under- development, as well as highlight the contribution of geographers to this literature. In large part, underdevelopment, when dealt with at the international scale, is a geographic concept − underdevelopment implies a *geographic* differentiation in income or whatever measure of well-being is thought appropriate. When we say a nation is underdevel- oped we mean that people living in a particular *place* are disadvantaged *vis-à-vis* people living in another place. Some theories designed to account for underdevelopment (for example, Wallerstein) are geo- graphic theories based on assumptions of transfers of value and econ- omic surplus between places. Yet we find that geographers as a whole have played a very small role in the development of underdevelopment theory. Moreover, looking at their growing contribution it is noticeable that it is very fragmented: some use dependency theory, some world systems theory, and all blend this with material on multinationals and the new international division of labour, but there is not, as yet, much coherency to the approach.

Another characteristic of the recent work on internationalisation is its focus on labour:

> In the literature this new international division of labour is some-times depicted simply as a crude reaction to the cheaper labour costs and more tractable workers to be found in the periphery, the whole process being set in motion as a result of various enabling conditions like new developments in transport and communications. Whilst this depiction is certainly an important component in current changes the reasons for 'relocation' are usually far more complex than this and stem from the fact that global corporations now have a world-wide character. They are therefore able to pick and choose loca-tions for particular production processes and react to prevailing political and fiscal conditions faster and more efficiently than previously in a continual process of *locational rationalisation* that causes the fixed capital of a production plant of a multinational corporation, although it may well be remunerative by its own standards, to be checked continuously against more profitable employment of capital elsewhere. (Taylor and Thrift 1982:6)

Finally, the literature discussed in this chapter focuses strongly on patterns of international organisation, to the neglect of the social and economic histories of particular places, the contemporary class struc-ture, and social and economic geography. It is to theories of underdevel-opment at a much smaller scale and which are place specific that we turn in the next chapter.

Notes

1. Though it is interesting to note that the experience of Russia in the second half of the nineteenth century led Marx to modify the 'necessary' component of this argument.
2. Lenin (1965) was written in 1917, while Luxemburg (1963) was first pub-lished in 1913.
3. Palma (1978:898-911) identifies three – the theory of underdevelopment (Frank), dependency as method (Cardoso), and the obstacles to development group (Sunkel).
4. Among the critics of Frank or Wallerstein are Laclau (1971), Taylor (1974), Lall (1975), Regan and Eliot-Hurst (1976), Roxborough (1976), Brenner (1977), Leys (1977, 1978), Skocpol (1977), Palma (1978), Petras and Trachte (1979),

Browett (1980b), George (1980) and Gülalp (1981). By contrast, Bienefeld (1980:5) puts the view that 'as concerns the essence of the approach [of dependency theory much of the critique is misplaced and misconceived'.

5. See, for instance, Kaplan (1978), Goldfrank (1979), Hopkins and Wallerstein (1980). For a favourable summary of Wallerstein's contributions see Alexander (1980).

6. See Magdoff (1969, 1978), Barratt Brown (1974), Kiernan (1974), Mack, Plant and Doyle (1979), Bell (1980) and Mommsen (1981). Both Kiernan (1974) and Mommsen (1981) include discussions of bourgeois theories of imperialism.

7. Examples include Jalée (1968, 1969), Rhodes (1970), Szentes (1971).

8. Amin (1974a, 1976, 1977, 1980a) has made a substantial contribution to underdevelopment theory, distinguishing between capitalist development at the 'centre' which is 'self-centred' and links the production of mass consumption and capital goods, with the 'disarticulated' production in the periphery which concentrates on exports and luxury goods. For an early statement of the model see Amin (1974b), and for its application to Black Africa see Amin (1972). For useful summaries and critiques of Amin's work see Leaver (1979), Brewer (1980: 233-57), Jonas (1980), Smith (1980) and Schiffer (1981).

9. For a brief summary and critique of Emmanuel's theory of unequal exchange see Brewer (1980:208-32) or Johnstone (1980). For more lengthy comment see Bettelheim (1972), Evans (1976) and Sau (1978).

10. A handful of geographers have used a Wallersteinian framework to examine the most recent phase of industrialisation. For example, see Ehrensaft and Armstrong's (1978) work on New Zealand, Taylor and Thrift's (1981) analysis of the Australian space economy and Rogerson's (1981) examination of South Africa. Characteristically, the prime focus of this work has been 'semi-peripheral' countries and their relations with the core and the periphery.

11. For a history of crisis theories see Shaikh (1978).

12. The recent, edited collections of Hamilton and Linge (1979, 1981) and Rees, Hewings and Stafford (1981) are an indication of the sort of work being tackled by industrial geographers, while the book edited by Taylor and Thrift (1982) focuses particularly on the multinational corporation.

13. Several articles on the semi-periphery are useful, including Seidman and O'Keefe (1980) and Rogerson (1981, 1982) on South Africa, and Perrons (1981) on Ireland. Work on peripheral countries includes Britton (1982) on tourism in Fiji, Forbes (1982) on energy imperialism in Indonesia, and Newfarmer and Topik (1982) on Brazil's electrical industry.

5 POST-DEPENDENCY THEORIES OF UNDERDEVELOPMENT

The literature on the 'articulation of modes of production' grew in parallel to dependency theories but, following the latter's failure to tackle Marxist analysis of production relations or provide a focus for the micro-analysis of underdevelopment, articulation research has come to occupy a more central position in the debate on underdevelopment.[1] Briefly, this literature is based upon a theory of imperialism which sees the securing of cheap labour supplies as the dominant impulse in the expansion of capitalism outwards from the centre. In the main though, it focuses on the articulation of capitalist and pre-capitalist modes of production in peripheral social formations, demonstrating the dominant role of capitalism within articulation and the way in which this dominance is used to 'conserve' and 'dissolve' the pre-capitalist modes of production. As Leys (1977:104) explains

> it transforms them from modes of production subject to their own 'laws of motion' to modes of production whose motion is primarily determined by the laws operating in the capitalist mode of production, and hence also progressively transforms the content, and eventually the form, of their relations of production.

Various forms of indigenous production (subsistence production, the housing sector, petty production) are able to persist in Third World nations, not because of their own dynamic but, largely because they are useful to the operation of the dominant sector (for example, squatter housing keeps low the cost of labour) or they perform a necessary task which the capitalist sector would find unprofitable to provide (for example, the distribution of fresh food and vegetables in the city). At the same time, however, these forms of activity are at the mercy of the dominant mode. Should capitalist firms be forced into the area previously the preserve of non-capitalist enterprises, they would invariably destroy the competition quickly and effectively through their superior resources and marketing strategies, and if necessary, through the support of the government.

The Articulation of Modes of Production

Like dependency and world systems theories, articulation theories also have roots in either the work of Marx and Engels on pre-capitalist modes of production[2] or the capitalist mode of production,[3] and antecedents in the work of earlier generations of classical Marxist theorists such as Lenin and Kautsky.[4] However, it was really Althusser and Balibar's project on Marxism which paved the way for the recent resurgence of research. It was Balibar, in fact, who tried to put together a theory of history using concepts and tools, such as mode of production and social formation, which had been sharpened by Althusser:

> we can say that the first problem for a history as a science, for a theoretical history, is the determination of the combination on which depend the elements which are to be analysed, i.e. it is to determine the structure of a sphere of relative autonomy, such as what Marx calls the process of production and its modes. (Balibar 1979:250)

He argued that history should be constituted as 'a science of discontinuous modes of production' (Balibar 1979:257). Within the theory of transition from one mode of production to another:

> the *dislocation* between the connexions and instances in transition periods merely reflects *the coexistence of two* (or more) *modes of production in a single 'simultaneity', and the dominance of one of them over the other*. (Balibar 1979:307)

The concept of articulation was, therefore, an 'anatomical metaphor' for the ways in which different modes of production are linked together, and the focus of articulation research the 'laws of co-existence and hierarchy' of the constituent parts of the social formation (Foster-Carter 1978:52-4).

Although this work was not directed specifically to underdevelopment theory, a theory of history clearly had great importance for an understanding of the protracted transition to capitalism in the periphery. The relevance of this work was first made clear by the critique which Laclau launched against Frank.[5] Essentially, his complaint was that Frank's sweeping description of all styles of production in the modern world as capitalist was quite false. Laclau insisted that feudal relations still existed in many parts of Latin America (and had even been resurrected) precisely because of their articulation with capital which had, in fact, preserved them because they were of greater use to the capitalist mode in their original or near-original form (Leys 1977:103-5). The focus of the articulation literature on the structure of production rather than exchange marked a significant shift within underdevelopment theory and directed it more specifically towards the mainstream of Marxist literature, which had always scorned the so-called 'market Marxism'.

The proliferation of literature adopting an articulation of modes of production approach has been dealt with elsewhere.[6] Suffice it to note here that it was originally closely associated with French economic anthropologists, such as Meillassoux, Terray, and Rey,[7] and later came to be the focus of the 'new economic anthropology' in the English-speaking world, attaining prominence in journals such as *Economy and Society* and *Critique of Anthropology*. In more recent years the articulation approach has been used to enlighten a much greater range of concrete research, including imperialism, urban petty commodity production, peasants, uneven spatial development and so on.

The most comprehensive recent attempt to develop a theory of the articulation of modes of production is by Taylor.[8] He rejects the concept of underdevelopment and substitutes the notion of a transitional social formation 'which is dominated by an articulation of (at least) two modes of production – a capitalist and a non-capitalist mode – in which the former is, or is becoming, increasingly dominant over the other' (Taylor 1979:101-2). The result is that peripheral social formations are characterised by a series of dislocations between levels of the social formation.

> As opposed to the previous period of determinancy in the last instance by a particular non-capitalist mode, in which the different levels were *adapted to one another*, the latter are now *dislocated with respect to each other, and with respect to the existing economic structure itself.* Imperialist penetration intervenes economically, politically and ideologically within these dislocated levels in order to ensure the increasing dominance of the capitalist mode of production, and to create [a] restricted and uneven form of development. (Taylor 1979:103)

Thus Taylor substitutes a notion of restricted and uneven development for underdevelopment, and illustrating his argument with empirical evidence from the agricultural, extractive and manufacturing sectors concludes:

> there exists a pattern of development characterised by a highly
> uneven sectoral configuration, in which a dominant yet externally
> dependent sector restricts the development of other sectors . . .
> Trade relations between industrial capitalist and Third World econ-
> omies constantly reinforce the reproduction of this restricted and
> uneven development, and its effects are manifest in a process of
> commodity exchange which enables a major transference of value
> from the Third World to the industrial economies. (Taylor 1979:69)

Taylor looks at capitalist penetration and at articulation during three
main periods. The first phase of capitalist expansion occurred during
the period of dominance of merchant capital. To a large extent expansion was restricted by feudal constraints, but did allow for the accumulation of money capital and, hence, provided a platform for later capitalist expansion. During this phase the pre-capitalist modes of production in the periphery were not much altered, although some were
strengthened and new modes were created. The second period commenced when the capitalist mode of production became dominant in
Europe. A declining rate of profit created a need for new markets, and,
gradually, through the exchange of non-equivalents, there came about a
transfer of resources from the periphery to capitalist countries. This
period also marked the commencement of massive disruption within
the pre-capitalist modes in the periphery and, notably, the beginnings
of the widespread separation of producers from the means of production. The third period came about with the bringing together of industrial and banking capital to create finance capital, which, in the Leninist
sense allowed the export of capital and the beginnings of the age of
imperialism. Separation of pre-capitalist producers from the means of
production was speeded up, and capitalist relations were created, but a
pattern of uneven development resulted because imperialism is selective
in its interests.

An example drawn from research in Indonesia illustrates some of the
detailed concrete research associated with the articulation literature.
The case is a study by the anthropologist J.S. Kahn of small-scale production, chiefly blacksmithing, in the highland zone of West Sumatra.[9]
One of Kahn's aims was to examine the articulation of the three main
modes of production in West Sumatra: large-scale commodity production (the capitalist mode), small-scale commodity production and subsistence production. His purpose was to demonstrate that the domin-

ance of the capitalist mode was expressed through the orientation of the subordinate modes to the reproduction of capitalism.

The critical process in this articulation is the transfer of value from small to large scale production primarily through the mechanism of 'unequal exchange'. The essence of the process is that returns to petty producers are less than the minimum wage-rate which is based on the cost of reproduction of labour power. This is so, Kahn claims, because labour is not entirely independent of the large subsistence mode of production; subsistence production bears the brunt of the cost of the reproduction of labour and, thus, allows the cash returns to labour to drop below the minimum value necessary to reproduction (Kahn 1975: 22-7). The result is that the exchange-value of the petty commodity production is lower than its (use-) value which, together with the fact that the output of capitalist production is generally priced higher than its value, means that exchange results in a transfer of value (that is, labour-time) from petty to capitalist production (Kahn 1978:113-14). The articulation of capitalist, petty commodity and subsistence modes of production brings about stagnation in the last two, whilst keeping the capitalist production strong.

Petty production, however, does not simply remain unchanged. It goes through cycles of expansion and contraction, but the forces of articulation are too strong to allow these cycles to bring about increased productivity through the revolutionary transformation of the forces of production. The mechanisms in Kahn's study area have worked in at least two ways. Crises in world commodity prices in the early 1920s led to an expansion of petty commodity production in West Sumatra, primarily through an amalgamation of small enterprises and increased efficiency due to economies of scale. However, this success induced migration to the productive areas which meant that the labour available to agriculture decreased. This, in turn, brought about increases in the price of rice. Combined with stagnation in world commodity prices it was sufficient to cripple the expanding petty commodity sector which returned to atomised production. The cycle was repeated in the late 1950s and early 1960s, but this time the cause of amalgamation and increased scale of production in the petty commodity sector was the weakening of the capitalist sector which Sukarno's erratic economic policies had brought about. With the reimposition of capitalist interests after 1966 the petty commodity sector again returned to atomised production. Thus Kahn argues that the small scale of petty production is not a permanent characteristic, but a product of the particular process of articulation at a point in time

(Kahn 1975:146-55).

A Critique of the 'Articulation' Approach

Whilst attempting to illustrate the emergence of a distinctive literature on the articulation of modes of production, it would be incorrect to impute too great a degree of homogeneity to this research. The literature has both strengths and weaknesses. On the one hand, the articulation approach has overcome the problem of scale implicit in the dependency and world systems research. Witness the paper by Bradby which was one of the earlier articulation studies. It drew together two major themes: what are the motivating forces behind capitalist world expansion, and, more importantly as far as the criticism of underdevelopment theory is concerned, how does the structure of the pre-capitalist mode of production influence the process of articulation (Bradby 1975)? Similarly, Kahn's work illustrates the importance of looking at the conjuncture of capitalist and pre-capitalist modes, not as unilateral penetration but as a reciprocal meeting of systems whose interests seldom correspond. Equally, though, the empirical studies cited above are guilty of giving pre-eminence in explanations of the underdevelopment of petty production to exchange mechanisms and the transfer of value which these bring about. As Brenner (1977) has argued, dependence on the flow of surplus across space puts stress on a quantitative process producing underdevelopment and masks the qualitative processes behind it. Just as accumulation begs the question of why the accumulated surplus should be used for productive investment, so the loss of economic surplus cannot provide the only explanation for the poverty and low productivity of the petty producers. Kahn recognises this and has pointed to themes which would help diversify the explanation. Included among the additional factors that need to be considered are the role of the state (and incidentally the influence of external forces upon it), the influence of the world economic policy, and the ideology of development.[10] Despite this, the original point stands — we should beware of allowing the concept of transfer of value to become the main pillar of the argument.

However, technical problems of this sort are really subsumed by a more fundamental series of questions which ask — What is meant by a mode of production? Has the articulation literature fallen into the trap of economic determinism? What place do the various classes occupy within this analysis?

Friedman has cast his net wide by criticising the use of concepts of mode of production in the method of historical materialism itself. His objections are threefold. First, much of this work, in his words, is guilty of 'mechanical materialism':

> that is direct determination of social forms by the productive process, by the organisation of the immediate work processes or by the 'fundamental distribution' i.e. social form of appropriation (relations of production), of nature and/or extortion of surplus. (Friedman 1976:3)

Second, taking the state or the society as the unit of analysis allocates the ideology of political independence an unearned legitimacy and autonomy. Both the international division of labour and the interdependence of production and reproduction specifically negate the validity of this level of analysis. Third, as neither production nor reproduction is, or can be, effectively contained by national boundaries it is false to seek socialist development through the pursuit of redistribution within the nation (Friedman 1976:3-8; 1974:444-89). In sum, Friedman is critical of the concept of mode of production because it fails to embrace the totality of a system of reproduction which he feels is the essence of Marxist analysis:

> Mode of production as relations of exploitation-appropriation + relations of production can never be a system. As relations of exploitation-appropriation + relations of realisation, circulation + forces of production it does become a system of reproduction. But then, it may contain numerous local production processes at different technological levels, as well as a plurality of relations of exploitation-appropriation, thus contradicting the fundamental tenet of orthodox theory. (Friedman 1976:15)

Banaji (1977), similarly, feels much of the articulation literature adopts a reductionist approach to the concept of mode of production. It transforms a complex and all-embracing phenomenon to a simplistic abstraction of an empirical observation, based on the delineation of the form of exploitation or the labour process. This reductionist error is responsible for the tendency to treat articulation as a form of dualism, in which non-capitalist modes are defined as a specific kind of subjugation of labour, deprived of their own laws of motion. This:

has the consequence that the complex conjuncture of the world economy becomes reduced to an undifferentiated 'capitalist' (Frank) economy or is simply divided into that economy and homogeneous 'pre-capitalist' entities based on formal appearances. (Wolpe 1980:30)

Instead, Banaji (1977:10) would prefer to define a mode of production as 'a definite totality of historical laws of motion'. What we can learn, then, from Banaji's argument is that we need to incorporate the laws of motion into a conceptualisation of a mode of production. This theme will be returned to later.[11]

Related to the reductionist tendency in the conceptualisation of mode of production is the accusation that articulation theory has often been reduced to crude economic determinism.

Reification aside, too little attention has been paid to other 'instances' and 'practices' than the economic: notably the political, not to mention those areas (ideology, religion, kinship ideas) which correspond to peoples' own consciousness of their position. (Foster-Carter 1978:77)

Mouzelis' criticism of Taylor echoes this point. He asks why it is only the economic instance which is theorised in the articulation literature and calls for the 'relatively autonomous theorisation of the political', avoiding both:

(a) the *reductionist* explanation of political institutions and developments in terms of the reproductive requirements of capital, or as mere 'conditions of existence' of the economy;
(b) the relegation of the study of politics to the residual spheres of *conjunctural* analysis (Mouzelis 1980:369-70).

Finally, the failure of articulation studies to adequately tackle class formation is a reflection of the economism implicit in this tendency.[12] Class structure is crucial because it is the mediator between the mode of production and human action. Leys is critical of this failing both in the mode of production literature, and in underdevelopment theory. The concentration on the economic leads to an overlooking of the political: of the importance of class domination, class struggle and the role of the state (Leys 1977:105). To this list can be added human agency. By failing to develop this the mode of production literature is rendered as sterile as previous versions of underdevelopment theory because it implicitly accepts the mechanistic determinism of economic forces and provides no basis for human action. Where class is considered it is assumed to be a derivative of immediate economic forces, without a history and puppet-like in its response to deeper, hidden structures.

Class and the Response to Economism

It has been argued in this and the previous chapter that an explicit analysis of class has been conspicuously absent from both the dependency/world systems and the articulation literature; even though, in the case of the latter at least, the class structure component of the social relations of production is clearly a key element of the concept of mode of production. Yet without an explicit understanding of class structure, this literature betrays a fundamental theme of Marxist research and, effectively, it has been argued, prevents us grasping uneven- or under-development. To be more precise, class analysis makes a particular contribution to at least three main aspects of underdevelopment theory. First, it is only through an historical class analysis that we can give due recognition to, and properly put into perspective, the role of people, their sufferings and struggles, and the reciprocal relationships they maintain with the mode of production and the social formation. Second, class analysis is basic to an understanding of underdevelopment because the core of this process is the method of appropriating surplus by the dominant class. Thus we pose the problem of underdevelopment as one of exploitation between classes and ask why it is that dominant classes depend largely on the extraction of absolute surplus labour rather than relative surplus labour. Why are the dominated classes not exploited (strictly in the Marxist sense) more, through reinvestment and increased productivity, and, hence, developed?[13] Part of the answer lies with the method of integration into the world capitalist economy, but part lies also in the history of class formation within the social formation. It is the latter which has been neglected in the recent critical literature and to which class analysis can contribute.[14] Third, a class analysis provides a basis for the explanation of recent political events in underdeveloped social formations and, more importantly, provides an analysis which has some use in the fight against underdevelopment. Earlier versions of underdevelopment theory led to either a fatalistic acceptance of underdevelopment or naive talk of autarky. Class analysis, whilst based on an understanding of the power of economic forces, ultimately locates the force of history in class struggle and, therefore, allocates to women and men a strong influence on their destiny.

Such a sweeping, optimistic set of assertions may overstate the case, but hopefully not, for it must be borne in mind that there are many conceptual problems still to be tackled. Not least among these is agreement on the meaning of the concept of class, which is used in a variety of ways.[15] Another problem arises from the fact that the social formations of the underdeveloped world are by no means 'pure' modes of production, so that economic classes are the products of capitalism and its articulated relationships with pre-capitalist modes of production. This means that whilst the primary contradiction is, as in the capitalist mode, between bourgeoisie and proletariat — accumulators of capital and 'free labour' respectively — the middle or intermediate classes are far more numerically significant than under capitalism. It has resulted in all sorts of difficulties. Breman's (1976:1939-41) attempt to specify the class formation in cities characterised by extensive petty commodity production, led to him suggesting the existence of not only a labour elite (or proletariat), but also a petty bourgoisie, sub-proletariat and a lumpenproletariat. However, the Indonesian PKI (Partai Komunis Indonesia) recognised four main rural classes: landlords, rich peasants, middle peasants, and poor and landless peasants.[16] Both these classifications suffer from their failure to grasp the significance of the social formation as a whole. The urban-rural distinction is a superficial one and the categories which have been built upon them are static and trivial (for example, the distinction between a sub-proletariat and a lumpenproletariat). If class analysis is to contribute to the reformulation of underdevelopment theory then it must transcend these difficulties.

Class analysis, in the context of underdevelopment in general, has meant quite different things to different people.[17] Amin, for instance, is representative of the attempt to reconcile class analysis and his own distinctive version of dependency/world systems theory. He tackles class from an international perspective arguing that the unequal international division of labour and an international class structure are both products of the contemporary imperial system. Underdevelopment, then, is a product of the superexploitation of labour in the periphery. Superexploitation is the transfer of surplus labour which occurs as a result of the poor remuneration to labour in the periphery which, in turn, is proportionately much lower than the productivity of labour in the periphery relative to labour in the centre (this is a sort of class-

based 'unequal exchange'). Amin concludes that the indigenous bourgeoisie play a dependent role in this process: the local exploiting classes
are merely intermediaries, subordinate allies, in this process of exploitation.

> That is precisely where their 'responsibility' lies − in their collusion
> with imperialism. And it is precisely because imperialism profits by
> this superexploitation that it operates through these international
> class alliances. (Amin 1980b:21)

Whilst invoking a methodology based on exploitation and class struggle,
Amin sees the role of international capital as supreme, and the
domestic bourgeoisie as relatively unimportant.

Rey, on the other hand, has attempted to reconcile class analysis and
articulation.[18] Though the roots of his approach to articulation are
firmly in the tradition of Althusser and Balibar his chief concern is to
see the articulation of the feudal (though not lineage) and capitalist
modes of production through the relations between four classes: capitalists and workers in capitalist production, and landlords and peasants
in feudal production. In the first stage of articulation an alliance of
capitalists and landlords occurs. The latter expel peasants from the land
in response to opportunities for higher rents, forcing them into wage
labour. From others they demand cash rents, thereby forcing peasants
to produce for the market and simultaneously create a demand for cash
goods. Capitalism is established in the second stage, but though 'all the
bourgeoisies of the world burn with desire to develop the "underdeveloped" countries' (Rey 1973:16), capitalism's penetration is uneven
and incomplete. Rey, rather controversially, suggests extra-economic
means, such as violence, are used during this stage to ensure the
continued breakdown of the feudal mode and a steady supply of labour
for the capitalist mode. When, finally, capitalism is able to take over all
agriculture, the third stage is reached, and the transition from feudalism
to capitalism is complete.

In addition, Rey has also concerned himself with the somewhat
different case of the articulation of the lineage mode of production with
capitalism. In Rey's view, capitalism is 'homificent' − its demands are
constant. Therefore, the protracted transition to capitalism is the
product not of capitalism (as in Frank's work) but of the particular composition of the pre-capitalist mode and the way this articulates with
capitalism. Basing his interpretation on empirical research in Congo-
Brazzaville, Rey argues that the lineage mode of production produces

two classes: chiefs and their dependents. Articulation is then inter-preted through these class relationships, enabling Rey to demonstrate:

> that the lineage mode of production was very well suited to gener-ating a supply of slaves for export during the period of the slave trade, rather poor at producing goods for export, and quite incapable by itself of generating either a proletariat or a marketable supply of food to support a proletariat. (Brewer 1980:192)

The nascent, indigenous bourgeoisie emerges out of the group that organises and controls the slave trade, but development remains fettered by the persistence of the benefits which the capitalist mode derives from its subordination of the lineage mode.

While both Rey and Amin attempted to locate class analysis within prevailing structuralist analyses, other authors have tried to dispense with much of this support and to focus primarily on class itself. In so doing, by contrast with Rey and Amin, both Petras and Trachte, and Leys, give the domestic bourgeoisie much greater prominence in their class analyses. Petras and Trachte (1979) argue that the critical set of relationships in the periphery is the triangular set which links the process of capital accumulation, the class structure and the state. Whereas the 'old' contradiction lay in the mechanisms for the direct extraction of surplus by the imperial power, the 'new' contradiction is the critical social strata which lies between imperial capital and the labour force. The keys to understanding underdevelopment are the class alliances that are formed within the periphery, and between it and the centre states, and the important role played by the imperial and peripheral bourgeois state in formalising class alliances and facilitating capital accumulation.

Similarly, Leys has revised his analysis of the dependent underdevel-opment of Kenya, lamenting his previous failure to give due prominence to class formation and the domestic bourgeoisie:

> Instead of seeing the strength of the historical tendency lying behind the emergence of the African bourgeoisie I tended to see only the relatively small size and technical weakness of African capital in face of international capital, and to envisage the state as little more than a registrar of this general imbalance; rather than seeing the barriers of capital scale and technology as relative, and the state as the registrar of the leading edge of indigenous capital in its assault on these barriers. (Leys 1978:252-3)

The implications of Ley's revisions are enormous. Whereas with his dependency framework the persistence of underdevelopment through peripheral capitalism appeared likely, his closer examination of the history of capital accumulation of a domestic bourgeois class led him to believe that:

> capitalist production relations may be considerably extended in a periphery social formation, and the productive forces may be considerably expanded within and through them, for reasons having primarily to do with the configuration of class forces preceding and during the colonial period. (Leys 1978:261)

Briefly, the reassertion of their dominance during the 1960s by a pre-capitalist accumulating class, combined with the creation of a proletariat during the colonial period by the settler plantation owners, created a set of economic relations in which appropriation of surplus labour increasingly depended upon increasing relative surplus labour (that is, productivity) rather than absolute surplus labour. Leys uses Kenyan data to illustrate the Brenner argument about the importance of class formation and qualitative changes in the structure of production in an explanation of capitalist development. Needless to say, there are other studies which have focused on class formation in an explanation of underdevelopment, but space forbids elaboration here.[19]

Concluding his critical review of Frank, Browett states unequivocally that the analysis of underdevelopment can only proceed in one of two directions: through Marxist analysis or through a reconstituted reformism. Dependency theories no longer provide, as they once did, a third alternative.[20] One may agree with this proposition, as far as it goes, but what are its implications? As Leaver (1979:325) has pointed out, Marxism is fast becoming the exemplar of pluralism, so where does that lead us? Should underdeveopment theory be pursued through a critical examination of the laws of capital accumulation (Amin) or the articulation of modes of production (Rey), through painstaking theorising (Althusser) or national liberation (Caldwell). Or, alternatively, is it that a theory of underdevelopment cannot be reached through a single methodological strategy or a single research focus? The problem is far more complex than that. There are no easy solutions to underdevelopment, nor will reconstitution be simple. The primary task is to attempt a synthesis of the needlessly polarised structuralist and class analysis viewpoints on underdevelopment. As Foster-Carter (1978:7) points out, we must eschew crude eclecticism, nevertheless:

it does seem to be true, and wrong, that the very recrudescence of Marxist analysis is tending, like a tide going out, to create little rock pools increasingly unconnected to one another, in which narrowly circumscribed issues are discussed separately and without thought of their mutual implications.

The excesses of economism contained within the articulation literature have already been discussed. Equally, the instinctive appeal of a return to class analysis must be balanced by an appreciation of its limitations. Mouzelis (1980:372) has been critical of what he terms class reductionism:

> the tendency to elevate classes and class struggles to a universal principle of explanation, and to forget that, especially in the third world, there are social conflicts which are not exclusively or principally based on class but on other types of cleavages (ethnic, tribal, religious, etc.).

In a more general sense, the methodology of class analysis has been said to lead to a 'formless historical relativism'. Yet, even more importantly, putting the structuralist and class analysis approaches into the perspective of the social sciences as a whole, it is clear that both have strengths and weaknesses and are the focus of much attention at the present time. The question then is not whether synthesis is necessary, but what is to be synthesised and how it is to be achieved.

It is true that we need to reassert the method of historical materialism, yet both the Marx of *Capital* and the Marx of the pre-capitalist modes of production have their supporters within the literature. However, we should begin with a critical evaluation of the main trends within both the current and the historic literature, not one or the other. An ideal beginning is to look at the literature on imperialism. The rejection of the dependency and world systems concepts, as they were used by Frank and Wallerstein, does not mean that the world scale of analysis should also be discarded. Quite the contrary. The pattern of world capital accumulation is still among the primary forces determining the pattern of world development. What we must guard against is the oversimplification of this role. As Amin has pointed out, the world capitalist system cannot be reduced to the capitalist mode of production; moreover capitalist expansion takes different forms over time and over space, with the result that the periphery also fulfils varying roles. This essential complexity was often lost in earlier theorising. More specifically, the integration of the world system through market relations and the subsequent transfers of surplus between social formations does not provide the basis for an explanation of underdevelopment, so we must reject Frank's 'contradiction of continuity through change'. Clearly, at certain stages there has been a substantial net flow of surplus from the poor nations to the colonial and neo-colonial powers, but at other times the flow has been reversed, either by the heavy cost of colonial administrations or extensive investment by multinational corporations in resources or manufacturing industry (Leys 1978:259-63). The main point is that we must keep the world system thrust in perspective. Charges of reductionism can be avoided by not basing underdevelopment on quantitative process but on qualitative change. This, in turn, means rejecting 'market Marxism' as the prime focus of our analysis (though of course it has some historically specific validity), and concentrating attention on the organisation of production on a world scale, and the articulation of the capitalist and pre-capitalist modes of production.

The danger here is that the approach lapses into a mechanical materialism, the mode of production being reduced to an abstracted description of empirical data. This is complemented by the criticism expressed by Friedman which warns of the danger of misinterpreting Marx's concept of production and in so doing failing to recognise the significance of reproduction. Clearly, these are important criticisms, but in themselves do not constitute a rejection of the method as such, but a warning as to its frequent misuse. The analysis of the mode of production – that is, the forces of production, the social relations of production (about which there is more below), politics and ideology – must remain a constituent part of the analysis of underdevelopment It is incumbent upon researchers to appreciate both the significance of the criticisms of Banaji, Friedman and others, and also the relationship between a mode of production and world capitalism on the one hand, and class structure and history on the other. The structured analysis which I have outlined so far constitutes two distinct but related foci of analysis, the material on imperialism looking at the evolution of the world economy through its successive historical epochs, and the articulation analysis relating these developments to the contradictory path of the pre-capitalist modes. It represents a structured methodology for tracing the flow of surplus product and surplus value through an economy, and provides the raw techniques upon which to develop an understanding of the economics of underdevelopment.

Yet a grasp of the economics of underdevelopment does not provide sufficient understanding to produce a general theory of underdevelopment. The call for a class-based analysis of underdevelopment is suggestive of a need to transcend the narrowly economic analyses that currently hold sway in political economy, and to focus studies of development and underdevelopment on historical research that has at its core the processes of class formation. This need parallels developments in other areas of Marxist research (see Thompson 1978; McLellan 1979; Preston 1982), where it is often felt that abstract, economistic Marxism has achieved the upper ground. Two aspects to the calls for a new direction are of particular interest. First, there is an emphasis on empirical research at the level of the society. It is appropriate, at this level, to concentrate on the specifics of class formation, the role of the domestic bourgeoisie, the importance of class alliances and exploitation, and the role of the state. What we should be attempting to do is ground our theoretical grasp of social and geographical transfers of value in the real relationships between individuals and classes within a particular social formation. The problem, however, is not with the endeavour, nor with the techniques of data collection and analysis, but in determining an adequate theory which enables us to satisfactorily relate class analysis, and particularly human agency, to the structures talked about above.

Second, the aim of a class analysis is to sensitise explanations of underdevelopment to the diversity of the underdevelopment experience, and the role of conscious and unconscious human action in these processes. We need to understand more than the dynamics of production – we need to try and grasp the dynamics of social reproduction. Why do people go on being exploited? Why is it that the poor in the Third World continue to work for a pittance, often amidst luxury? How is it that underdeveloped societies are able to reproduce themselves when the conditions of existence of such a large proportion of their populations are so degraded? It is probably true to say that we have a fair grasp of the basic economic processes associated with development and underdevelopment, but we have a rather poor understanding of the dynamics of these processes and the way they are embedded in society. These are the sorts of issues to which development geographers should increasingly turn their attention.

Conclusion

The purpose of this part of the book has been to summarise the growing critique of dependency and world systems theory, to discuss and criticise briefly the approach of those studies which concentrate on the articulation of modes of production, and to propose a synthesis of aspects of these approaches along with an equally important emphasis on social reproduction and class relations. It should be recognised that we are dealing with an exceedingly complex process upon which a relatively simple set of tools (for example, class analysis) can have little impact. Hence, we need to look at a series of interrelated processes – imperialism, articulation, historical development, social reproduction and class formation – simultaneously. At the same time we must be aware that they represent different levels of analysis and that the theoretically defined relationships between the structured abstractions – imperialism and articulation – and the concrete class processes and struggles are far from understood.

The following three chapters specify some of the theoretical issues which geographers are currently confronting in trying to build a geography of underdevelopment upon principles derived from political economy and contemporary social theory. It is tackled by an examination of different approaches to three aspects of the urbanisation process in the Third World – regional uneven development, rural-urban migration and circulation, and urban informal labour markets and urban class formation. Implicit in the argument is the need to restore balance to underdevelopment research by shifting it away from political economy and towards the complex array of social processes within which underdevelopment is embedded. This is surely the purpose of class analysis, to better grasp the way in which humans, individually and collectively, manage their own lives in conditions not of their own making.

Notes

1. The development of Marxist analyses of 'primitive' societies is a recent phenomenon. Terray (1972:95) argues that the publication of Meillassoux's *L'Anthropologie economique des Gouro* in 1964 may have been the turning point.
2. Marx (1964) and Marx and Engels (1979). See the discussion in Wolpe (1980:1-6).
3. The main texts here of course are the three volumes of *Capital*. Taylor (1979) is a strong advocate of using Marx's analysis of capitalism rather than his more peripheral work on pre-capitalist formations.
4. Lenin (1956). See Banaji (1980) for a comment on Kautsky.
5. Laclau (1971:19-38). For summaries of the disagreement see Alavi (1975: 1243-51), Barbalet (1976) and Foster-Carter (1978:50-1).
6. See Clammer (1975, 1978) Bradby (1975), Foster-Carter (1978), Seddon (1978), Wolpe (1980) and Kahn and Llobera (1980). For a recent review see

Wolpe (1980:1-43) and Forbes and Thrift (1981).

7. See, in particular, Meillassoux (1972), Terray (1972) and Rey (1973).

8. Taylor (1979). By way of background see Taylor (1972, 1975, 1976).

9. Kahn (1974:1-35, 1975:137-58, 1976:64-95 and 1978:103-22).

10. Kahn (1974:28-9). The significance of ideology is examined in Kahn (1978:103-22).

11. After Wolpe (1980:31). It should also be noted that Hindess and Hirst (1975) advocated the use of the concept of mode of production for the analysis of pre-capitalist social formations, but in a later auto-critique (Hindess and Hirst 1977) abandoned the concept altogether in favour of social formation.

12. Rey is notable among the exceptions to this rule, and will be considered in the following section.

13. This is the question posed by Kay (1975). Exploitation, of course, is measured by the amount of time worked minus that which needs to be worked to reproduce labour.

14. On the other hand, the bulk of the bourgeois analysis of underdevelopment has favoured 'internal' obstructions to underdevelopment almost to the exclusion of the 'external'.

15. Part of the problem is that Marx died before he was able to write more than a page or so on class — Marx (1959:885-6). However, people such as Ollman (1968:573-80) have spelled out in more detail Marx's use of class, whilst others have developed sophisticated definitions of class with their roots in historical materialism (Poulantzas, 1975:13-15).

16. Incidentally, these social classes seem to be borrowed intact from Mao Tse-tung (Mortimer 1972:3-4; Gordon 1978:211-13).

17. But almost nothing to development geographers, with a few exceptions such as Slater (1975a:172-3), McGee (1976:1-38) and Buchanan (1970). Slater (1977:19-20) laments the failure of geographers to consider spatial problems from a class perspective.

18. Rey (1973, 1975, 1979). For brief summaries and critiques of Rey see Bradby (1975:142-52), Copans and Seddon (1978:31-6), Foster-Carter (1978: 56-66) and Brewer (1980:Ch. 8).

19. Shivji (1975:10-20), Amarshi, Good and Mortimer (1979:97-160). Mamak and Ali (1979).

20. Browett (1980b:19-23). By contrast, see the earlier reviews of Foster-Carter (1976) and Goldsworthy (1977).

PART THREE:
REGIONALISM, URBANISATION AND UNDERDEVELOPMENT

Where do correct ideas come from? Do they drop from the skies? No. Are they innate in the mind? No. They come from social practice.

Mao-Tse-tung (Robinson 1971)

I am confined to using some already available threads of knowledge and to see what kind of tapestry I can weave from them. In this sense, I shall grope for synthesis by employing what has been called 'recollection as epistemological faculty'. I adopt this approach because I think there is less need for new data and more need for re-evaluating what we think we already know.

(Olsson 1975)

6 SOCIAL THEORY AND REGIONAL UNEVEN DEVELOPMENT

Earlier chapters of this book looked at aspects of the emergence of the geographic study of development, and the growth of neo-Marxist underdevelopment theory. Empirical research has sometimes been used to illustrate these themes. Here, an attempt has been made to demonstrate the links between changing material conditions and the growth of social and economic ideas, but essentially the argument has been abstract. The purpose has been to review theoretical trends within the study of geography and development and to point to criticisms that have been made of them. It has been necessary to steer a path between a relativist approach to research on development, which would simply give approximately equal weight to competing views, and a hard-line rejectionist approach which would characterise one approach as correct and all others incorrect. All ideas are ultimately a product of particular formative geographic and historical forces upon human thought. This does not mean we cannot differentiate between particular viewpoints, for, as has been argued, the best of the radical thought on underdevelopment shows a rigour and depth of analysis all but absent from much conventional work. Nevertheless, we need to keep firmly in mind that ideas are constantly changing just as societies are constantly changing. There are social limits to knowledge that consistently keep in check our grasp of the reality of human social evolution.

One way in which we are constantly reminded of the context of knowledge is through reference to the history of thought. Yet reviews of theoretical trends in the study of geography and development are in themselves only the first stage in constructing theory. Criticism and review alone do not constitute theoretical development even though they are the base upon which theory is constructed. Creative theoretical work is inseparable from empirical research and social practice. These elements are intertwined in a complex manner and can only be temporarily and artificially separated.

This and the following two chapters attempt to make some progress on the construction of a critical and radical geography of underdevelopment by contrasting the application of different theoretical perspectives to three substantial, closely-linked geographical issues, namely regional underdevelopment, population mobility and urban class formation. The central question is: what can geographers contribute to an understanding of development and underdevelopment? This chapter begins by looking at approaches to regional development. It is followed by an examination of the concept of space in Marxist geography and the regional political economy approach, which is illustrated by a case study of Peru. The final parts of the chapter discuss a critique of political economy, and the way new approaches to regions and space might be used to raise new questions about underdevelopment. Chapter 7 goes on to look at explanations of peasant migration and urbanisation in Indonesia, criticising conventional interpretations and applying the structurationist viewpoint to the issue. Chapter 8 examines the growth of the Third World city, the emergence of an informal labour market, and the process of urban class formation.

The Regional Question

The regional question has provided an arena for considerable debate and disagreement among contemporary geographers, regional planners, regional scientists, and social scientists in general. Regional development has been an important focus of development geography during the post-war period, a trend closely related to the incorporation of regional planning goals in the five-year plans of many peripheral capitalist societies since the 1960s. Three main approaches have predominated in the non-Marxist literature. The first examines regional issues through neo-classical principles of economic equilibrium. This 'marginalist' approach emphasises the importance of allocating resources through the market, and views regional inequality as a transitory phenomenon. With economic development and the integration of factor markets regional inequalities are reduced. A form of self-balance is achieved, which, it has been caustically observed, is 'an analog to the outcome of equilibrium in the price determination model of neo-classical economics' (Wilmoth 1978:45). A second approach could be labelled 'institutionalist'. Based on principles like 'circular and cumulative causation', it recognises the tendency towards spatial inequality in the operation of the capitalist market:

> Once regional inequalities develop, the workings of the market —
> and the migration of capital and labour in particular — tend not to
> result in the reduction of the inequalities. Contrary to the general
> prediction of neo-classical economics, any tendency toward regional

balance is offset by powerful counter-tendencies toward imbalance. (Stilwell 1978:20)

In order to counter tendencies towards regional imbalance, government intervention was deemed necessary. The key writers on this issue include Hirschman (1958), Myrdal (1957), Perroux (1950) and Friedmann (1966). Third, the diffusionist approach, illustrated by the geography of modernisation research (see Chapter 3), has been of some significance. The emphasis in modernisation theory has been upon the 'spatial diffusion of growth generating innovations throughout the space-economy from initial "bridgeheads" ' (Ede 1982:27).

Friedmann and Weaver (1979) have sketched out the complementary evolution of regional planning doctrine, based largely on the North American experience (Table 6.1). They argue that a major shift in thinking occurred with the emergence of regional science in the early 1950s. Up until then regional planning combined an emphasis on Utopian planning with comprehensive river basin development plan-

Table 6.1: The Evolution of Regional Planning Doctrine, 1925-75

1925-35	Utopian planning: bio-synthesis and a new culture; cultural regionalism	Territorial Integration
1935-50	Practical idealism: comprehensive river basin development	
1950-75	Spatial systems planning: A. Spatial development in newly industrialising countries (growth centres) B. Backward regions in industrially advanced countries	Functional Integration
1975-	Selective regional closure: the new utopianism? Agropolitan development	Territorial Integration .

Source: Friedmann and Weaver 1979:8.

ning, approaches which stressed territorial integration. The new approach, by contrast, stressed functional integration:

Along one dimension, it emphasized the problem of *spatial organization*; accordingly, it was preoccupied with urbanization, industrial location, and the creation of strong inter-city ties. The principal targets of this dimension were the newly industrializing, post-colonial countries. Here regional planning was associated with 'nation-building', central planning, and the spatial integration of the national economy . . . The second dimension of the new doctrine of regional planning concerned the problems of *backward regions* in industrially advanced countries. (Friedmann and Weaver 1979:6)

The single, most influential concept of regional development during the 1960s and 1970s was undoubtedly the 'growth pole'. It was a term originally associated with the work of Perroux (1950, 1971), whose primary concern was with interactions among industrial sectors. Economic growth, it was argued, was generated through a series of dominant sectors or poles in the economy. These propulsive firms, which would tend to be large and oligopolistic, would have a strong influence on their suppliers and clients. Growth poles, therefore, were located in economic, not geographic space, and were essentially an idealisation of the way in which inter-industry linkages worked and how they could be manipulated to provide the maximum multiplier effects. Boudeville (1966) and others assisted in applying the concept of the growth pole to geographic space, whereby they became known as growth centres. These development poles became the range of activities which located around the original propulsive activity. Spatial development, and economic development, became concentrated on an urban growth strategy, in which 'stress upon a few dynamic sectoral clusters and upon urban-industrial growth [was] the key to more generalized development' (Hansen 1981:19).

Three attractions account for the widespread use of the concept (Friedmann and Weaver 1979:125). First, growth centre strategies made sense in that they advocated a focusing of public and private investment on a particular place, rather than allowing a scattering of inputs. Second, they accord with development experience as observed in western developed countries, where urban and industrial growth have been paired and remain central to capitalist development. Third, the growth pole/growth centre concept emerged from a 'hard' discipline – economics – and therefore could be propounded with the full force of technocratic authority.

Yet, despite the importance attached to growth centre strategies, a number of empirical studies have questioned their effectiveness, pointing out that spread effects are small and, in some cases, less than the backwash effects, and asking whether, if the main purpose is to promote development in the small towns and rural areas, it would not be better to invest in them directly (Nichols 1969; Wong and Saigol 1984). The response from supporters of the growth centre strategies ('development from above' or 'centre-down' models as Stöhr and Taylor (1981) refer to them) has been to point out that the evaluations of the strategy have been unfair. Time-horizons have been far too short; it is necessary to wait 15-25 years before a proper evaluation can be made. Moreover, it is argued that growth centre strategies need to be seen as one aspect of comprehensive economic planning, they need to be adequately implemented, which they have often not been, and they need to be supported by a package of other policies. As Hansen (1981: 36) concludes:

> one may say of the centre-down paradigm what Shaw said of Christianity: it is not necessarily wrong; it has simply never been tried . . . despite their faults, economic dualism and growth pole strategies will keep gross national product growing more rapidly than would be the case under alternative strategies.

Nevertheless, many would disagree (for example, Coraggio 1975). The basis of the disagreement strikes at the very root of the distinction (mentioned in Chapter 3) between a compositional and contextual approach to human organisation. To be more precise, the search for functional integration of the space economy came to be challenged by calls for territorial integration, decentralisation and regional autonomy (Table 6.1). Before this is considered approaches to regionalism in the radical literature are discussed.

Regional Political Economy

Geography in recent years has begun a transformation from an essentially descriptive, atheoretical discipline, to one whose momentum is more and more closely linked to broad shifts in social theory. The growth of a Marxist geography has been one, if not the most important, aspect of this change. Peet's (1979) definition is as follows:

> marxist geography is one specialization within a marxist science based in historical materialism. Hence, marxist geography begins by accepting the characterization of social process as being essentially the production and reproduction of the material base of life; in the capitalist mode, the labour/wage capital relation is reproduced in the interest of the continuing self-expansion of capital. But this process has a number of aspects, or moments, and marxist geography

merely specializes on two of these – the environmental relations, natural and spatial.

This is elaborated in another paper:

> A mode of production generates a typical set of relations with the physical environment, and a territorial structure, which reflects the relations of production (especially the purposes of the owners of the means of production) and the level of development of the productive forces. Social formations structured by the same mode of production thus have generally similar geographies. But a given mode of production expresses itself differently under varying physical conditions or in areas of varying cultural transmission from decayed modes of production, producing variations between and within the social formations it generates. . . Geographic relations thus play extremely important mediating roles between modes of production and the social formations which appear on the earth's surface. (Peet 1979:166-7)

These tracts serve as both a definition of Marxist geography and a theoretical justification – Marxist science is made up of partly autonomous but dialectically interrelated parts, each of which focuses on the relations between instances and the societal whole.

This particular conception has, however, been criticised by geographers who deny the validity of a division of labour within Marxism that corresponds so closely to bourgeois social science. Slater simply argues that acceptance of historical materialism requires a totally new beginning. The criticisms of Eliot-Hurst (1980:3) centre around the division of epistemological space implicit in Marxist geography which he regards as '. . . their most important and constraining commonality'. The perpetuation of a division represents a theoretical ideology – adjectival geography – which is at the core of geography's inability to transcend wishy-washy radical interventionism and bourgeois non-materialist forms of thought and progress to a true Marxist science.[1]

The key to Eliot-Hurst's argument is the inappropriate ontological autonomy which he believes the 'Marxist geographers' (here including Peet, Soja and Walker) give to space:

> Far from being a 'separate', distinct object, 'space' is simply one aspect of a *single relationship* in which unevenly developed concrete patterns on the earth surface can direct us to that abstraction, space,

not vice-versa. The notion that 'space', an abstraction, produces spatial patterns by auto-dominant auto-genesis, even if wrapped in the guise of 'uneven development', is an example of Hegelian idealism, and in the last resort, unscientific and ideological. (Eliot-Hurst 1980:11)

The argument is echoed by Smith (1979:375-6) who recognises the need to consider the spatial aspects of capitalism but who feels that 'the emphasis on space soon proves a barrier, not a catalyst, to further theoretical development'.

Despite the problematic status of space for Marxist theorists, regionalism — 'the analysis of intra-national spatial differentiation' (Massey 1978:106) — has attracted some of the best contemporary geography researchers to its debates. A number of distinctive approaches to regionalism have emerged, most claiming some fundamental affinity to the main corpus of Marxist writing, yet separated by methodological chasms of considerable width. All share a fundamentally different view of space to the non-Marxist regional scientists:

The regional scientist views spatial analysis as a highly specialized examination of one aspect of social behavior — especially economic behavior. The regional political economist explains spatial organization as a manifestation of the logic of the social system itself. . . To understand how. . . struggles to gain, maintain, and increase control over surplus operate over space is to understand the logic behind the development of spatial organization in a society. Spatial organization reflects those struggles and the underlying social relations of production. (Salinas and Moulaert 1983:4-5)

Massey (1978) has distinguished three approaches to regional political economy (see also Jensen-Butler 1982). The first has sought to identify general abstract laws concerning the spatial form of capitalist development. Lipietz (1977), for instance, has pursued a 'law of value over space'; Castells (1977) has separated space into the urban — the sphere of capitalist consumption — and the region, the space of production; and Marx (1959, 1973), it has been pointed out, saw a tendency towards spatial concentration evident in the capitalist mode of production.

A second group of writers has drawn on underdevelopment theory to explain intra-national regional inequality (Edel *et al.* 1978). Carney, Hudson, Ive and Lewis (1975), for instance, drew on dependency theory to explain the problems of the north-east of England. The law of unequal exchange has been used by Lipietz (1977) in a regional context. Several other geographers have used the internal colony model as a means of bringing theories of imperialism to the understanding of intra-national patterns of domination and exploitation (Drakakis-Smith and Williams 1983).

Third, Massey (1978) advocates an approach which focuses on the imperatives of capital accumulation, shifts in the spatial division of labour, and the subsequent creation of spatially uneven development:

> In any given period, new investment in economic activity will be geographically distributed in response to this pattern of spatial differentiation. . . The term 'spatial division of labour' is meant to refer to the *way* in which economic activity responds to geographical inequality in the conditions of accumulation – the particular kinds of use made by capital of such inequality. (Massey 1978:114)

The approach is illustrated by discussion of rounds of new industrial investment and empirical research on the nascent spatial division of labour in the electronics industry. Changes in the structure of production in the electronics industry has led to the splitting of functions and their allocation to different locations. Thus, control functions and research and development are confined to central metropolitan regions, employment requiring skilled labour is concentrated in industrial cities, and the depressed areas are left with the role of supplying semi-skilled labour. This new use of space is combined with old patterns to produce a regionally specific economy and class structure.

For our purposes one of the key problems with this literature is that it has tended to address regional uneven development in capitalist countries of the core (for example, Massey 1979; Clark 1980; Simon 1980; Carney, Hudson and Lewis 1980) or semi-periphery (Lewis and Williams 1981; Jensen-Butler 1982; Stilwell 1982), rather than in the underdeveloped world. Another problem is that uneven development is a topic undergoing rapid theoretical development, so it is difficult to summarise a position common to all approaches.

Nevertheless, we can draw on analyses by Salinas (1977, 1983) of the Peruvian experience to illustrate the way in which capital accumulation structures space in the underdeveloped countries. Between the fourteenth and sixteenth centuries Peru was spatially reorganised due to the growth of the Incan Empire. Prior to this period the population was widely scattered in tribal villages but, with the emergence of the

Incas and the spread of their territorial domination into modern-day Bolivia, Chile and Ecuador, a spatial hierarchy of settlements was formed. The Incan empire was based on the town of Cuzco in the southern highland *sierra*. A group of secondary cities (Jauja, Cajamarca, Chan Chan) was formed to maintain territorial domination in association with an elaborate system of administration, and the territory of the Incas was spatially integrated through the development of a system of stone paths. The logic of the system was the effective extraction of surplus from the subordinated peoples. The spatial structure which developed during this period facilitated capital accumulation by the Inca ruling classes, while this domination was secured through a common ideology emphasising economic reciprocity and religious representation. Production was increased in parts of the empire by the introduction of new technology such as the establishment of an irrigation system in the south.

The entrance of Spanish mercantilists into the Peruvian economy in the sixteenth century marked the beginning of a new phase of capital accumulation. Demand in Europe was for luxury goods, but when gold and silver were found near Ayacucho, Arequipa and Potosi, precious minerals became the focus of mercantilist interest. A system of forced labour was developed to work the mines, and agricultural production in the *sierra* conserved, but the surplus was diverted to the Spanish. Spatial reorganisation occurred in line with the needs of the new ruling class. The Incan transport network was reinforced, and new cities were established. Lima developed as the major urban place, and a new set of secondary cities — Trujillo, Lambayeque, Tumbes — emerged, initially serving as centres of control but later, and more importantly, as transshipment points and administrative centres.

From the beginning of the eighteenth century there was a shift in the colonial economy away from minerals to agricultural products. The *latifundios* became the dominant mode of organisation in commercial agriculture, generating a surplus for export. This led to the further growth of colonial port cities due to their enhanced role as foci of export trade and, with the integration of the colonial economy, the development of internal trade. Moreover, the emergence of a new elite, made up of colonial mercantilists and the *latifundistas*, created a demand for manufactured imports, thus further building up the colonial ports. Yet the establishment of a new dominant class also helped to increase the demand for independence, which was achieved in 1821.

Independence corresponded with further changes in the world

economy, particularly the growth of industrial capitalism. England replaced Spain as the dominant external power in the Peruvian economy, and there was a further shift in the external trade patterns, with the growth of exports of guano and nitrates, and in the 1870s cotton and sugar. A bureaucracy was formed. On the whole the spatial organisation inherited from the colonial period remained, though the coastal cities expanded (especially Lima), transport links between the cities and the major mineral deposits were developed, and a new town, Iquitos, grew in the upper reaches of the Amazon.

The USA began to replace Britain beginning with the expansion of monopoly capitalism at the turn of the century. Initially, American companies bought into the extractive sector, strengthening the minerals industry in the *sierra* and agriculture along the coast. In turn, this had the effect of reinforcing the financial and commercial role of Lima. After the Second World War the further growth of an urban elite meant that the main cities grew as centres of consumption, while the *sierra* was further peripheralised. Investment location decisions were controlled by three fractions of the bourgeoisie. The monopoly capitalist fraction, producing for export, could usually attract a labour force and, therefore, tended to locate close to raw material supplies along the coast. In contrast, industrial capitalists produced for the domestic market which was largely concentrated in Lima, where wages could be kept lower than in the enclaves along the coast. Finally, the bureaucratic bourgeoisie was located mainly in Lima, but made various attempts through the 1960s and 1970s to decentralise (Hilhorst 1981). Most programmes, however, proved ineffectual, and so the wishes of the two dominant fractions of the bourgeoisie − the foreign and the 'grand-export' bourgeoisie − prevailed, and development and industry remained concentrated in Lima and along the coast.

Although this has been a very general account of the evolution of the spatial structure of Peru, it illustrates the sorts of considerations that a viewpoint on regionalism based in regional political economy takes into account. It is an historical approach, contrasting the forms of spatial organisation during the pre-Incan, Incan, mercantilist and capitalist periods. The focus of the analysis is on the means of extraction of surplus and the processes of capital accumulation, class formation and rivalry between class fractions. External powers − Spain, England and the USA − are demonstrated to be important in understanding the place of Peru in the world economy, and this relationship is, in turn, via the medium of a foreign bourgeoisie, shown to explain the emerging spatial structure of the country. Regions that were central to one mode

of production, such as the *sierra* during the period of Incan domination, become peripheral during periods when another (that is, capitalist)
mode of production predominates. Thus we have space being restruc-
tured during particular historical epochs in conjunction with, and to
better facilitate, the processes of capital accumulation. The dominant
classes are able to conceptualise and implement strategies in line with
the logic of capital, and the state, reflecting these interests, assists in the
process. Conflict occurs over the contradictory interests of the ruling
fractions of the bourgeoisie and its rivals, but this has not resulted in
significant alteration to the prevailing trend.

A Critique of Political Economy

A comprehensive assessment of the regional development and the
regional political economy viewpoints would be beyond the scope of
this chapter. Instead, three areas of concern common to the work on
development and underdevelopment in geography and political
economy are highlighted. First, much work on underdevelopment has
been characterised by an economistic approach to the problem, yet
there is a growing feeling that explanations of underdevelopment
should be orientated more to the examination of social relations, class
conflict, and reproduction, or, in other words, the social context of
exploitation. This concern is related to a widespread dissatisfaction with
structuralist explanation, an excessive faith in economic determination
by the laws of capital, and the failure to understand the role of human
agency in social change. A new problematic is emerging in geography
which is concerned with shifting social enquiry away from functionalist
explanations of social and economic change. It aims to conceive of
human beings 'as *partially* knowledgeable agents and not just as "cultural
dupes", and as able to initiate action which can *transform* social structure' (Thrift 1982:1281). Paralleling this concern is a feeling that we
should be looking more at what people can do about development and
underdevelopment, and why they might or might not be doing it.

Second, a large proportion of the work on underdevelopment theory
has been pitched at an abstract level. This trend probably reached its
peak in the discussions of the articulation of modes of production literature, but was also evident in much of the Marxist debate. The importance of the primacy of theory was closely and unnecessarily linked to
abstract discussion. Many of the empirical investigations that were
undertaken were reductionist in that they seemed to squeeze informa-

tion from a great diversity of experiences into a universalist framework. Research work often failed to differentiate, in time and space, processes linked to colonialism and underdevelopment. Instead, these processes were conflated to reinforce general principles of surplus extraction and domination. At the same time, the holistic approaches which characterised pre-war development studies were replaced by a broad spatial differentiation between core and periphery, between the developed and the Third World. Recent thinking calls for the reinstatement of an approach which makes no *a priori* or static distinction between developed and underdeveloped countries, but which instead focuses on a single, complex world economy and the relationships between the various small and large social and economic entities of which it consists. At the same time this approach aims to disaggregate and would seek to differentiate the experience of underdevelopment in time and space, and highlight the complexity of the overall pattern.

Third, the growth of economistic and abstract thought was accompanied by the increasing domination of compositional over contextual knowledge. Theories sought an understanding of processes outside of the context of place. Specialisation based on themes and universal theories predominated over specialisation in the study of places, and 'development studies' grew in stature *vis-à-vis* 'area studies'. Concurrently, a discipline-based approach has seemed to give way to the multi-disciplinary and even inter-disciplinary study of development, but in many ways this has simply reinforced the major social science disciplines. The middle-ground of 'political economy' has become overcrowded, while questions on areas such as the environment and the organisation of space have received relatively sparse treatment. In other words, the predominance of the political economy of underdevelopment has centralised and focused interest on a relatively small number of issues, and drawn critical researchers away from a wide variety of related research.

Parallel criticisms of Marxian political economy have come, in recent years, from several disciplinary and ideological viewpoints, moreover, many are characterised by a maturity not present in the ignorant and destructive – in fact, reactionary – attacks evident in the literature during the 1970s. Within the field of urban studies Elliott and McCrone (1982) have argued for a shift of interest away from Marxism towards 'left-Weberianism'.[2] They believe that Marxists are preoccupied with the significance of holistic theory, fail to escape the caricature of human action as determined by supra-human forces and, rather surprisingly, have taken insufficient account of history and class conflict. Duncan and

Ley (1982) have offered an assessment of Marxist work in human geography and are highly critical of: its pretentious holistic philosophy, tendency to reify theoretical structures, the reductionist aspects of its central concern with economic forces, and its failure to adequately assess the status of individuals and the place of empirical evidence in social research. Finally, Thrift (1983) has identified four common concerns which unite the proponents of the structurationist viewpoint, and which put them in opposition to the standardised political economy treatment of social change: they oppose functionalist explanation; they are concerned that explanation be neither based on structural determinism nor voluntarist principles; they see the need for a theory of practical action which is absent in most social theory; and time and space are central to all social interaction but are absent from much contemporary theory. Many more arguments could be cited, but to do so would be repetitious.

Probably the most important attack on theoretical Marxism delivered in the last decade was by Thompson (1978), which caused us to recognise very clearly that there are (at least) two Marxisms (Gouldner 1980). These have been variously labelled: scientific and critical Marxism, theoretical and historical Marxism, and structuralist and humanist Marxism (Duncan and Ley 1982:31). Underdevelopment theory (like urban studies and human geography) has been much more closely associated with the scientific, theoretical or structuralist Marxism, that is, Marxist political economy.[3] Even so, the recent volume by Harvey (1982), surely the most comprehensive statement of the relationship between Marxian political economy and space, ended on a note which left the reader wondering about the limitations of political economy. He concluded in an 'Afterword':

> The crucial commodity for the production of surplus value, labour power, is itself produced and reproduced under social relations over which capitalists have no direct control . . . the labourers themselves are human beings possessed of all manner of sentiments, hopes and fears, struggling to fashion a life for themselves that contains at least minimal satisfactions. The conditions of production and reproduction of labour powers of different quantity and quality exist at the very centre of that life. And though susceptible of all manner of influence through bourgeois institutions and culture, nothing can in the end subvert the control workers exercise over certain very basic processes of their own reproduction. Their lives, their culture and, above all, their children are for them to reproduce. (Harvey

1982:447)

It is very clearly recognised in this passage that there is much to understand about human society that falls outside the sphere of control of the capitalist, outside the direct influence of capitalism, and, consequently, outside the grasp of political economy. This is not to deny the validity of a political economy which reveals hidden economic relationships, but it is a direct challenge to the holistic claims of political economy explanation.

Harvey apart, it would be all too easy to interpret these criticisms as a total rejection of materialist methods of analysis, which they are most explicitly not. As Elliott and McCrone (1982:20) recognise:

> we shall not try to raise an 'idealist' banner in opposition to a 'materialist' one . . . The task is to encourage appreciation *both* of the realities of material life – the real differences of experience and interest of different groups and classes – *and* the constellations of ideas and sentiments with which men (sic) make sense of their lives.

More specifically, Thrift advocates the 'marriage' – or 'interpenetration' – of the structurationist school and Marxist social theory. Though appreciative of the difficulties of bringing the two together, he believes there is a fundamental (though largely unrecognised) agreement that 'the point of historical materialism is to allow conscious, directed, and reflexive human agency to become the social structure', the main thrust of the structurationist school (Thrift 1983:34). Doubtless the task of 'interpenetration' will be seen by some as heretical – yet more evidence of the eclectic nature of theory-building in geography.[4] But it is not so easily dismissed.

Society, Space and Underdevelopment

From the diverse array of criticisms discussed above two can be focused upon. First, the structure/agency issue, and second, the compositional/contextual dichotomy. The structure/agency dichotomy has its origins in nineteenth century capitalism and social theory. The divergent demands of industrial capitalism led to a redefinition of individuals and their relationship to society and the creation and perpetuation of a duality. A growing sphere of mass production became juxtaposed against a view of the individual as an object of scientific knowledge:

In capitalism these two tendencies come together as a major contradiction between socialized production and private appropriation.
Capitalist societies are both collectivist and individualistic. On the
one hand, each individual lives in a highly socialized world; on the
other, each individual lives in a privatized world. (Thrift 1983:26-7)

Forms of explanation have polarised and congregated around the
extremes of this duality. Structuralist explanations incorporate strong
notions of determination built upon assumptions of the significance of
universalist processes in social changes, and all but ignore the creativity
of human practice. In contrast, voluntarist-based social theory has a
very weak notion of determination, seeing social change as an accumulation of human practices and an expression of human volition.
    Closely related to this dichotomy, social theory has also tended to
align with either a compositional or contextual framework of knowledge:

In the compositional approach . . . human activity is split up into
a set of broad structural categories founded on the property of
'alikeness' and derived via a formal-logical method based on the
tool of abstraction. These categories are then recombined as an
explanation of society or, at least, of parts of it. In the contextual
approach . . . human activity is treated as a social event in its immediate spatial and temporal setting and the categories so derived are
based on a property of 'togetherness' that must not be split asunder.
(Thrift 1983:27-8)

Both sets of dichotomies are represented along axes in Table 6.2,
and some of the approaches and theories of development examined
in this and earlier chapters are plotted on them. Such representation
inevitably simplifies, and may even distort, some of the material discussed, but it is a useful means of identifying differences between
approaches to underdevelopment. A distinction between two different
types of theory illustrates this.
    The first group of approaches to be considered occupies some sort
of polar position according to the two variables represented in the
Table. Vidalian regional geography and, perhaps to a lesser extent, the
area studies focus on the third world (Chapter 3) are characterised by a
combination of voluntarist assumptions and contextual analysis. A
strong association with fieldwork and empirical research, an emphasis
on unique experiences, and an apparent antipathy to generalisation and

Table 6.2: Theories of Development and Underdevelopment

	CONTEXTUAL	
● Class analysis		● Vidalian regional geography
		● Area studies
DETERMINIST		**VOLUNTARIST**
● Socio-spatial dialectic	● Structuration	
		● Territorial integration
● Marxist geography		
● Capital accumulation theories of regional underdevelopment	COMPOSITIONAL	
● Political economy of development		● Regional development

theoretical discourse, mark much of this work with a distinctive flavour. In contrast, the literature on regional planning and regional development reviewed earlier in the chapter, shares the voluntarist assumptions of regional geography, but is characterised by the domination of compositional over contextual explanation (growth centre theory, for instance, is an abstraction removed from the context of place). Marxist geography, capital accumulation theories of regional uneven development, and the whole political economy of development (discussed in Chapters 4 and 5) are all characterised by strong notions of determination, no matter whether perceived at the international level (as in world systems theory) or at the regional level (regional uneven development), or even at the local level (the articulation of modes of production). Concurrently, this work is compositional by virtue of its emphasis on abstract laws and its lack of historical and geographical specificity. Finally, the class analysis critique of underdevelopment theory, discussed in Chapter 5, has been assigned a position which emphasises its strong notions of determination, at the same time recognising the historical specificity of the analysis. The class analysis approach in development studies is a specific application of the second, and hitherto less important, historical or humanist Marxism referred to by Duncan and Ley (1982).

More important than the schools of thought which occupy the polar positions on Table 6.2, however, are those attempts to shift towards a theoretical understanding of human social, spatial and economic organisation which balances the determinist/voluntarist and contextual/compositional forces. Three attempts to do so will be briefly considered. The first is Soja's specification of the socio-spatial dialectic (Soja and Hadjimichalis 1979, Soja 1980, 1981), which, as is evident from Table 6.2, made a serious attempt to consider both contextual and compositional processes in human social evolution, albeit within a strong determinist-Marxist framework. Soja (1980) believes there are three main approaches to spatial analysis in Marxism. One asserts that class analysis is the core process, the beginning and the end of understanding social process. The second presents space as important, but tends to defer to the overriding significance of aspatial social class:

Wallerstein depicts the capitalist world system as revolving around two basic 'dichotomies', one of class (bourgeoisie vs. proletarian) and the other of 'economic specialization' within a spatial hierarchy (core vs. periphery) . . . [yet] after positing what appears to be a dialectical relationship between social (class) and spatial (core-periphery) structures, the spatial structure is subordinated to the social and viewed largely as a manipulation of space which does not affect class hierarchies. (Soja 1980:222)

The third view, which Soja holds, and with which he associates Lefebvre (1974, 1976) and Mandel (1976), takes the view that 'social and spatial relationships are dialectically inter-reactive, inter-dependent: that social relations of production are both space-forming and space-contingent' (Soja 1980:211).

The socio-spatial dialectic is a concept which attempts to draw attention to the fundamental significance of space in human society:

The spatiality of capital is a . . . 'social hieroglyphic', a carrier and encapsulation of the social history of capitalism, a congelation of social relations and class conflict, a repository of labour power and appropriated value . . . What appears as a thing-like collection of physical properties and attributes — . . . deteriorated inner cities and

repetitive suburbs, more and less 'developed' regions . . . — is in
essence a socially created field of relationships between individuals
and classes congealed and concretised to maintain and perpetuate
the exploitive dominance of those who control the means of production. (Soja 1981:18)

History and geography are reinstated in materialist method in approximately equal balance:

the vertical and horizontal expressions of the relations of production
under capitalism (i.e. relations of class) are, at the same time, homo-
logous, in the sense of originating in the same set of generative structures (e.g. the relations between labor and capital); and dialectically
linked, in that each shapes and is simultaneously shaped by the other
in a complex interrelationship which may vary in different social
formations and at different historical conjunctures. (Soja 1980:225)

Space is critical to modern capitalism. The need to reduce the circulation costs of capital, labour and commodities originally contributed
to the geographical centralisation of production in towns and cities.
Once established, the urban hinterlands were transformed into dependent regions 'as markets for urban products, as reserves of labor, and
increasingly as sources of super-profits' (Soja and Hadjimichalis
1979:9). Thus, the exploitative relationship between town and country
— between centre and periphery — became the basis for the reproduction of the economy during the period of competitive industrial capitalism. However, contradictions in this spatial pattern emerged, for the
extant built environment prevented capital mobility and the periphery
became better organised politically. The result was an expansion of
capitalism away from the centre and into the non-capitalist world.
Imperialism expanded the geographical range of capitalism and reorganised centre-periphery relations on a world scale. The geographical transfer of value, via the mechanism of unequal exchange, from periphery
to core was now based on the exploitation of colonised peoples. Labour
reserves in the economically depressed areas were the chief motive of
imperial expansion, though increasingly colonies and neo-colonies were
seen as significant markets for surplus production in the capitalist core.
Ultimately, however, the limits of capitalist expansion were reached —
there were no more 'underdeveloped' peoples who could be brought
into the periphery of capitalism, causing another crisis of accumulation.
At this conjuncture an expanded role became necessary for the state,

especially through increased control of economic organisation, so that the state and space are combined to assist in the reproduction of late capitalism.

Regional uneven development under capitalism is, first, a reflection of the natural environment and the 'crude physical spatiality of human existence' (Soja 1981:20). Second, and more importantly, it is 'socially and historically produced . . . rooted in and shaped by evolving relations of production, technological change, and political struggle' (Soja 1981:20). The patterns of regional differentiation so produced are evident in regional differentials in labour productivity, rates of profit, the organic composition of capital and the costs of variable capital, which includes both wage rates and the costs of reproduction of labour power. Exchanges between regions produce a geographical transfer of value, and this, in turn, reinforces differential rates of accumulation and realisation of value. Yet contained within capitalism are contradictory processes towards spatial differentiation and spatial equalisation, the former a product of capitalism's need for regional unevenness to ensure its reproduction, the latter evidence of the homogenising capacity of capital. Nowhere is this more clearly illustrated than in capitalist expansion on a global scale, where in many parts of the Third World the contradictory forces of development and underdevelopment are combined in such a stark form in the major cities.

Regional politics are important to the transformation of capitalist space, for Soja sees an intersection between the struggle of social classes and territorial political conflict, yet it is here the weakness of the analysis, for our purposes, can be pinpointed:

> The two forms of class struggle [i.e. social and regional] can be made to appear in conflict, especially with the manipulation of territorial identities under bourgeois nationalism, regionalism, and localism. But when territorial consciousness is based on the exploitative nature of capitalist relations of production and reproduction, and not on parochialism and emotional attachment to place, it is class consciousness. The production of space has indeed been socially obfuscated and mystified in the development of capitalism, and this has allowed it to be used against the class struggle. (Soja 1980:224)

The attachment of the analysis to strong, Marxist notions of determination is amply evident in this view of politics. A recursive relationship between structure and agency simply does not exist — political struggle, even when it takes a regional form, is a class reaction. It is implicit that other forms of regional politics are relatively unimportant, compared to the conflict between economic classes. More important, however, is whether Soja's conception of space is consistent with the need to understand both compositional and contextual explanations. On the one hand, there can be no doubt about the significance of space to his analysis, nor of the stress he places on empirically determining the nature of the socio-spatial dialectic in particular places and at particular times. On the other hand, the balance of the analysis tips towards abstraction and compositional theory, for there is no attempt to understand forces of determination external to capitalism, nor to theorise the specific or the role of mediating institutions in the shaping of the specific.

The second departure from the norm in regional studies is the shift in regional planning away from functional integration and towards territorial integration, which was discussed briefly earlier in the chapter. Labelled by Hebbert (1983) the 'new decentralism', territorial integration is at bottom 'a basic needs strategy for territorial development' (Friedmann and Weaver 1979:193). Whereas functional integration is essentially the centralised control and distribution of resources over a given space – that is, is fundamentally compositional in context – territorial integration stresses the significance of human relationships in space, self-reliance, and the need to develop these resources contextually. Moreover, this approach has dropped the universalism of earlier theories, and opted instead 'for a plurality of approaches based on the needs, history and prevailing conditions of the individual countries concerned' (Lo and Salih 1981:123). Being a practical means of bringing about development the emphasis of territorial integration is on the 'maximum mobilization of each area's natural, human, and institutional resources' (Stöhr and Taylor 1981:1). A brief summary of aspects of territorial integration is given in Table 6.3.

A key focus of strategies of territorial integration is the agropolitan district. These small communities are the basic building blocks of society, and are intended to be self-organising and responsible for themselves. Agropolitan districts are based on individual interaction, incorporate rural-urban linkages which are symbiotic and equal, and are to be ecologically appropriate units. In peasant societies or societies dominated by small-scale handicraft production the purpose of an agropolitan strategy would be to protect and enhance the cellular structure of society. By contrast, in capitalist societies the agropolitan structure would need to be created. An alternative use-value (or parallel)

Table 6.3: The Conditions for Agropolitan Development

Basic conditions	1. Selective territorial closure
	2. Communalisation of productive wealth
	3. Equalisation of access to the bases for the accumulation of social power
Territorial framework	1. Agropolitan districts (15,000-60,000 people)
	2. Agropolitan neighbourhoods in cities
Economic expansion	1. Diversifying the territorial economy
	2. Maximum physical development constrained by the need for conservation
	3. Expanding regional and interregional (domestic) markets
	4. Following principles of self-finance
	5. Promoting social learning
Role of the state	1. Agropolitan district is self-governing
	2. The central state is strong

Source: Based on Friedmann and Weaver 1979:194-204

economy based on domestic-market orientated, small-scale production units in decentralised locations would need to be formed through policies of regional closure (Friedmann and Weaver 1979; Lo and Salih 1981; Weaver 1981; Hebbert 1983).

A strategy of selective regional closure is an important component of agropolitan development, but it is also central to related, less-Utopian, programmes for regional development. The issue which this strategy addresses is:

the leakage problem in a spatial context . . . how can net rural-urban transfers of resources be channelled to favour the growth and development of rural areas? More narrowly, how can the agricultural surplus be retained in the rural areas, preventing it from flowing excessively to the urban areas to be reinvested for its own development?. (Lo and Salih 1981:147)

Proponents of such a strategy advocate supply and demand-side policies as well as political and administrative decentralisation (Stöhr and Todtling 1978). More specifically:

this could be done by control of raw material or commodity transfers which contribute to negative terms of trade and/or by control of factor transfers (capital, technology), and by the retention of decision making powers on commodity and factor transfers in order to avoid the underemployment or idleness of other regional production factors, or major external dependence. (Stöhr 1981:45)

In sum, the strategy of selective regional closure is aimed at minimising the outflow of investible surplus, while creating self-sufficient, self-reliant territorial units. External economic relations for the region would, as much as possible, be limited to the 'export' of those commodities in which the region has a comparative advantage.

Aspects of the agropolitan strategy may appear, from this brief sketch, to be Utopian, but the concept of territorial integration, decentralisation and regional closure is now very important to regional policy-making. Yet being a theory of policy, as distinct from a theory of explanation, means that the concept of determination is given scant consideration in much of this work. Moreover, the eclectic nature of the territorial integration writings further confuses attempts to reconstruct the nature of determination. On the one hand, there can be little doubt that neo-Marxist political economy underpins the whole conception of spatial transfers of surplus. On the other hand, Weaver (1981: 93-5) talks of the force of 'wilful community action' in social change, and believes the political victories in Ireland, India and Algeria 'a matter of will'. This voluntarist perspective sits uneasily with the determinist nature of political economy, not because of any fundamental incompatibility between the two, but because there is no attempt to recognise or reconcile the fundamental structure/agency dichotomy.

The attitude to space implicit in territorial integration further distances this body of writing from the main thrust of contemporary literature. Space is conceptualised in a way that has more in common with the humanist writers of the between-war years such as Patrick Geddes, Lewis Mumford and Howard Odum than with later writers in regional science and regional studies. Human relationships in space take on a meaning quite different from those normally conceived: 'class interests are divergent, territorial interests tend ... to be self-regulating and harmonious' (Hebbert 1983:13). While the failure to consider class conflict (not to mention gender and racial conflict) seems to push territoriality towards Utopianism, at the same time the underlying assumptions that communities in space need to be understood in terms of the order which that space gives to the community, and that these communities cannot be effectively split apart, accords in principle with the stress which is placed on space from a contextual viewpoint. Yet neither the socio-spatial dialectic nor theories of territorial integration overall deal adequately with the structure/agency or compositional/ contextual dichotomies. In seeking to explain different aspects of human spatial relations, both have embraced a strong view of the significance of space, but without sufficient explicit attention to the related structure/agency issue.

It was recognised in Chapter 5 that the political economy of underdevelopment, represented in the various world-scale systems approaches and in the articulation of production approach, lacked sensitivity to the diversity of experiences which collectively make up the Third World, and in terms of explanation, focused too heavily on structural and economic determinism. One way out of this blind alley was to revert to 'class analysis', reasserting a supposedly historical and place-sensitive mode of analysis that was as much based in historical materialism as the approaches it was meant to replace. Another alternative owed more to the type of critical sociology generally associated with the Frankfurt school (Preston 1982). Using the study of regional development and underdevelopment, this chapter defined more precisely two critical problems associated with the main approaches to development and underdevelopment – recursiveness and contextuality – and showed how the concepts of territorial integration and the socio-spatial dialectic have attempted to shift ground from the polar positions on these two axes. However, while they have succeeded in reasserting the importance of contextuality in explanation, neither have explicitly tackled the question of the recursive structure/agency relationship. For this reason the remainder of the chapter focuses on some of the contemporary work on 'structuration' and, in particular, the attempt by human geographers and others to specify the contexual or spatial aspect of structuration.

Sustained criticism of structural theory – objectivism – and of the various forms of subjectivist theory (stemming from the methodology of phenomenology and the like) over the last few years has given rise to a number of attempts to articulate an alternative approach to social theory.[5] While the conceptual focus of the structuration school on the interrelatedness of human agency and social structure is now widely debated in social theory, I will confine myself largely to the meaning of structuration as it is revealed in the works of Giddens (1979, 1981, 1982a, 1982b), Gregory (1981, 1982), Pred (1981a, 1981b, 1982), Sayer (1981, 1982, 1983), and Thrift (1981, 1982, 1983, forthcoming). Briefly, the theory of structuration holds that:

all social action consists of social practices, situated in time-space,

and organised in a skilled and knowledgeable fashion by human
agents. But such knowledgeability is always 'bounded' by unacknow-
ledged conditions of action on the one side and unintended consequences of action on the other. (Giddens 1981:19)

The key to structuration is the argument that social structures are,
at one and the same time, the medium and the outcome of social
practices. Neither the subject (that is, the human agent) nor the
object (society and social institutions) has primacy – human action
presupposes institutions but, by the same token, social institutions
presuppose human action. Human actions are constrained by social
structures, such as polite modes of behaviour and deference to authority; they are also enabled by social structures, language being the
example usually cited. Crucially, though, these structures must be
produced and reproduced by human actions, for they cannot exist
independently. Humans behave in ways that have both intentional
and unintentional consequences, sometimes reproducing and trans-
forming social structures. The unintentional consequences of human
agency are as significant to the structurationist interpretation as the
intentional. Giddens is particularly concerned with two aspects of
human action; 'capability', or the option to act in another way, and
'knowledgeability', 'all those things which the members of the society
know about that society, and the conditions of their activity within
it' (Giddens 1982:9) (see also Thrift, forthcoming).
    Entwined with the theory of structuration in the work of Giddens
is the development of a logic of inquiry which he terms the 'double
hermeneutic'. He rejects positivist methodology and criticises aspects
of hermeneutics:

neither the positivistic view that laws in natural and social science
are logically identical, nor the hermeneutic notion that causal
laws have no place in the social sciences at all, are acceptable . . .
Laws in the social sciences are intrinsically 'historical' in character:
they hold only given specific conditions of 'boundedness' of know-
ledgeably reproduced systems of social interaction. (Giddens 1982b:
15)

Yet there has been some criticism of the notion of determination
implicit in the structurationist debate. Thrift (1983:33) comments
on 'an unresolved ambiguity about the relative importance of economic
determination which sometimes allows structurationist models to

appear far more individualist and voluntarist than is the intention'. Sayer (1983:111-12) is a little more charitable, believing that Giddens' criticisms of economic reductionism and his concern not to rule out some determination by 'non-economic social forms' are points well taken. The degree to which the relationships given by historical materialism can be qualified, however, can be determined through historical investigation.

Mediating concepts provide a point of contact between agency and structure. In the work of Bourdieu this is:

> a 'semistructure' called 'habitus' consisting of cognitive, motivating ('reason-giving') structures that confer certain objective conditions and predefined dispositions on actors based on the objective life-chances which are incorporated into the strategies involved in particular interactions, these interactions being improvisations regulated by habitus. (Thrift 1983:30)

Giddens discusses three mediating concepts. Structures are 'recursively organised rules and resources', systems are 'reproduced relations between actors or collectivities, organised as regular social practices' and social institutions, which are 'structured social practices that have a broad spatial and temporal extension' (Giddens 1982:34). The social institutions are the basic building blocks of this argument, for these are the everyday means by which subjects reproduce systems and structures. Moreover, it is these social institutions that human geographers (or, more specifically, time-geography) have been interested in, for the most significant of these institutions – home, work, school, leisure – are situated in and reflect socially structured space (Thrift 1983:31).

Giddens (1981:30) argues that time-space relations must be made central to social theory, for time and space are constitutive features of social systems, 'implicated as deeply in the most stable forms of social life as in those subject to the most extreme or radical nodes of change', and present and significant from the beginning. He uses the term 'time-space distanciation' to refer to 'how social systems are embedded in time and space' (Giddens 1981:4-5). Historically, non-capitalist societies were characterised by high 'presence-availability', a situation where 'there are relatively few social transactions with others who are socially absent' (Giddens 1981:5). While contemporary capitalist societies have experienced time-convergence (through, for instance, improvements in transport), 'presence-availability' has decreased with, for example, spatial differentiation and specialisation. Both Giddens and

Pred (1981b) have discussed the way time-geography, through its study of life-paths, permits the elaboration of the way in which social practices are related to social structure, but Gregory (1982:210-11) sounds a warning:

> although these recurrent space-time intersections . . . constitute a necessary medium of social reproduction, they do not provide a sufficient condition for the constitution of social structure . . . the concept of spatial structure [is not] equivalent to, and delimited by, a system of spatial interaction . . . the contingent and differential engagement of the modalities of structure *depends upon* and is *structured by* a definite spatial structure of social relations.

This is a timely reminder of the ultimate significance of economic forces in determining aspects of human behaviour, a corrective to the drift towards voluntarism in the 'structurationist' literature.

Thrift (1983) has strongly argued against the implied voluntarism of time-geography and, as well, has tried to illustrate the significance of contextuality to the 'structurationist' argument by discussing concepts such as 'locale' and region. Broadly speaking, his project for a 'reconstructed regional geography' aims to develop a workable understanding of the dynamics of regional class formation and its potential as an instrument for transformation and, ultimately, human emancipation. Parallels can be drawn between the contextuality of Soja's socio-spatial dialectic and the class-focused development theories discussed in Chapter 5, but Thrift's conception is both class and region-based, without being reduced to the mere sum of the two. Social activity within a region is conceived as a:

> continuous *discourse*, rooted in a staggered series of shared material-situations that constantly arise out of one another in a dialectically linked distribution of opportunity and constraint, presence and absence. A region is lived *through*, not in. (Thrift 1983:38)

The profile of a region's population is shaped in a number of ways. Processes amenable to a compositional analysis – topography, the organisation of production (especially the labour process), class structure and the form of the state – are part of the 'regional setting'. More important, in a contextual analysis, are the 'locales', or 'settings for interaction'. In capitalist societies the dominant locales are the home and school (reproduction) and work (production). Other locales, such as leisure facilities, are dependent, but by no means insignificant, while in other societies other locales (the example given is religion in Bali) may be dominant.

> Such locales have five main effects. First, they structure people's life paths in space and time . . . Second, these institutions can have effects on *other* people's life paths through the constraints they place on a person's ability to interact with other people engaged in activities within them. Third, they provide the main arenas (in time terms) within which interaction with other people takes place . . . Fourth, they provide the activity structure of the day-to-day *routines* that characterize most parts of most people's lives . . . And fifth, they are the major sites of the processes of *socialization* (seen in the active sense) that take place from birth to death, within which collective modes of behaviour are constantly being negotiated and renegotiated, and rules are learned but also created. (Thrift 1983:40)

Another set of 'counterinstitutions', often embedded in conservative locales, challenge the orthodox socialisation processes and generate a means of social transformation. Thrift (1983:42-8) discusses three aspects of social action: personality formation, the availability of knowledge, and the 'institutional context of sociability' — that is, the particular forms of regional social institutions and organisations and whether they tend to favour social action or not. These threads are brought together:

> as part of a closely interrelated inquiry into the nature of conflict and the *capacity* of particular social groups living through particular regions to carry on class conflict and other forms of conflict. Capacity [is] the ability of different social groupings . . . to organize and then to carry on various historically and geographically specific kinds of opposition to other social groupings . . . Capacity is clearly a function of the ability of a social grouping to produce transformative individuals (personality formation), particular forms of knowledge, and particular forms of sociability, each of these being inseparable from the others. (Thrift 1983:48)

This development of the theory of structuration deals very explicitly with both recursiveness and contextuality. Moreover, it is orientated towards social action — both in historical explanation and in a prescriptive sense — and although this is not explicitly discussed in the structuration literature, it is highly relevant to the main, current issues in development studies. Specifically, it positions the sort of call for a class analysis framework mentioned in Chapter 5 in a more clearly defined context. The structurationist debate not only allows us – and this is particularly relevant to geographers – to locate the class-based analysis of underdevelopment in a regional study that is cognisant of the broader implications of geographically specialised research, it stresses the significance of the geographical context to meaningful understanding of human society and, ultimately, effective transformation.

Conclusion

The regional question, and the significance of space itself, has in the last few years been dismissed by some radical writers as epiphenomenal or even as a fetish. I have strongly argued against this assumption suggesting that some of the key problems of both the orthodox and political economy approaches to regional underdevelopment stem, in part, from a failure to understand the cohesive significance of space and place. This point, together with the polarised positions of pre-existing theories of determination/voluntarism, characterise much of the recent work on development and underdevelopment. In contrast, the concepts of territorial integration and the socio-spatial dialectic, and the work on human geography and structuration, try to shift the focus of explanation away from the orthodox polar positions plotted in Table 6.2. Such a shift is not intended to replace the basic insights of the political economy approach to underdevelopment. These must remain as a sort of platform of current wisdom. Rather, the aim is to build into regional political economy a means of recognising the significance of human action in space. The following two chapters focus on two concrete aspects of underdeveloped societies – labour migration and urban informal labour markets – drawing largely on experience in Indonesia. Their purpose is to demonstrate different approaches to particular aspects of the changing nature of regions and cities in Indonesia, and point to ways in which we might seek to reinterpret these societies in the light of developments in contemporary social and economic theory.

Notes

1. Both Eliot-Hurst and Smith ground their disagreements with Peet in the

environmental relation closest to them all – namely, space – and, significantly, not in the natural environment.

2. In urban studies, see also Mingione (1981) and Saunders (1981).

3. Underdevelopment research, human geography and urban studies have all drawn heavily upon Althusser's interpretation of Marx, rather than interpretations, such as those of Thompson and Giddens, which have been discussed in history and sociology respectively.

4. The pitfalls of eclecticism, or more precisely the attempt to combine Marxian categories with empiricist science or non-materialist abstract science, are dealt with by Fincher (1983).

5. See, for instance, Bourdieu (1977), Touraine (1977), Thompson (1978), Bhaskar (1979) and Layder (1981).

7 MIGRATION, CIRCULATION AND URBANISATION IN INDONESIA

Wide-scale, sustained urbanisation is one of the most significant geographical processes of the last two centuries. In Europe the shift of population from the rural areas to the towns and cities was closely associated with the emergence of industrialisation (Hobsbawm 1974). That did not make it any less traumatic for the agricultural workers displaced from the land, nor did the growth of industry guarantee a good life in the city. Many were forced into the informal labour market, working in domestic service or in petty trade, while factory conditions for the industrial workforce, and housing standards in general, were very poor. The urbanisation process in the Third World lagged behind Europe but, particularly in the last three decades, has grown at a very fast rate. The incorporation of rural societies into the world economy precipitated a destabilisation of village economies, redirecting and amplifying an innate restlessness in rural populations and leading to large-scale permanent and temporary shifts of population to the towns and cities. Zelinsky has termed this process a 'mobility transition'. He argues:

> There are definite, patterned regularities in the growth of personal mobility through space-time during recent history, and these regularities comprise an essential component of the modernization process. (Zelinsky 1971:221-2)

In other words, he has pointed to a general shift in the nature of mobility as society evolves from a premodern traditional society through transitional stages to an advanced society (Table 7.1).

While there are certain clear parallels between urbanisation in Europe and in the contemporary Third World, they occurred in different historical epochs and, therefore, can be compared only with great caution. In the immediate post-war period the growth of cities in Southeast Asia was labelled 'pseudo-urbanisation' because it was thought the generally slow economic development which prevailed in the region had failed to provide adequate industrial employment for the urban population (McGee 1967, 1971). Others, however, argued that employment opportunities were being increasingly created, a trend

Table 7.1 The Mobility Transition

Phase I – The Premodern Traditional Society
(1) Little genuine residential migration and only such limited circulation as is sanctioned by customary practice in land utilisation, social visits, commerce, warfare, or religious observances.

Phase II – The Early Transitional Society
(1) Massive movement from countryside to cities, old and new.
(2) Significant movement of rural folk to colonisation frontiers, if land suitable for pioneers is available within country.
(3) Major outflows of emigrants to available and attractive foreign destinations.
(4) Under certain circumstances, a small, but significant, immigration of skilled workers, technicians, and professionals from more advanced parts of the world.
(5) Significant growth in various kinds of circulation.

Phase III – The Late Transitional Society
(1) Slackening, but still major, movement from countryside to city.
(2) Lessening flow of migrants to colonisation frontiers.
(3) Emigration on the decline or may have ceased altogether.
(4) Further increases in circulation, with growth in structural complexity.

Phase IV – The Advanced Society
(1) Residential mobility has levelled off and oscillates at a high level.
(2) Movement from countryside to city continues but is further reduced in absolute and relative terms.
(3) Vigorous movement of migrants from city to city and within individual urban agglomerations.
(4) If a settlement frontier has persisted, it is now stagnant or actually retreating.
(5) Significant net immigration of unskilled and semiskilled workers from relatively underdeveloped lands.
(6) There may be a significant international migration or circulation of skilled and professional persons, but direction and volume of flow depend on specific conditions.
(7) Vigorous accelerating circulation, particularly the economic and pleasure-oriented, but other varieties as well.

Phase V – A Future Superadvanced Society
(1) There may be a decline in level of residential migration and a deceleration in some forms of circulation as better communication and delivery systems are instituted.
(2) Nearly all residential migration may be of the interurban and intraurban variety.
(3) Some further immigration of relatively unskilled labour from less developed areas is possible.
(4) Further acceleration in some current forms of circulation and perhaps the inception of new forms.
(5) Strict political control of internal as well as international movements may be imposed.

Source: Zelinsky (1971:230-1.

reinforced by the selective growth of industry in the region during the last few years (McGee 1981, 1982a, 1982b). Nevertheless, the changing nature of the world economy has meant that demand for labour, structure of production, and even commitment to a particular place are far different from last century. The point is that urbanisation in the contemporary Third World cannot be assumed to follow the same course as in Europe.

The purpose of this chapter is to examine different interpretations of migration and circulation in Indonesia, with a view to developing an alternative framework for analysing the geography of mobility.[1] In the first part, three means of examining circular migration are discussed and criticised. They are: the descriptive-empirical research carried out chiefly in West Java, the mobility and tradition models which have been developed to explain West Sumatran migration, and the political economy models of mobility. The second section of the chapter considers key concepts, such as structuration, with which we might attempt to build a new theory of mobility; and the third section illustrates these concepts by examples drawn from the Indonesian experience.

Explanations of Migration and Circular Migration

Empirical Models

Until the early 1970s the three main foci of mobility research in Indonesia were transmigration policy, the so-called peripatetic groups such as the Minangkabau, and urbanisation. It is only in the last few years that researchers have broken away from these traditional topics and looked at population circulation as a whole. This has proved a significant step forward for which we should be grateful to the meticulous local level studies of people like Hugo[2] (1978a, 1978b, 1982) in rural West Java, and to a lesser extent, the Jakarta-centred research of Critchfield (1970), Jellinek (1978a, 1978b), Papanek (1975), Temple (1974, 1975) and others. Some of the insights they have provided into circulation can be summarised by drawing on three themes from the literature: the extent of circulation, the nature of employment in the town, and the impact of circulation on the village.

First, the extent of circulation. Hugo (1979:204-6) makes the point that the extent of circulation far exceeds that which we might expect from the Census figures. The reason is that the Census deals in the category of permanent migration, which is defined as movement resulting in a return journey more than six months later. In focusing on permanent migration there is no accurate measure of either commuting or circular migration, defined as a movement from village to city that results in a return migration at least once every six months. The focus on permanent migration Hugo characterises as a concern with the 'tip of the iceberg'. In 10 of the 14 West Javan villages he examined, circular migration was dominant. Up to 15 per cent of the income of migrants in the cities of Jakarta and Bandung could be spent on transport to and from villages, whilst Hugo found that 90 per cent of so-called permanent migrants returned on a visit to villages at least once each year.

Second, the majority of West Javan migrants, according to Hugo (1978b:26-9), find urban employment in petty production, or as it is otherwise known, the informal sector. The type of petty production depends on the village of origin – Hugo (1977:64) shows how migrants from one village will ride trishaws, those from another hawk groundnuts, and so on. Not all jobs are in petty production; Hugo points out that migrants also work in airline offices and hotels, or for the government or the army, or in factories or hospitals. By and large, though, petty production is the most frequent form of urban employment; the hours of work are flexible, its absorptive capacity is greater than wage-enterprises, and the overall low urban wages require a flexibility of commitment that is only catered for by petty commodity production.

Looking at circulation from the city end, Papanek (1975:17-19) found that around two-thirds of his sample of petty producers made a yearly visit home, whilst over half of that group visited two or more times. The people who earned the lowest incomes, and those with the least attractive jobs, usually did not return to the village. However, over two-thirds of the trishaw riders and petty traders returned to the village each year.

Third, Hugo (1979:206-10) elicited that the pattern of circulation had a significant impact on the rural villages of West Java. Remittances accounted for some 60 per cent of income in households containing a commuter, whilst circular migrants contributed about 50 per cent of total household income. The bulk of remittances was spent on basics, mainly food and clothing, whilst some money was spent on education or invested in housing. Out-remittances from villages were relatively insignificant by comparison, mainly being money sent to support students in the town.

The social impact of circulation is far more mixed, according to Hugo, for on balance the social costs of circulation may well outweigh the social benefits. On the one hand, the villages had problems of raising labour for *gotong-royong* (mutual-help) projects; circulation produced problems of selecting village leaders, the absence of young people detracted from the village social climate, and divorce rates among migrants were higher than the average. On the other hand, the return of a better-educated, more respected group of migrants with new ideas for the village was insufficient compensation for the social dislocation caused by out-migration.

In sum, the value of this work is the rich detail it has provided about the mobility of relatively small groups of Indonesians. However, there are epistemological limitations to the inductive methodology which characterises this research. The meticulous documentation of the patterns of mobility in West Java has provided a sound descriptive basis for the investigation of an explanation of mobility, but it is critical to appreciate its limitations. We observe the careful exposition of the *situation* of mobility, but there is little attempt to come to terms with the *setting* or the context within which migration occurs (Mitchell 1978). What we require now is a consolidation of this data in the light of our understanding of the nature of change throughout Indonesian society — that is, the way in which mobility is both a cause and a reflection of economic, political and social change, and not simply one or the other.

To illustrate this critique two critical aspects of Hugo's analysis are examined. The first is his generation of a typology of migration. He divides spontaneous migrants into seven categories, and forced migrants into two categories based on three criteria: the characteristics of the move; commitment to the city; and commitment to the village (Hugo 1978b: Table 5). It is this sort of taxonomic exercise which can lead us into a cul-de-sac, for it imposes a theoretical significance upon a description. If we accept, for example, a sevenfold division of spontaneous migration then we will inevitably be committed to a complex, fragmented explanation of each. In other words, the form of the mobility determines the form of the explanation; this contradicts the argument that mobility is an epiphenomenon, reflecting the unity of the structure of society.

Second, the dominance of form is reflected in the unbalanced explanation Hugo (1977:62, 1978:Ch. 8, 1979:206, 210) offers for circulation. On the one hand, the explanation of 'aggregate' factors is quite clearly located in economic forces, but these are little more than touched upon. He concludes:

> . . . the gradient of population flow is away from areas where
> ecological pressures are greatest and opportunities to earn a liveli-
> hood are least, and toward areas of relative economic expansion.
> (Hugo 1978a:297)

These are, of course, influenced by socio-cultural factors '. . . super-
imposed on and inter-related with regional economic differentials'
(ibid). In general, these deliberations are not developed — how long
have these economic forces been important, and what has given rise to
this pattern of uneven development? These are the sorts of questions
that need to be more thoroughly considered.

On the other hand, the discussion of the behavioural dynamics of
mobility is far from complete, being located in the balance of centri-
petal and centrifugal forces. The economic pressures of village life have
given rise to mobility, based on expectations of work in the cities.

> Opposing this force is a strong environmental preference for the
> village especially because of its function as the locus of fundament-
> ally important family ties and loyalties. (Hugo 1978a:297)

Circulation is a product of these two processes. However, there are
also 'intervening variables' which modify the raw economic pressures.
These include the degree of uncertainty which surrounds the migrants,
the socio-cultural pressures within the village, and the personal characteristics of the migrant, specifically, stage in the life-cycle, skills and
psycho-social attributes (Hugo 1978a:297-8).

This section has argued that we cannot continue to depend solely on
detailed empirical research on mobility. The value of the existing micro-
research cannot be doubted because it has provided us with a valuable
resource bank of data on mobility, far exceeding in accuracy and
quality previous data sources such as the Census. Nevertheless, this
inductive empirical approach to mobility research has resulted in an
uneven development of our explanations of mobility. A typology of
mobility is an unsatisfactory starting point for the development of a
theory of mobility because it is essentially atheoretical and fragments
the underlying structural unity of forces of change in Indonesia. The
inevitable result is detailed exposition of local forces in migration (the
situation) but a poor development of the broader aggregate economic,
political and social forces (the *setting*) which are at the core of change
in contemporary Indonesia.

Mobility and 'Tradition'

A second important focus of mobility research in Indonesia has been directed towards those groups who are seen to be particularly prone to *merantau* or circulation. This provides a useful opportunity to raise some questions about another, apparently more recent, trend in mobility studies. It is the tendency to point to long histories of mobility among groups as evidence of a certain continuity in forces that have given rise to mobility. A parallel argument is noticeable in recent literature on mobility in Melanesia. Chapman (1977:1) for instance stresses:

> . . . the antiquity of circulatory forms of movement and [thereby] to challenge the common assumption that these are transitory kinds of behaviour linked to particular processes and phases of socio-economic change – notably urbanization, modernization, and industrialization.

Similarly, Ward (1980:11-16) was puzzled by the readiness of Papua New Guinea highlanders to volunteer for work in the Highlands Labour Scheme in the 1940s. His surprise, he argues, reflects the common (albeit hidden) assumption that highland societies were static. Once we realise that pre-colonial societies were not static but constantly changing and characterised by well-established mobility patterns then the readiness of highlanders to move is understandable.

The importance of pre-colonial mobility patterns is apparent, but there are two aspects of this argument which may be questioned. The first is the assumption that because the form of behaviour known as circulation occurred both before and after direct colonial intervention in Indonesia or Papua New Guinea, then we can assume that the forces which gave rise to that mobility are relatively constant. The second issue which follows from this is that the 'traditional' forces within a society are the most important in explaining a pattern of mobility. This is the sort of argument compiled by Watson (1970:107-24) who, based on evidence from Papua New Guinea, puts the proposition that the contemporary dynamics of population movement can only be interpreted in terms of an historical social structure essential to certain human communities. No one would deny, it appears, that mobility reflects both factors internal and factors external to a society; the disagreement is over the relative balance of these factors. The argument to be challenged is well summarised by Chapman and Prothero (1977:7) when they say: 'Circulation has endured but has been modified; its incidence has been greatly magnified; but this in turn serves only to emphasize customary patterns of mobility.'

These issues can be aired in an examination of Minangkabau mobility, perhaps the group best known in Indonesia for their proclivity to *merantau*. Naim (1976:149-50) defines *merantau* as:

> leaving one's cultural territory voluntarily, whether for a short or long time, with the aim of earning a living or seeking further knowledge or experience, normally with the intention of returning home.

Minangkabau are not the only group in Indonesia with a reputation for *merantau*: as Hugo has shown it is also important to the West Javanese, a people often assumed to be without much desire for circulation. Some other well known *merantau* are the Batak, Banjarese, and Bugis. Although the Minangkabau have a long history of overseas migration, in recent years the pattern of *merantau* has changed. Almost all circulators now move to urban areas and take up occupations quite unlike those which they left.

> Though most of the people come from rural villages where the families engage in agricultural activities, practically none of them repeats the same occupation in the *rantau*. Instead, they engage in trade, services and intellectual occupations, which, in terms of financial return may also be considered as upward economic mobility. And yet, the old economic system, that is subsistence agriculture, is always there to receive them back whenever failure or hardluck is encountered in the *rantau*. (Naim 1973:27)

Because of the long history of Minangkabau mobility, explanation has tended to rely on the distinctive character of Minangkabau social organisation. Swift (1971:255-67) is one who has explored those aspects of Minangkabau society which appear to have brought about circulation. In essence, Swift's explanation concentrates on the 'traditional' pressures within Minangkabau society, pointing out that their significance has increased with the changes brought about within the colonial and post-colonial society.

> In the past, temporary migration and achievement in the *rantau* offered some escape from the tight status restrictions of the homeland, and the role of religious leader seems to have offered mobility to a few. The Dutch colonial period opened up a much wider range

of opportunities for individual status improvement. Economic change increased trading opportunities, and the Minangkabau had an aptitude for trade which some local people lacked. (Swift 1971:267)

Whilst Swift argues that a complex of factors gives rise to circulation, the crux of his explanation relies on the so-called traditional aspects of Minangkabau social organisation. Notably, these include the rivalry induced by *adat* (customary) status differences, the cultural exclusiveness of the Minangkabau which supports individuals away from home, and the matrilineal extended family, which encourages economic prosperity in the *rantau* whilst channelling the wealth acquired towards traditional prestige ends. The Minangkabau ideal personality is an individualist, strongly orientated towards competition and achievement, unlike, according to Swift, his Malay counterpart. The result is that he is more likely to be mobile than people in cultures without the same 'traditional' pressures.

Others have considered this same aspect of Minangkabau. Naim, for instance, has argued that *merantau* is institutionalised into the Minangkabau social system.

The Minangkabau man normally has no role to play in either his mother's or his wife's lineage. His position is rather weak: in his mother's lineage (to which he actually belongs) he is not provided with a compartment or *bilik* for his private use, unlike all the female members, while in his wife's lineage he only visits her at night. He does not as a rule inherit a portion of the lineage property of either side. As a male member of his mother's lineage he functions as protector and guardian (*mamak rumah*) and as such it is his duty also to enlarge and enrich the lineage properties.

Because of this precious position he is apt to travel anywhere he wants. Before marriage he is even encouraged to go away and prove to himself that he can earn money and stand on his own feet. *Merantau* then can also be viewed as an initiation into manhood and as a social obligation upon the man to leave his village to acquire wealth, further his knowledge and gain experience. (Naim 1973:31)

The difference is that Naim argues that this is one among a complex of pressures changing over time. Social pressures, even though they may be institutionalised, are not regarded as the determining force of circulation.

A critical reaction to the 'traditional social organisation' argument focuses on the two points raised earlier. First, there is the question of the importance of these 'traditional' forces in circulation. Kahn (1976:64-95) has examined Minangkabau matrilineal organisation and asks whether the term 'traditional' has been used in an appropriate way. He commences by pointing out that many important decisions are now made in West Sumatran villages outside the matrilineal structures. Among these are economic decisions (particularly due to the declining importance of subsistence agriculture), some political issues, and the sphere of marriage arrangements. These are cited as evidence of the declining significance of matriliny, yet *merantau* continues. More importantly, though, Kahn argues that the commonly used meaning of matrilineal organisation derives not from the 'traditional' or pre-colonial society, but from the early colonial nineteenth century society. Kahn argues, in fact, that it was the Culture System of forced export crop production that was responsible for many of the important features of matrilineal organisation.

The results of the Culture System were: 'the relatively static, seg-mentary system of clans and lineages with corporate land ownership often taken to be the hallmark of the "traditional" Minangkabau matrilineal system' (Kahn 1976:88). In other words, Kahn argues that the demand made upon Minangkabau society by the Culture System brought about a solidifying of the matrilineal structure. Moreover, he believes that this process was necessary to the success of the Culture System in West Sumatra. The result was that, as on Java, aspects of earlier Minangkabau social structure were built upon by the colonial power so that whilst the outward form appeared unchanged, in effect, they no longer deserved the label 'traditional'.

If we accept Kahn's analysis, then it is misleading to consider socio-cultural forces as 'traditional'. More importantly, though, it challenges the conceptual basis of the explanation. If the political and economic changes which were wrought by the Culture System can be seen to have considerably altered the social structure, then surely an explanation of mobility must search out these causal forces through an analysis of the underlying political and economic structure. The discussion of so-called traditional forces makes for an incomplete explanation.

The second question concerns the continuity of patterns of mobility before, during and after the colonial period.[3] The danger is that we take a continuous pattern of mobility to be evidence that the under-lying causes of mobility have similarly been continuous. This is a false assumption. The structure of all parts of Indonesian society is in constant change and periodically alters in some fundamental dialectical manner. Naim (1973:410) recognises an aspect of this when he discusses the complex of causes which bring about Minangkabau mobility. Between 1900 and 1970 the form of Minangkabau migration remained more or less constant, but the forces producing this pattern were constantly changing. Some (for example, political unrest) were only significant at particular periods, others increased steadily in significance (ecological, demographic, economic, education, urban attractions) whilst still others remained constant throughout the period or declined in significance (geographical and social-systemic). This demonstrates that a constant form of mobility, at the aggregate level, should not necessarily be assumed to imply a consistent structural cause of mobility.

However, we can take the argument further. Kahn (1976:90) explains that in West Sumatra the abolition of the Culture System in 1908 created an entirely new social formation. The *merantau* form of mobility continued through this period but the structure of causation was not the same prior to and after 1908. To assume so is to fail to appreciate the fundamental changes wrought by the colonial power through its major changes of policy. The abolition of forced cultivation, together with a gradual decline in the amount of land under colonial ownership, signalled the beginning of a chain of events which included the production of rice as a marketable commodity and drastic changes in the structure and output of the subsistence sector as a whole. These, in turn, were the catalysts of further far-reaching social changes among the Minangkabau. Yet throughout, the Minangkabau pattern of *merantau* persisted. Our task in the historical analysis of mobility is not simply to relate different patterns of mobility to different social structures, but to go further and also identify the critical changes which societies undergo, even when these do not immediately and obviously correspond with changes of the form of mobility.

A criticism of this approach to mobility research is that once again it leads us into a cul-de-sac. Naim (1976:179) also develops a typology of migration focusing on ethnic groups and characteristics of mobility such as class of migration, mode of movement, occupational orientation and so on. The problem is not the accuracy or the thoroughness of such an exercise (though we might well question aspects of it) but rather its epistemological value. If we wish to progress in mobility research then we must take a new tack and look to the organisation of the society in general. Moreover, we should be wary of those studies which search out traditional forces as explanations of mobility. 'Traditional' often becomes synonymous with 'natural' forces which reflects a poverty of ideas, and can also be misused as an apology for colonialism.

The Political Economy of Migration

Some of the boldest ideas to emerge on the political economy of mobility have come from Africa. Samir Amin (1974c:65-121) has argued that modern labour migration in West Africa can best be understood through the uneven impact of capitalist expansion upon tribal societies. Mobility reflects, according to Amin, an aspect of proletarianisation. The spatial impact of capital in West Africa has been to produce three broad types of regions:

(1) those organised for large-scale export production have already entered the capitalist phase, which implies private appropriation of the land and the availability of wage labour; (2) those formed as a result of colonial economic policies which have continued to be followed after independence, serving as reserves, which supply this salaried labour, and finally (3) those which are not as yet part of the system, or to be more precise those which are still only marginally so and serve only as auxiliary reserves. (Amin 1974c:94)

The development by capital of certain regions, and the corresponding underdevelopment of others have, in themselves, not always been sufficient to cause such widespread mobility. Different policies have been applied in different regions in order to ensure a supply of labour, ranging from coercion and the imposition of taxes to more subtle strategies of urban-oriented education. The process, though, according to Amin, has got out of hand:

it has gone beyond its intended objective as a result of its own dynamism, and beyond the society which tried to enclose it; in other words the 'rural-exodus' has become uncontrolled, uncontrollable and explosive. Such is the law of the development of social contradictions that, what is 'functional' at one stage becomes 'dysfunctional' at another, that is, it puts in jeopardy the social organization from which it grew. (Amin 1974:98)

Thus, for Amin, migration is a direct result of the reorganisation of West African society brought about by the expansion of capitalism and its need for physical resources and, more importantly, labour.[4]

Titus (1978:194-204) has examined the appropriateness of Amin's model in Indonesia by means of a macro-statistical analysis of migration patterns. He classifies Indonesia's provinces into three broad categories according to lifetime migration rates, based on data extracted from the 1971 Census. Category I includes places, such as DKI Jakarta, which are characterised by high mobility rates and high in-migration. Category II provinces (for example, South Kalimantan) are characterised by low rates of mobility, and Category III provinces (West Sumatra) have high negative (that is, out) mobility.

His second task is to categorise provinces by a contrived measure of regional inequality. This is based on scores of the province's centre or periphery status, and includes measures like the presence of big urban centres and the extent to which the province is dependent upon a single export. On this basis provinces are categorised as Centre (C1 and C2 – Jakarta, North Sumatra) and three levels of periphery – P1 South Sulawesi, P2 East Kalimantan and P3 Nusatenggara, respectively less and less centre-like.

Titus then cross-correlates the two sets of data, and comes up with three results:

The greatest mobility together with net in-migration is to be found in . . . the economic 'boom' provinces of both the centre type (Jakarta, N. Sumatra) and the relatively developed periphery type (S. Sumatra, Riau, E. Kalimantan) . . .

The lowest mobility and a zero-migration balance is to be found . . . in the isolated and still largely self-sufficient periphery type of province, i.e. E. and W. Nusatenggara . . .

Finally the highest mobility together with net out-migration appears . . . in the highly integrated but stagnating peripheral provinces close to the centre regions (W. Sumatra, C. Java, Yogyakarta). (Titus 1978:200)

Titus concludes that this evidence is sufficient to confirm the relevance of Amin's work to Indonesia, though he cautions that the 'socio-economically more complex intensely colonised regions' of Indonesia need to be taken into account.

Titus's paper (or for that matter, Amin's theory) is important because it points to the need to examine the process of uneven development in Indonesia, the forces which have given rise to this process, and the forces which seem to be perpetuating it. The concessions to 'regional development' in the second and third five-year plans notwithstanding, the spatial economy of Indonesia is as yet imperfectly understood. Titus has compiled a prima facie case that demands greater attention. The approach is, however, incomplete because it fails to look beyond the macro-organisation of space. It shifts the focus of Indonesian migration from detailed, empirical micro-research to a general model of regional uneven development and the broadly correlated population mobility, but does not come to grips with the complex way in which humans respond to changes in the political economy of the region. Generally speaking, a critique of this approach to migration research could easily echo the critique of underdevelopment theory summarised in Chapter 6: it overplays the importance of structural economic deter- minist forces in explaining migration and underplays the role of human agency; it is an overly abstract and generalised explanation that ignores the complexity of human society; and it fails adequately to tackle the time-space dimensions of migration, especially detailed patterns of regional homogeneity and diversity.

Although the above three sets of critiques apply particularly to the conceptual problems of research work on Indonesian migration, it is also evident that there is much dissatisfaction with conventional approaches to mobility, both from the point of view of theorists of human spatial organisation (Santos 1979) and from writers with regional interests in Papua New Guinea (Curtain 1980), Africa (Swindell 1979) and South and Southeast Asia (McGee 1978b).

The dispute common to most of this work can be distilled into two issues. First, in the past, much work on mobility has tended to be descriptive, eschewing the need to develop theories of human mobility and instead elaborating particularist explanations of mobility. This has necessarily resulted in detailed investigation of case study material focusing, in particular, upon the individual decision-maker and assuming that mobility patterns are best seen as the sum total of these decisions. The bulk of research energy has been directed towards the individual, which explains why structural forces have merited such superficial treatment. Second, those theories which have attempted to explain mobility have been too naive and mechanical. They have endeavoured to generalise from the example of the individual – expect- ing migrants to migrate simply because of urban-rural wage differentials (Harris and Todaro 1970) – or they have been pitched at the world scale and have assumed that societies pass through a series of lineally- arranged stages, each associated with a specific pattern of mobility (Zelinsky 1971). Alternatively, they have been general political economy models which have accounted for broad shifts in population but have been unable to explain detailed and complex patterns of migration with any precision.

Towards a Theory of Mobility

The task is to reconcile some of these divergent trends and channel them towards investigations which are likely to produce a set of theories of mobility. We need to overcome the false dichotomy that has emerged between particular and universal forces, or to be more precise, 'the individual, his family and the local community on the one hand and the larger political economy on the other' (Swindell 1979:255). Most studies have acknowledged the need for this type of approach, either implicitly or explicitly. Equally, few studies have achieved either a balance or a true integration of these levels of analysis. In an attempt to explain why this may have been the case, three aspects of this methodology are elaborated.

The Individual and Society

There are several ways of viewing this relationship. Mobility research has been, more often than not, marked by implicit notions of voluntarism in which society is assumed to be the sum product of the intentional actions of individuals. By contrast, radical research in Third World countries has sometimes gone to the other extreme and been guilty of reification; society is assumed to be external to the individual and imposes massive constraints upon behaviour. In these studies mobility is seen as wholly a product of the political economy. Neither set of assumptions appears to be true. The voluntarists are as guilty of over-simplification as are the structuralists, for both overlook the complexity of the relationship between the individual and society.

An alternative framework for analysing this relationship is suggested by the concept of 'structuration' (Bourdieu 1977; Giddens 1979). As discussed in the previous chapter, the term refers to a complex set of relationships between individuals and society in which society is a product of historical practice, and is constantly reproduced and transformed by it, and yet at the same time shapes historical practice. Thrift (1981:77) refers to it as: 'the continued "hyperdialectic" between society and individual, in which the individual reproduces and/or transforms society and society simultaneously socializes the individual'. The significance of the concept of structuration is that 'the structural properties of social systems are both the medium and the outcome of the practices that constitute those systems' (Giddens 1979:69). Thus the '*structure is not a constraint on or a barrier to action but is instead essentially involved in its reproduction*' (underlined in the original) (Gregory 1981:10).

This is an important formulation because it begins to prepare the ground for developing a theory of mobility based on dual levels of analysis – that of the individual and society. Clearly though, it requires much work. What is society? To what extent can we use categories like political economy or mode of production and how are they related to structure? Are there relations of determination between the individual and society? If there are, what are they? Finally, of particular importance in the Indonesian context, there is the question of whether a concept of structuration is applicable in peripheral capitalist societies, remembering that it was based on work done in advanced capitalist societies where the concepts of economy, culture and society can be somewhat different. Much remains to be considered before we can progress far; nevertheless we can press on and explore this framework.

Structure and Process

The major spatial rearrangements of population, which all countries have experienced at some time throughout the past 200 years, are associated with the establishment and expansion of the capitalist mode of production. The starting point for an analysis of this process is the world economic system, whilst the leading edge of the human mobility process is labour migration. In order to relate these processes directly to mobility patterns in Indonesia we need to look at the development and spread of capitalism throughout the archipelago. We find that its spatial development is uneven, concentrating on cities and towns and a few other special regions such as those well endowed with resources. Migration was once thought to be an equilibrating mechanism that reallocated factors of production (predominantly labour) to these regions, reflecting the need for a redistribution of population to fit the uneven distribution of natural resources. However, this is clearly not the case. For example, there is a significant and growing concentration of population in Jakarta and the other major cities of Indonesia; yet, the majority has not been drawn into productive capitalist enterprise. Quite the reverse. A significant proportion of their immigrant workforces is occupied in low productivity petty commodity production, contributing primarily to their own subsistence and reproduction rather than economic development through the expansion of productive enterprises.

Taking a more critical look at the expansion of capitalist production we see that its impact is uneven in two important ways. First, it creates a socially uneven pattern benefiting certain groups and classes at the expense of others. Second, it creates a spatially uneven pattern benefiting certain regions and not others. The configuration of this pattern depends on both the nature and direction of capitalist expansion (itself a product of the relationship between forces of production such as technology, and relations of production such as the class formation) and on the resilience of the existing economy – in Indonesia almost always peasant subsistence agriculture.

In a general sense, the products of this articulation are twofold. On the one hand, specific groups and classes and specific regions become poles of accumulation and may experience temporary or, occasionally, permanent economic growth. The nature of this growth will differ from place to place. On the periphery it is more likely to be associated with major natural resource projects whereas in the large urban centres it will be a combination of the effects of a growing bureaucracy, a concentration of entrepreneurs and the spin-offs from the growth of manufacturing industry. On the other hand, regions and classes will suffer disarticulation as the shock-waves of capitalist expansion reverberate through the country but bring no real change to the economic structure. The pre-existing order is eroded both directly – for example the marketing of cheap consumer durables undermines local craft production – and indirectly – in the sense that expectations are aroused which cannot be fulfilled.

Human mobility is closely connected with these processes. Populations are redistributed towards the centres of accumulation and away from those of disarticulation; the fact of movement away from areas of disarticulation serves to undermine them further. The distinction between permanent and circular migration becomes increasingly important. Permanent migration is dominant in those societies where the bulk of the population fit into the broad classes of bourgeoisie and proletariat; circular migration is characteristic of those transitional societies where the capitalist mode is dominant qualitatively but not quantitatively. Large sections of the population have a dual dependence (Burawoy 1976), or are interdependent, on city and village but are unable to gain an adequate income from either. Circulation continues to enjoin different sectors of the economy and thus plays a vital role both for the individuals affected and the economy as a whole.

Outlined very briefly here are the broad economic processes which characterise the current epoch in Indonesia – using loosely defined terms such as the capitalist mode of production, peasant production, and categories of population such as class. Whilst these categories illuminate patterns of mobility at the macro-level of analysis, a theory of mobility requires a theoretically sound amalgamation with insights gained from an examination of the individual and his or her local circumstances.

The Individual and Process

A critical weakness common to both the voluntarist and structuralist approaches to migration research is a failure adequately to conceptualise the relationship between the individual and the economy and society. Nevertheless, the existing stock of micro-level data on Indonesian mobility – the criticisms sprinkled throughout this essay notwithstanding – is of considerable value in sketching the set of circumstances which confront villagers in different areas. In fact, one of the criticisms often made of researchers working on Indonesian topics, such as mobility, is that they frequently overlook the available data resources and opt instead for new data collection. However, this type of research might be supplemented – possibly even replaced – by the more explicit methodology associated with time-geography. In essence, time-geography is an attempt by geographers (originally in Sweden but increasingly in other parts of the world) to analyse the space-time behaviour of individuals (organisms) and artefacts (things). By focusing on an individual's trajectory through space and time, scholars are able to write 'the geographical biography of the population within a constrained environment' (Parkes and Thrift 1980:246). This approach stresses, at the present time, the social constraints upon the individual's trajectory – for example, capability constraints, coupling constraints and authority constraints – as well as those which space and time themselves make upon the trajectory. The value of the approach, which, incidentally, was a product of Hagerstrand's early work on Swedish migration patterns, is that it provides a systematic methodology for the collection of longitudinal micro-data on human behaviour over time and space. It has had occasional use in contemporary mobility research. Chapman (1976), for instance, has documented the time-geography of individuals over periods of up to seven months in the Solomon Islands.

But more importantly, how can this sort of exercise, which works from the individual up, be integrated with the macro-approach which works downwards to the individual? The key lies in ensuring the compatibility of the sets of assumptions about the influence of structures – whether socio-economic at the level of political economy or spatially and temporally at the level of the particular place – upon the behaviour of individuals. In essence, the concept of structuration defined a two-way dialectical relationship between the individual and society in which they transformed and reproduced one another. As a result, we need to ensure that we approach the time-geography analysis of the individual not from the point of view of the way time, space, and society (in its broadest sense) *constrain* the behaviour of the individual, but from the way in which time, space, and society selectively *influence* the individual, and, just as importantly, the way the individual *feeds back* into (and, ultimately, *reproduces*) the society and transforms it. Similarly, when we approach the analysis from the political economy standpoint we are not talking about a simple process of *determination*, but a process which individuals and classes can and do *transform*, *opt out of*, or *avoid*. In other words, a complex socio-economic process which, like society as a whole, depends upon people to reproduce it and which, in turn, is shaped and reproduced by it. While these proposals cannot be said to have solved the disjuncture between scalar levels of analysis, they do illustrate how mobility research can confront some of the main pitfalls of integrating the study of the individual and society.

Migration and Circulation in South Sulawesi

The patterns of circulation which characterise petty producers in the provincial city of Ujung Pandang, capital of the province of South Sulawesi, are a useful illustration of the patterns of mobility in Indonesia.[5] Almost three-fourths (73.8 per cent) of petty producers were born outside the town, almost all in the rural areas of South Sulawesi. Around half, possibly two-thirds, of migrant petty producers keep in contact with their villages by regular trips back. The most mobile group are the trishaw riders, nearly half of whom make two or more trips to the village each year. The return to the village for the harvesting of the rice is the most notable component of circulation. Some 59.8 per cent of trishaw riders returned to plant the rice crops, whilst 68.0 per cent returned for the harvest. Other petty commodity producers were a little less diligent, the corresponding overall figures being 36.4 per cent and 42.4 per cent.

It is almost always males who migrate to exploit employment opportunities with a view to circulation. Partly this reflects the greater range of socially-acceptable work restrictions placed upon free female movement. The effects of the bi-locality of the family are widespread. Most (36 out of 58) trishaw riders who were active circulators lived with their spouses in Ujung Pandang, but a significant proportion, 38 per cent, had left their spouses in the village. By contrast nearly all pedlar's families lived with their spouses in the city. This raises an interesting point about the significance of family structure in mobility. Bi-locality would appear to take two different forms. On the one hand, it consists of a sexual division of labour in which the female remains in the village, presumably keeping on with subsistence work on village rice-land. On the other, there appears to be a generational division of labour. In this case the entire nuclear family circulates, while older relatives (parents, uncles and aunts) remain in the village and are the recipients of remittances etc.

The underlying causes of migration to the town were complex, but to most migrants reflected economic pressures (rural poverty), political conflicts and upheavals, and socio-cultural changes (for example, social dislocation). They in turn were a product of both the expansion of capitalism and internal tensions within the pre-existing society. There are three processes of some importance. First, capital has brought about a process of uneven development of the forms of production (a 'ruralisation' of the rural areas, according to Merrington, 1975); it has 'underdeveloped' the subsistence sector both by the extraction of resources and by allowing the stagnation of the economy, but also by the creation of new wants that cannot be met by 'traditional' means. Second, the result has been that labour has moved to take advantage of any available alternative employment opportunities. As the demands for wage labour have been quickly satisfied, so migrants have been forced into the only alternative form of employment in petty production. Third, petty production is partly geared to service the needs of wage labour, but incomes are restrained by the slow growth of the wage labour-force, and more importantly, by the large number of migrants in the city and the way in which this sphere is articulated with the dominant capitalist sphere of production in the city (Forbes 1981b). As a result, migrants are unable to break the vital link with the rural sector. Spatial mobility is a response to this pattern of integration.

Among Ujung Pandang's trishaw riders, the continuing links with the village were important in sustaining the rider in the city, the assistance taking both a tangible form (exchange of rice) and an intangible form (the use of the village for rest and recreation). In the same way, the village also depended on circulation. Remittances are an important component of household income, as Hugo (1979:206) has shown, and the seasonal flow of labour is critical to a successful harvest. The overall importance of circulation is impossible to gauge precisely, but it is possible to argue that this practice represents a significant dampener on structural change in the villages. The poverty of a proportion of the rural population, and simultaneously increasing expectations, can be met, albeit inadequately, through circulation, and does not necessitate the sale of land and permanent migration. Thus circulation suspends the capitalisation of the rural sector, preserving inefficient peasant landholdings through subsidising their owners and workforce. Hugo (1979:207) has shown that a large proportion of remittances are spent on necessities such as food and clothing, whilst Crystal (1974:119-152) notes the heavy spending on ceremony by the Toraja. Remittances are generally not invested in land, and so they are not contributing to land consolidation, but rather to temporarily preserving smallholder subsistence agriculture.

Conclusion

The argument presented above is related to the more far-reaching discussion of the 'conservation' and 'dissolution' of the pre-capitalist economy in the modern world system (see Bettelheim 1972:271-322). Mobility, it has been argued, is one among several human practices which serve to conserve the pre-capitalist forms of production in the underdeveloped countries. By contrast, permanent labour migration has the opposite effect, reflecting in the process of urbanisation the expansion of capital in the city and having the effect of hastening the spread of capital through the country. The distinction between permanent and circular migration therefore is a critical one. Circulation is significant in the preservation of both petty commodity production and peasant subsistence production. It is not, however, an independent force. It is a critical link in the socio-economic structure of a society. For instance, it has been argued that in parts of Africa the lack of any urban employment has meant a decline in circular migration, and this has meant, in turn, the increasing capitalisation of agriculture as potential urban migrants turn to cash crop production (van Binsbergen and Meilink 1978:11). Human agency, manifest in the decision of the individual to migrate or not to migrate, is important because of its two-pronged character. On the one hand, it reflects fundamental changes in the socio-economy; on the other, it has a substantial impact on the nature and direction of change in the socio-economy. Migration and circulation is the product of human responses to a particular situation which is itself the product of further human action, and so on. But just as importantly, the practice of migration and circulation aids the reproduction of the conditions of impoverishment which caused it in the first place. In the following chapter a different aspect of this framework is examined through a discussion of informal labour markets in Third World cities. Whereas in the above discussion circular migration was portrayed as a reasonably ordered response to changing material conditions in the villages and cities, the next chapter looks at urban conflict and urban class formation.

Notes

1. Parts of this chapter are drawn from two earlier publications, Forbes (1981b, 1981c).

2. A summary of Hugo's work can be found in Hugo (1978b) and Goldstein (1978).

3. A related point was made by Titus (1978:194-204) who argued there is little evidence for assuming an intrinsic, culturally determined difference in the propensity of Indonesians to migrate. He rejected the contrast between the:

> relatively low level of mobility among inland peoples with closed corporate social systems with the high mobility of coastal people with a commercial 'pasisir' culture and more loosely structured social systems. (Titus 1978:202)

because, he argued, the highland Toraja are now just as mobile as the lowland Bugis. Thus the assumption that different levels of mobility reflect different social systems is, according to Titus, a false one.

4. Such a brief summary gives an oversimplified view of the Amin analysis. Apart from the original paper the reader is also referred to the collection of essays in *African Perspectives*, 1978 No. 1 for a detailed examination of both theoretical and empirical aspects of this type of approach to migration.

5. This section is based on Chapter 8 of my doctoral thesis (Forbes 1979). By petty producers in this case is meant pedlars (specifically of fish, fruit and vegetables and ice-cream) and trishaw riders. The statistical data are drawn from a sample of 320 interviews.

8 CONFLICT AND CLASS IN THE CITY

The growth of urban settlements in the Third World during the last two centuries has varied in time and space according to the manner in which they have been incorporated into the world economy. Generally speaking there have been two significant phases of urban growth (Roberts 1982). The first phase commenced with the colonial expansion designed to incorporate the products of the colonies — mainly agricultural products and minerals — into the world capitalist system. The urban centres that emerged during this period were charged primarily with administering to the trade in raw materials, policing the populations involved, and supplying the commercial and transport functions to enable the trade to carry on. As a result of these roles the cities that developed during this time were usually located at service sites on export routes or, in the case of major mining concerns, at the point of production. Latin America was one of the earliest regions incorporated into the world economy, and as a consequence, urbanised more rapidly than comparable regions in Asia and Africa. On the whole, however, urbanisation during this period fluctuated in pace. During one period India even appeared to be 'deurbanising' when the British colonial rule undermined the indigenous industrial system.

The second phase of urbanisation corresponded to industrialisation in the Third World, but again individual colonies and countries were spread across a long time horizon. Argentina, for example, began to industrialise in the nineteenth century whereas many Asian and African countries did not commence until the last few decades, and some not at all. Yet practically all countries experienced an upsurge in urban population after the Second World War. In 1920, 5.8 per cent of the population of the less developed regions lived in towns and cities with populations in excess of 20,000: 20 years later this had only increased to 8.6 per cent, but then by 1975 some 20.3 per cent of these regions' populations were expected to be living in urban places (Table 8.1). There is a clear differentiation between the experience of Latin America and East and South Asia and Africa. In 1920, 14.4 per cent of the population in Latin America were urbanised, climbing to 40.5 per cent in 1975. By contrast, only 4.8 per cent of the African population lived in urban places in 1920 and this grew to 18.1 in 1975, less than half the proportion living in towns and cities in Latin America.

164

Table 8.1 Percentage of the Population of the World and of Each World Region that is Urban (in places of 20,000 or more) (%)

	1920	1930	1940	1950	1960	1970	1975
World Total	14.3	16.3	18.8	21.2	25.4	28.2	29.7
More Developed Major Areas	29.8	32.8	36.7	39.9	45.6	49.9	52.1
Europe	34.7	37.2	39.5	40.7	44.2	47.1	48.2
Northern America	41.4	46.5	46.2	50.8	58.0	62.6	65.4
Soviet Union	10.3	13.4	24.1	27.8	36.4	42.7	46.4
Oceania	36.5	38.0	40.9	45.7	52.9	57.9	57.1
Less Developed Major Areas	6.9	8.4	10.4	13.2	17.3	20.4	22.2
East Asia	7.2	9.1	11.6	13.8	18.5	21.7	23.7
South Asia	5.7	6.5	8.3	11.1	13.7	16.0	17.4
Latin America	14.4	16.8	19.6	25.1	32.8	37.8	40.5
Africa	4.8	5.9	7.2	9.7	13.4	16.5	18.1
More Developed Regions[a]	29.4	32.6	37.0	40.0	46.0	50.5	52.8
Less Developed Regions[b]	5.8	7.0	8.6	11.4	15.4	18.5	20.3

Note: a. More developed regions refers to Europe, Northern America, Soviet Union, Japan, temperate South America, Australia and New Zealand.
b. Less developed regions refers to East Asia without Japan, South Asia, Latin America without temperate South America, Africa and Oceania without Australia and New Zealand.
Source: Roberts 1978:7.

The significant geographic concentration of problems – poverty, poor housing, pollution, inadequate services – in the city have been constructively and critically analysed in a number of books on Latin American cities (Roberts 1978; Portes and Walton 1981), Africa (Sandbrook 1982), Southeast Asia (McGee 1967) and the Third World in general (Gilbert and Gugler 1982). This chapter focuses on interpretations of one key aspect of Third World cities: employment, and particularly the informal labour market and urban petty production. Definition and measurement problems make difficult an accurate estimate of the size of informal employment, but both the statistical and qualitative evidence support the belief that in many Third World cities over half the workforce is in informal employment (Table 8.2). Discussion in this chapter is in four parts: the first part of the chapter looks at the emergence of interest in the 'informal sector'; the second looks at the critique of informal sector research and the subsequent emergence of a petty production approach; the third looks at the importance of conflict in the formation of a class of petty producers; and the fourth and final part points to the significance of class formation in the discussion of underdevelopment.

Table 8.2: Estimates of the Size of the 'Informal Sector'

Place	Date	Criterion of employment	Total employed	Per cent in informal sector
Bombay	1961	Employment reported to Director of Employment and Training	1,687,000	55
Jakarta	1971	Registered establishment	⟩ 1,000,000	⟩ 50
Belo Horizonte	1972	Social security payment	?	69
Lima	1970	Size of establishment	619,000	53
8 cities in Peru	1970	Size of establishment	?	62

Source: Mazumdar 1976:659.

Employment and the Informal Sector

Corresponding to the growth of the 'basic needs' approach in development studies (Chapter 3), the decade of the 1970s witnessed the emergence of a new set of concepts by which to analyse small-scale enterprises in peripheral capitalist societies. The concept of the informal sector was coined by Hart in 1971 to describe urban workers outside the wage sector (Hart 1973). Paralleling this was the work of the International Labour Organisation (ILO) in the late 1960s and, in particular, the formation of its World Employment Programme in 1969. The point of the programme was to construct development strategies which were employment orientated. This involved a considerable redirection of the prevailing wisdom which had framed development strategies primarily in terms of an economic growth objective, with employment goals relegated to residual status. The first significant document to bring together the informal sector concept and employment orientated development strategies was the ILO report on Kenya (ILO 1972).

This report was compiled from the work of a large group of people, but the intellectual flavour owed much to research at the Institutes of Development Studies at the Universities of Sussex and Nairobi respectively. It argued in favour of equity, though not as a substitute for growth; the catchphrase was redistribution with growth (ILO 1972:3). The key employment issue, as far as the report was concerned, was not unemployment but the prevalence of low incomes among the so-called underemployed. It was calculated that 20 per cent of adult males and 50 per cent of females in the urban areas of Kenya lacked the opportunity to earn a reasonable income (ILO 1972:63). Yet, at the same time, they argued that the informal sector, where many of these people worked, had been grossly misunderstood:

> the bulk of employment in the informal sector, far from being only marginally productive, is economically efficient and profit-making, though small in scale and limited by simple technologies, little capital and lack of links with the other (informal) sector. (ILO 1972:5)

The result was a recommendation that vigorous action should be taken to promote the informal sector (ILO 1972:223). Essentially, they wanted reform of the harsh licensing laws which discriminated against informal sector activity, research concentrated on products suitable for manufacture or use in the informal sector and, most important of all, links encouraged between the informal sector, private business and State enterprises (ILO 1973:21-2). The point was to strengthen the linkages between formal and informal enterprises in the expectation that this would bring about: 'A transfer of incomes from the top income groups to the working poor [which] would result in new types of labour-intensive investments in both urban and rural areas' (ILO 1972:6-7).

The ILO country studies were followed in the World Employment Programme by city studies. Included among them was a study of Jakarta (Sethuraman 1975, 1976a, 1976b). The author noted the significance of the informal sector to Jakarta, comprising around half the workforce of over one million. He noted too that trade and service activities were the most prominent – unlike Africa where manufacturing was often of greater significance – and that informal sector operators usually worked without legal permits, with little capital and low earnings per worker. Like other studies of this type he also concluded that small-scale enterprises 'have virtually no connections with either the government of formal sector enterprises' (Sethuraman 1975:196). Finally, he drew attention to the fact that the informal sector was composed of a high proportion of newcomers to the town, which was attributed primarily to the high rate of unemployment in surrounding areas, and only secondarily to the rural-urban wage differential.

The policy emphasis of the Jakarta study echoed other World Employment Programme studies. Urbanisation needed to be slowed down by a combination of urban policy – the author saw the 'closing' of Jakarta to outsiders in 1970 as an arm of this — and rural policies designed to keep migrants at home. These were necessary to prevent the improvements in the city being swamped by new migrants. The key to the growth of urban employment was the development of policies to promote the urban informal sector. Current policies which discriminated against the informal sector needed to be reviewed or discussed. Following upon this, efforts were required to upgrade the technology used by informal sector enterprises and to promote the integration of the sector into the formal and public sectors. The informal sector was seen as an important sphere of production, not only because of its contribution to employment but also because it aided skill formation and ultimately the formation of human capital.

It was at about this time that the World Bank, concerned that the benefits of development were not reaching the target population of the bottom 40 per cent — the world's poorest — began to reorient strategies towards the rural and urban poor (Adler 1977). The Urban Poverty Programme had two thrusts. On the one hand, it aimed to deliver basic services to the mass of urban poor through programmes like the Kampung Improvement Programme in Indonesia. On the other hand, it aimed to generate productive non-farm employment opportunities at the lowest capital costs practicable (Jaycox 1978:12). The policy has since been spelt out in detail by the World Bank (World Bank 1978). Basically, this part of the programme is designed to channel assistance towards informal sector enterprises and markets, and to promote industrial and commercial development. Between 1973 and 1978 the informal sector programme received only 7.4 per cent of the funds allocated by the World Bank to its Urbanisation Project in Indonesia (shelter programmes received 51.7 per cent). Despite research evidence of the significance of the informal sector, it has proved difficult to implement policies which promote informal sector activities.

Nevertheless, the close relationship between informal sector theories and policy is demonstrated by the fact that the bulk of theoretical development was conceived either within the World Employment Programme, or outside it by scholars who worked closely with policy bureaux. McGee, for instance, a pioneer of informal sector research in Southeast Asia (McGee 1973, 1974, 1976) maintained close links with the Canadian-sponsored International Development Research Centre (IDRC 1975, McGee and Yeung 1977). This nexus between policy and theory started to erode around the middle of the decade when studies critical of the informal sector began to appear and a new framework — the petty production approach — emerged (Moser 1978). Nevertheless, these developments did not deter organisations like the World Bank from pushing on, as we have seen, nor did they have much impact on the many informal sector studies which have succeeded them.

Informal sector promotion is the latest round in a series of strategies designed to tackle the problems of the urban poor. The emphasis of this policy package on redistribution, together with its characteristic incorporation of rational and managerial techniques, contrasts strikingly with its punitive predecessors which were concerned mainly with the eradication of the informal sector (Baker 1980:4). Its emphasis is on the working poor and their ability to cope with the urban economy and, sometimes, to prosper and thrive. It celebrates the resourcefulness of individuals to adapt to difficult economic conditions, seeing urbanisation and the growth of an informal sector as an indigenous solution to the transition of societies through the peripheral capitalist stage. The main barrier to accumulation and the development of petty capitalism is clearly seen to be hostile government, ignoring the legitimate needs of small-scale enterprises and proposing instead mindless punitive policies designed to clear away the informal sector in order to present a picture of modernisation. Freed of these constraints, and assisted by benevolent policy, the inherent resourcefulness of the urban poor – amply demonstrated by their migration from the villages and quick entry into employment, ingenious solutions to the housing problem and informal enterprises – will quickly assert itself and result in growth and development. The vision was not always so Utopian. Some stressed that the promotion of the informal sector was only in lieu of any prospect of structural change and more fundamental redistribution (McGee 1976). Nevertheless, the promotion of the informal sector did appear to offer a great deal of promise.

The relationships between informal enterprises and the rest of the economy tended to be somewhat overlooked. The informal sector, we were told, relied on indigenous resources, on family labour, on skills acquired outside the school system and locally adapted technology (ILO 1972:6). In other words the independence and self-sufficiency of informal sector enterprises were stressed, as if somehow this whole area of economic activity had emerged in isolation and separate from the rest of the urban economy. But then, this marginal economic location was also seen to be a constraint upon the development of the informal sector. The lack of integration with the formal sector was frequently put forward as a barrier to growth. Recommendations invariably followed for the integration of the two sectors, the assumption being that it would prove of mutual benefit.

Finally, the policy emphasis of informal sector research is abundantly clear. It reflects two positions. One is a pragmatic, humane concern for the well-being of this great mass of humanity, for the 1970s was a time of heightened social consciousness in universities and planning bodies such as McNamara's World Bank. The other, more contentiously, is the fear that the pot might boil over. Informal sector policy was one means of maintaining the *status quo* and pre-empting collective action. The two have frequently been lumped together. This sort of policy has proved successful in that it appears likely to persist well into the present decade. Elites like it, as do planners and policy-makers. There are constraints upon policy implementation, not the least of which is the lack of funds, but the policy has the perceived advantage of ameliorating problems that seemed not too long ago to be intractable.

However, the informal sector approach has come in for a considerable amount of criticism since the mid-1970s. Broadly speaking, three main points have been made. First, it has been argued that the attempt to delineate the informal sector is wasted because urban enterprises more closely represent a continuum of scale and characteristics rather than the two-division cluster explicitly recognised by the informal sector (Missen and Logan 1977). McGee (1978a) argues that this has made for an unreal typology of small-scale enterprises. No matter what characteristic might be chosen to form the typology — for example, ease of entry, or reliance on local resources — it is not difficult to catalogue a handful of exceptions. The heterogeneity of forms of production has prompted Breman (1976) to argue there is no such thing as a separate informal sector. He proposes that small-scale enterprises reflect the fragmented nature of the entire labour market in Third World countries, which is consequently better viewed as a whole, rather than through the isolation of a single sector.

The second criticism of the informal sector concept highlights its inward-looking nature. Many studies of this type have tended to concentrate on the description of the character of informal sector enterprises, often in an attempt to draw out the peculiar characteristics of its workforce (Breman 1976; McGee 1978a). There has been little emphasis upon the integration of small-scale production into the whole economy. Some, such as Geertz (1963), discussed the close rural links of the informal sector workforce, but there have been few attempts to analyse these in detail, and none which have attempted to focus on the integration of the informal sector with other forms of economic activity within the city. As a result, the importance of undertaking of small-scale production both in terms of its internal structure and its external relations is a critical point which has tended to be lost in many informal sector studies.

The third criticism is that informal sector studies have been strongly associated with a conservative ideological framework. Moser (1978) believes that the use of the informal sector concept by social and economic planning institutions, such as the ILO, has encouraged the view that the problems of underdevelopment – poverty, unemployment and so on – are the consequence of economic structural imbalance and are amenable to treatment through a planning policy conceived within the existing economic, social and political order. The informal sector, whilst not necessarily taking a leading role in development planning, has been part of the ILO strategy for coping with urban poverty. The importance of this is that studies have been inclined to build up the positive aspects of the informal sector and play down the negative.

Class and Urban Petty Production

Petty commodity production is the label generally used in the literature to define 'that group of activities normally seen as lying outside the principal spheres of capitalist production in underdeveloped economies' (Gerry and Birkbeck 1981:128). Petty production:

> possesses no autonomous dynamic of its own and. . . the level of possible capital accumulation is constrained by structural factors embedded in the wider social formation. The urban economy is conceptualized in terms of a continuum of economic activities with petty commodity production recognized as a form of production existing at the margins of the capitalist mode of production integrated into it in a dependent or subordinate fashion. The persistent feature of stagnating incomes in petty commodity production is linked to its important role within the capitalist mode of production of keeping down the reproduction costs of urban wage labour.
> (Rogerson and Beavon 1982:250)

The defining characteristic of the petty commodity production approach is this stress on the interrelatedness of the urban economy. It is an approach which characteristically:

> focuses on the structural linkages and relationships between differ-

ent production and distribution systems (which include technical as well as social relations of production). . . This approach identifies the constraints on the expansion of small-scale enterprises, the levels of capital accumulation possible and the dynamics of production at this level, and the transitional processes, whether to capitalist production, or proletarianization. (Moser 1978:1061)

A number of studies have used the petty production approach to examine the emergence of an informal labour market. For instance, Le Brun and Gerry (1975) highlight the significance of integration in their work on urban areas in Senegal. In fact, they argue that capitalism has been largely responsible for the growth of many forms of petty commodity production. By creating a small wage workforce capitalism has formed a market for commodities; this has resulted in the importation of manufactured goods and has thus provided equipment for the domestic production of consumer commodities, as well as commodities for exchange. Moreover, they believe that many of the skills evident among petty commodity producers have been acquired in capitalist wage employment. This is not to deny that there is also a 'traditional' petty production sector made up of village craftsmen, such as weavers. Le Brun and Gerry stress, however, that though these craftsmen may not owe their emergence to capitalism, in recent years they have become integrated into the State, and in that way have been subordinated to commercial capital. Some weavers, for instance, now work in State controlled artisan's villages, producing commodities for the tourist market. Whilst weavers may represent a 'traditional' craft, their close links with capital have resulted in the organisational structure of production being transformed into capitalist relations of production.

In a later article, Gerry (1978) elaborates upon the impact of articulation. The processes retarding the development of a domestic capitalist class in Senegal are not the result of the 'backward' nature of indigenous production. Rather they are a manifestation of the dominance of capitalist production over all other forms of production. This domination is realised through a variety of processes. These include capitalist domination of large sections of production and distribution which forces petty production into the remaining less profitable areas of production and distribution. A notable instance of this is the capitalist control over the industrial sector. Another method of domination is through the capitalist sector's control of the institutions which facilitate capital transfer and accumulation such as credit sources, licences and contracts. Often instruments of the State, these institutions are firmly in the grip of that section of the domestic bourgeoisie whose interests correspond with those of the metropolitan capitalist class. The result is, it is argued, that petty production is forced into a dependent and peripheral status within the complex Senegal social formation. It is trapped in an 'involutionary impasse, able only to reproduce its conditions of existence, often at the expense of its own standard of living and labour remuneration' (Gerry 1978:1154).

The politico-ideological components of the exploitation of petty production, and the processes of class formation, have been examined by Gerry and Birkbeck (1981), making use of Wright's (1976) notion of a contradictory class location. Historically in capitalist societies, and at present in peripheral capitalist societies, the situation can be summarised as follows:

> with the constitution of an advanced and mature capitalism, PCP (petty commodity production) plays both a material and an ideological role: the former is to support capitalist industry materially, whilst allowing a considerable transfer of the burden of responsibility and cost to the lower echelons of production and distribution hierarchies; the latter is to convince a large section of the economically active population that only the maintenance and reproduction of the capitalist system offers them the chance of material wellbeing and the promise that the hardest-working and most innovative will reap the rewards of their past sacrifices and hardships. (Gerry and Birkbeck 1981:133)

Yet whereas petty commodity production is *relatively* insubstantial and insignificant in advanced capitalist societies, its function in the periphery – the provision of cheap food and consumer goods, maintenance of a reserve army of labour, the opportunities it offers for supplementing wage incomes and as a market for capitalist goods – is very important to capitalist production.

Class formation follows firstly from location within the relations of production. Here Gerry and Birkbeck are anxious to differentiate between the apparently self-employed working poor and settle on a threefold division:

1. Direct wage workers (for example someone working on a commission).
2. Disguised wage workers (for example, renting equipment).
3. Self-employed workers.

Wage workers, although they may not recognise themselves as such, by virtue of their relationship to the means of production are part of the proletariat. The self-employed workers, who in fact represent a smaller proportion of petty producers than is often thought, are considered a lumpen-capitalist fraction of the bourgeoisie. This group is called lumpen-capitalist rather than petty bourgeoisie because the possibilities of accumulation are more restricted. Disguised wage workers, according to Gerry and Birkbeck (1981), such as managers and semi-autonomous employees in capitalist societies, occupy a contradictory class location, embodying characteristics of bourgeoisie and proletarian, at least in terms of the relations of production. However, they caution that 'relations of production are only one determinant of class location. . . we must examine with equal rigour the politico-ideological level' (Gerry and Birkbeck 1981:142).

It is the disguised wage workers in the contradictory class location on which they focus. Essentially, Gerry and Birkbeck (1981) argue that the ideology characteristic of disguised wage workers is politically conservative, being based on illusions of independence, a preoccupation with simply getting work rather than the condition of work, a faith in individualism and a belief in miracles. Thus, collective political action seldom occurs, while ideology reinforces faith in the economic order. Like lumpen-capitalists, disguised wage workers possess so-called 'pygmy property' which permits them to do little more than reproduce their existing conditions. Far from having a viable stake in an exploitative system, in many cases they constitute the objects of exploitation (Gerry and Birkbeck 1981:151). Whereas the proletarianised wage worker might be best served by simply maintaining his or her ties with the capitalist system, the other major forms of petty producers requires:

> a return to the liberal, *laissez-faire* and highly individualist capitalism of the past. Pygmy property is thus compromised in that, rarely able to make the ideological leap to radical political action, it tends to lend its support to the parties of corporate bourgeois property — the very mode of production which blocks its development. (Gerry and Birkbeck 1981:152)

While recognising the significance of forces other than relations of production in the formation of classes, Gerry and Birkbeck (1981) still define classes in terms of these economic relations. Ideology is only important to the extent that it reinforces a clouded view of the objective economic position of the petty producer. This extends economic functionalism into the realms of politics and ideology. Petty producers are economically functional to peripheral capitalism, while their ideology through stressing individualism, a faith in miracles, etc. ensures their political quiescence. Although their argument is framed very cautiously, Gerry and Birkbeck (1981) argue substantially the same case as Portes and Walton (1981). Petty production is functional to peripheral capitalism – it is a structural feature of the economic organisation of society. Functionalism of course is a risk – perhaps the major risk – in any structuralist argument. After fleshing out the major structural forces in a society, it then becomes necessary to slot people into the categories within the structure. Whereas much of the work on petty producers in the 1970s stressed the individualistic entrepreneurial talent of this group, the more recent work has tended to swing too far in the opposite direction, denying petty producers any economic or political independence. While not refuting either the significance of the relations of production in class formation or the apparent political quiescence of petty producers, the next part of the chapter argues for the importance of understanding everyday forms of conflict in order to understand class formation.

Conflict and Class

Erik Olin Wright has somewhat ironically noted 'the analysis of class structure is intended not as the end point of an investigation, but as the starting point' (Wright 1980:365). Yet it is clear there is no consensus on the theoretical criteria for specific classes within the class structure of capitalist societies, nor is there agreement among Marxists on the precise class structure of contemporary capitalism. Nevertheless, it would seem that the underlying problem of a functionalist interpretation of class formation among petty producers is located within the non-recursive definition of class employed within this work. Class formation emerges from both the objective location of individuals within the general relations of production and the everyday practice – particularly that which is conflict-based – of those individuals.

As Poulantzas (1973) who is sometimes held to epitomise the structuralist view of class, has argued, there is a *double articulation* between form and behaviour which is important. He holds that 'economic, ideological, and political relations as a totality impose a structure upon class struggles, but they become transformed as effects of class struggles' (Przeworski, 1977:368). Class is not simply the material form of a structural category; the structural relations that constitute classes define *class places*, while at any conjuncture, classes adopt *positions*. These positions, of course, may not correspond to the attitudes and behaviour we might expect from the class places. Przeworski (1977:367) has taken this proposition further:

> *Classes are not given uniquely by any objective positions because they constitute effects of struggles, and these struggles are not determined uniquely by the relations of production.* . . . Class struggles. . . are structured by the totality of economic, political, and ideological relations; and they have an autonomous effect upon the process of class formation. . . classifications of positions must be viewed as imminent to the practices that (may) result in class formation. The very theory of classes must be viewed as internal to particular political projects. Positions within the relations of production, or any other relations for that matter, are thus no longer viewed as objective in the sense of being prior to class struggles. They are objective only to the extent to which they validate or invalidate the practices of class formation, to the extent to which they make the particular projects historically realizable or not.

In other words, classes cannot be read off from the mode of production as if from a wall-chart. Relations of production determine the class relation, but it is human behaviour and conflict which are the flesh and blood of class formation. An anecdotal illustration might aid in clarification. Working-class children are forced to attend school but while there, many adopt a stance hostile to the school. They rebel against authority within the school as a sort of semi-conscious rebellion against the structure of society as a whole, very much against the wishes of their teachers and middle-class society. A functionalist interpretation would have it that they need to be 'educated' to conform to society's need for a stable educated labour-force, but there they are struggling against 'the system'. Yet, ironically, the end result of their struggle is to ensure the reproduction of their working-classness because their lack of education practically guarantees that they are unemployable or suited only to the worst-paid jobs (Willis 1977). My argument tries to separate means from ends. In both a functionalist and a non-functionalist interpretation the main ends are the same — the reproduction of a class structured society — but the means towards those ends are quite different. In one behaviour is rigidly predetermined by objective structures; in the other behaviour both produces and reproduces the objective structure (Thrift: personal communication). As Gregory (1980:13) (and following Giddens and Habermas) would have it 'social systems are both the medium and the outcome of the practices that constitute them: the two are recursively separated and recombined'.

According to Nelson (1979:125-9) there are three main viewpoints on the political mobilisation of the urban poor. The first is the theory of the radical marginals which argues that the lag between urban growth and industrial progress radicalises these 'peripherals'; the second is the theory of the available mass which argues that the urban poor are atomised and alienated and therefore relatively easily mobilised; the third is the theory of the passive poor, in which the 'culture of poverty' is a force for conservatism. In recent years the general consensus has been that the urban poor have proved a fairly conservative force. Communist parties tend to draw 'virtually all their support from students, intellectuals, and (often fairly elite) segments of organised labour', while most revolutionary parties have focused their mass revolutionary action on the proletariat (Latin America, Vietnam prior to 1941) or the peasantry (China, Cuba, Vietnam) (Nelson 1979:344-5). But there have been notable exceptions: in Allende's Chile in the 1960s there was a strong attempt to court the urban poor; the Venezuelan Communist Party seems to have attracted quite a bit of support from *barrio* residents; while the Turkish Labor Party also tried to mobilise the urban poor. Clearly, the urban petty producers have not played a vanguard role in revolutionary conflict, but that does not mean they have had no role. For instance, strikes by pedicab drivers and other urban workers during the 1920s and 1930s in Vietnam played their part in the lead-up to the struggle for independence.

On the whole though, this stress on the quiescence of the urban poor has been part and parcel of the functionalist interpretation of their role in Third World cities. There are fragments of evidence which suggest that research on petty producers has tended to underestimate the significance of conflict among petty producers. A chief reason for this has been the use of what Cohen (1980:8-22) has called 'formula dichotomies'. Forms of conflict have tended to be dealt with from polar positions. Fanon, and some who followed, saw the lumpenproletariat as a revolutionary class, wheareas Marxists and non-Marxists alike have reacted by stressing the political conservatism of the urban poor. The emphasis on formula dichotomies forces us to take an either/or stand on political conflict.

It is very clear that researchers have tended to ignore the everyday forms of conflict – of consciousness, action and resistance. Cohen, Copans and Gutkind (1978:23) make the point that, historically, much of the day-to-day struggle of ordinary people is not at all well documented. Certainly there is very little published social history of the urban poor, nor does there appear to be much source material on the everyday existence of the urban poor. Yet it is the day-to-day conflict and patterns of behaviour which are the bread-and-butter of human history. As Cohen (1980:8) argues, for the African working classes, 'there has been too much reliance on data relating to strikes, unionisation and overt political militance, and for the most part a failure to discover and evaluate the silent, unorganised, covert responses of African workers'. Both non-Marxist and Marxist interpretations of Third World societies have tended to ignore this type of behaviour, implicitly dismissing it as insignificant. Conflict models have pointed to independence movements, break-away movements, labour strikes, religious movements and riots, but have not reached down to encompass criminal behaviour and everyday discord, whereas these are the most common forms of conflict and the ones in which urban petty producers are most likely to feature.

In the wake of the interest stimulated in urbanisation by organisations such as the ILO, and Southeast Asianists like McGee in the late 1960s and 1970s, there has emerged a growing bank of studies on Indonesian cities and especially the urban poor. This work has focused on issues like rural-urban migration, the formation of urban labour markets, urban kampungs, housing issues, urban subsistence production and petty commodity production (especially small-scale manufacturing, markets and trishaw riders) (Forbes 1981d). By and large these studies (which, incidentally, overwhelmingly focus on Jakarta and Yogyakarta) are essentially descriptive and are either accounts built around a statistical survey or detailed personalised descriptions of life in a kampung. Very little of this sort of material is set within an explicit theoretical framework. A characteristic feature of these studies is the argument in favour of the urban poor against their enemies, real or perceived. Consequently, most play up the stable, functional role of the urban informal sector and play down conflict. Nevertheless, it is possible to distinguish three different forms of conflict and resistance common to the informal sector.

There is evidence to suggest that urban informal sector workers have participated in broad social protest movements within the cities. Trishaw riders seemed to have a back-up role to students in the anti-Japanese urban riots in Jakarta in the 1970s and early 1980s, while it appears trishaw riders, especially, link in with semi-criminal (for example, prostitution) and criminal activities. It is also clear that petty producers come into conflict with the dominant forces in society in ways specific to this sector. It has recently been argued that petty and subsistence production may themselves be strategies for avoiding the wage labour relation. The corollary is that it is difficult to sustain empir-ically the argument that all informal sector production is functional to the cheaper reproduction of wage labour. The price of trishaw services, for example, is well above the price of transport on mini-buses. In other words, it could be argued that there are significant components of informal sector production which are clearly non-functional to the capitalist classes. If we were to study these groups' income earning opportunities then it would be to highlight strategies of employment independent of the wage labour relation. Resistance and conflict have also been central to the relations between the State apparatus and informal sector workers: trishaw riders avoid purchasing licences, petty government regulations on traders are flouted and officials bribed (Jellinek 1975, 1977). Finally, there is significant discord between different groups of petty producers. Often this reflects ethnic divisions such as conflict in Ujung Pandang between trishaw riders from diff-erent regions within the province (a hidden aspect of this is the closed shop nature of much small-scale production – access to employment is only available to people with specific place-links, such as villages). At the very least the disruption that this form of violence creates repre-sents significant resistance to the smooth operation of the urban econ-omy (although fighting is confined to nighttime when the disruption to others in the city is minimal).

Conclusion

There are three main points to be made about urban class formation in Third World cities. Attention must be diverted from economistic models of class structure and concentrated instead on the relationships between the economic class location and patterns of conflict in the city. This develops the structuration concept discussed in the previous two chapters. Following this, our expectations of what constitutes con-flict should be geared to encompass a whole range of practices from revo-lutionary behaviour down to everyday forms of discord and resistance. Significantly, it is the everyday forms of struggle which shape classes and class consciousness, as much as relationships to the means of production. Examining the everyday forms of conflict commom to petty producers raises questions about their perceived class status. Judging by the Indonesian experience there is evidence of an embryonic class structure forming among petty producers, and this leads me to dispute the 'politically conservative' label that has been heaped upon the urban poor. Instead, it seems likely that the political action taken by petty producers has taken different forms from those which the classical models of societal conflict have directed us to search out. Finally, it is beyond the scope of this chapter to consider whether urban conflict involving petty producers is 'part of an incremental chain of consciousness' (Cohen 1980:21) or simply a disorganised and individualistic response, but it is something well worth further consideration.

CONCLUSION

From beginning to end the arguments assembled in this book have shifted from the general to the specific. The volume began with a sweeping account of world history, followed by broad brushstrokes detailing the emergence of a geography of development (Part One) and a political economy of underdevelopment (Part Two). The last three chapters focused on particular places and issues, and concluded with a tentative statement about an aspect of class formation among a section of the workforce in the cities of Indonesia (or more particularly, one city, Ujung Pandang). This structure corresponds to the three main themes which the volume is intended to highlight. The first theme is the social context of knowledge. What we know, and what we need to know, changes as the material conditions of human society change. Understanding does not come from simply applying standardised concepts and theories to new information, as some economists and certain types of Marxists will sometimes argue. We need to be alert to the fundamental revisions necessary to our theories. Although this is a relatively straightforward argument, and is taken to much greater lengths in the recent literature on the sociology of knowledge, the boundaries to understanding imposed by the sociology of knowledge argument are not generally accepted by those working outside the main arenas of methodological debate. It does not mean we should abandon the classical literature (in fact, geographers, on the whole, would benefit from deeper contemplation of some key geographic thinkers from the past, and not only Vidal de la Blache), nor does it commit us to modernism and a rejection of earlier research work. Most importantly, it points geographers to the need for a critical awareness of changing material and intellectual conditions.

Second, and following on from this, I have argued that we are necessarily in the process of readjusting our approach to underdevelopment. It was said of the late Dudley Seers:

He had come to recognise that 'income is not welfare, nor even a proxy; it is one input into welfare, whereas the pattern and length of life are its dimensions'. 'The pattern of life': so in the end he had come round to a fully human view, beyond not only income growth or even income distribution but also beyond social indicators and

181

basic needs. (Singer 1983:4-5)

In order to better grasp the causes and consequences of underdevelopment it is the human dimension of the problem — 'the pattern of life' — to which we need increasingly to direct our attention. It means we need to increase our understanding of social processes *vis à vis* economic processes, and not just the social relations of production, but the whole complex process of social reproduction. Moreover, we will be required to shift our focus away from the building of grand theories of underdevelopment to time and place-specific empirical research, and to theorising at a different and much lower scale. Geography, as a contextual social science can, and must, be central to this project. Place, space and the environment are intimately associated with the shaping of people's lives, both actively and passively interrelating with life paths, daily tasks, exploitation, gender domination, reproduction of labour power and class formation. These relationships are able to be theorised; there is no doubting their significance — and thus the importance of geography — to a better understanding of development and underdevelopment.

Third, I remain committed to a radical interpretation of underdevelopment. The most appropriate and convincing explanations of underdevelopment are evident in the Marxist and neo-Marxist literature. Although much effort was expended in criticising aspects of the political economy of underdevelopment, there is no doubt that the basic building blocks of a coherent economic explanation of underdevelopment are apparent in this literature as a whole. More important, though, at the present time, are the questions which proponents of political economy are *not* asking — to be precise, why do these structures of economic exploitation persist? This should be another linchpin of a radical interpretation of underdevelopment. How do we expect the processes of human emancipation and transformation of the conditions of underdevelopment to occur? Ever since the 1930s the State, through its exercise of a benevolent public policy, has been seen as the key to development (Porter 1983). The Marshall Plan, the international aid agencies, the growth of development planning, regional planning and the emergence of large bureaucracies in Third World countries are all evidence of the faith placed in the transformative capacity of public policy. Yet the role of the State in any one society is dependent upon the class structure of that society and, more particularly, the relationship between the ruling class and the State. This relationship is problematic and place-specific — it cannot be assumed. The importance of the radical approach is that it recognises the significance of the politics of everyday life. It asks questions about how people actually organise themselves politically, and what they can achieve by bringing about fundamental shifts of power in society. Hence the significance of class formation among urban petty producers in the last chapter. Finally the interrelations between class and territorial (for example, city) based political organisations and their transformative capacity makes political geography increasingly central to the understanding of development.

A book such as this can only be open-ended. The project was primarily to review, and place in context, development geography in the past and to summarise and criticise current radical attempts to forge a geography of underdevelopment. It should be apparent from the argument that there are significant new questions which need to be tackled. Most significant in my view, is not the question of why so many people in the Third World are poor, but of why this condition continues to be reproduced; what are the obstacles to its transformation? The answers are, of course, manifold and complex, but for geographers one avenue of assault is to look more deeply at the relationship between human agency and social structure and, particularly, at the mediation of context – space and place – in the political process.

BIBLIOGRAPHY

Abdel-Malek, A., 1981, *Civilisations and Social Theory. Vol. 1 of Social Dialectics* Macmillan, London

Adler, J.H., 1977, 'Development theory and the Bank's development strategy – a review', *Finance and Development, 14,4,* 31-4

Alavi, H., 1975, 'India and the colonial mode of production', *Economic and Political Weekly*, Vol. 10, special number, pp. 1235-62

Alavi, H. and Shanin, T. (eds.), 1982, *Introduction to the Sociology of 'Developing Societies'*, Macmillan, London

Alcaly, R.E., 1978, 'An introduction to Marxian crisis theory' in Union for Radical Political Economics (ed.), *U.S. Capitalism in Crisis*, URPE, New York, pp. 15-22

Alexander, M., 1980, 'Structure and process in the modern world-system. The world system theory of Immanuel Wallerstein and its predecessors' in R. Peet (ed.), *An Introduction to Marxist Theories of Underdevelopment*, Department of Human Geography Monograph 14, Australian National University, Canberra, pp. 113-22

Amarshi, A., Good, K. and Mortimer, R., 1979, *Development and Dependency. The Political Economy of Papua New Guinea*, Oxford University Press, Melbourne

Amin, S., 1972, 'Underdevelopment and dependence in Black Africa – origins and contemporary forms', *The Journal of Modern African Studies, 10,4,* 503-24

Amin, S., 1974a, *Accumulation on a World Scale*, Trans. B. Pearce, Harvester Press, Sussex

Amin, S., 1974b, 'Accumulation and development: a theoretical model', *Review of African Political Economy, 1*, 9-26

Amin, S., 1974c, 'Modern migrations in Western Africa' in S. Amin (ed.), *Modern Migrations in W. Africa*, Oxford University Press, London

Amin, S., 1976, *Unequal Development*, Harvester Press, Sussex

Amin, S., 1977, *Imperialism and Unequal Development*, Harvester Press, Sussex

Amin, S., 1980a, *Class and Nation. Historically and in the Current Crisis*, Monthly Review Press, New York

Amin, S., 1980b, 'The class structure of the contemporary imperialist system', *Monthly Review, 31,8,* 9-26

Amnesty International, 1981, *Amnesty International Report 1981*, Amnesty International Publications, London

Arndt, H.W., 1972, 'Development economics before 1945' in J. Bhagwati and R.S. Eckaus (eds.), *Development and Planning: Essays in Honour of Paul Rosenstein-Rodan*, Allen & Unwin, London

Arndt, H.W., 1980, 'Economic development; a semantic history', *Economic Development and Cultural Change, 29,3,* 457-66

Baker, A.J., 1979, *Anderson's Social Philosophy, The Social Thought and Political Life of Professor John Anderson*, Angus and Robertson, Sydney

Baker, D., 1980, 'Understanding urban poverty', *Prisma. The Indonesian Indicator, 17,* 3-9

Baker, J.N.L. (ed.), 1963, *The History of Geography*, Blackwell, Oxford

Balibar, E., 1979, 'On the basic concepts of historical materialism' in L. Althusser and E. Balibar (eds.), *Reading Capital*, Verso, London, pp. 199-308

Banaji, J., 1977, 'Modes of production in a materialist conception of history', *Capital and Class, 7,3,* 1-44

Banaji, J., 1980, 'Summary of selected parts of Kautsky's *The Agrarian Question* in H. Wolpe (ed.), *The Articulation of Modes of Production*, Routledge and Kegan Paul, London, pp. 45-92

Barbalet, J.M., 1976, 'Underdevelopment and the colonial economy', *Journal of Contemporary Asia, 6,2,* 186-93

Barr, K., 1979, 'Long waves: a selective, annotated bibliography', *Review, 2,4,* 675-718

Barratt Brown, M., 1974, *The Economics of Imperialism*, Penguin, Harmondsworth

Becker, J.F., 1977, *Marxian Political Economy. An Outline*, Cambridge University Press, Cambridge

Bekki, A., 1966, 'Regional studies in foreign countries of Japanese geographers – Part 1' in A. Bekki *et al.* (eds.), *Japanese Geography 1966. Its Recent Trends*, Association of Japanese Geographers, Tokyo, pp. 157-60

Bell, M., 1980, 'Imperialism: an introduction' in R. Peet (ed.), *An Introduction to Marxist Theories of Underdevelopment*, Department of Human Geography Monograph 14, Australian National University, Canberra, pp. 39-50

Berdoulay, V., 1981, 'The contextual approach' in D.R. Stoddart (ed.), *Geography, Ideology and Social Concern*, Barnes and Noble, New Jersey, pp. 8-16

Berger, P.L. and Luckmann, T., 1966, *The Social Construction of Reality. A Treatise in The Sociology of Knowledge*, Doubleday, New York

Bernstein, H., 1979, 'Sociology of development versus sociology of underdevelopment?' in D. Lehmann (ed.), *Development Theory: Four Critical Studies*, Cass, London

Berry, B.J.L., 1972, 'Hierarchical diffusion: the basis of developmental filtering and spread in a system of growth centres' in N.M. Hansen (ed.), *Growth Centres in Regional Economic Development*, Macmillan, London, pp. 108-38

Bettelheim, C., 1972, 'Appendix I. Theoretical comments' in A. Emmanuel (ed.), *Unequal Exchange: A Study in the Imperialism of Trade*, NLB, London, pp. 271-322

Bhaskar, R., 1979, *The Possibility of Naturalism*, Harvester, Brighton

Bienefeld, M., 1980, 'Dependency in the eighties', *Institute of Development Studies Bulletin, 12,1,* 5-10

Blaut, J.M., 1979, 'The dissenting tradition', *Annals of the Association of American Geographers, 69,1,* 157-64

Blussé, L., Wesseling, H.L. and Winius, G.D. (eds.), 1980, *History and Underdevelopment*, Leiden University Press, Leiden

Boeke, J.H., 1942, *The Structure of the Netherlands Indian Economy*, Institute of Pacific Relations, New York

Boudeville, J.-R., 1966, *Problems of Regional Economic Planning*, Edinburgh University Press, Edinburgh

Bourdieu, P., 1977, *Outline of a Theory of Practice*, Cambridge University Press,

Cambridge

Bowman, I., 1934, *Geography in Relation to the Social Sciences*, Report of the Commission on the Social Studies, Part V, Scribners', New York

Boxer, C.R., 1965, *The Dutch Seaborne Empire 1600-1800*, Pelican, Harmondsworth

Boxer, C.R., 1973, *The Portuguese Seaborne Empire 1415-1825*, Pelican, Harmondsworth

Bradby, B., 1975, 'The destruction of natural economy', *Economy and Society, 42,2,* 127-61

Breman, J., 1976, 'A dualistic labour system? A critique of the "informal sector" concept', *Economic and Political Weekly, 11, 48, 49, 50,* 1870-6, 1905-8, 1939-44

Brenner, R., 1977, 'The origins of capitalist development: a critique of Neo-Smithian Marxism', *New Left Review, 104,* 25-93

Brewer, A., 1980, *Marxist Theories of Imperialism. A Critical Survey*, Routledge and Kegan Paul, London

Britton, S.G., 1982, 'International tourism and multinational corporations in the Pacific: the case of Fiji' in M.J. Taylor and N.J. Thrift (eds.), *The Geography of Multinationals*, Croom Helm, London, pp. 252-74

Broek, J.O.M., 1942, *The Economic Development of the Netherlands Indies*, Institute of Pacific Relations, New York

Bromley, R.D.F. and R. Bromley, 1982, *South American Development: A Geographical Introduction*, Cambridge University Press, Cambridge

Brookfield, H.C. (ed.), 1973, *The Pacific in Transition. Geographical Perspectives on Adaptation and Change*, ANU Press, Canberra

Brookfield, H.C., 1975, *Interdependent Development*, Methuen, London

Brookfield, H.C. with D. Hart, 1971, *Melanesia: A Geographical Interpretation of an Island World*, Methuen, London

Browett, J.G., 1980a, 'Development the diffusionist paradigm and geography', *Progress in Human Geography, 4,1,* 57-79

Browett, J.G., 1980b, 'Into the cul-de-sac of the dependency paradigm with A.G. Frank' in R. Peet (ed.), *An Introduction to Marxist Theories of Underdevelopment*, Department of Human Geography Monograph 14, Australian National University, Canberra, pp. 95-112

Browett, J.G., 1981, 'On the role of geography in development geography', *Tijdschrift voor Economische en Sociale Geografie, 72,3,* 155-61

Browett, J.G., 1982, 'Out of the dependency perspectives', *Journal of Contemporary Asia, 12,2,* 145-57

Brown, E.H. (ed.), 1980, *Geography Yesterday and Tomorrow*, Oxford University Press, Oxford

Buchanan, K., 1968, *Out of Asia. Asian Themes 1958-66*, Sydney University Press, Sydney

Buchanan, K., 1970, *The Transformation of the Chinese Earth*, Bell, London

Burawoy, M., 1976, 'The functions and reproduction of migrant labour: comparative material from Southern Africa and the United States', *American Journal of Sociology, 81,5,* 1050-87

Caldwell, M., 1977, *The Wealth of Some Nations*, Zed, London

Capel, H., 1981, 'Institutionalization of geography and strategies of change' in D.R. Stoddart (ed.), *Geography, Ideology and Social Concern*, Barnes and

Noble, New Jersey, pp. 37-69

Carlstein, T., 1982, *Time Resources, Society and Ecology. Vol. 1: Preindustrial Societies*, Allen and Unwin, London

Carney, J., Hudson, R., Ive, G. and Lewis, J., 1975, 'Regional underdevelopment in late capitalism: a study of the north-east of England' in I. Masser (ed.), *Theory and Practice in Regional Science*, Pion, London

Carney, J., Hudson, R. and Lewis, J. (eds.), 1980, *Regions in Crisis*, Croom Helm, London

Castells, M., 1977, *The Urban Question*, Edward Arnold, London

Chapman, M., 1976, 'Tribal mobility as circulation: a Solomon Islands example of micro-macro linkages' in L.A. Kosinski and J.W. Webb (eds.), *Population at Microscale*, New Zealand Geographical Society, pp. 127-42

Chapman, M., 1977, 'Circulation studies at the East-West Population Institute, Honolulu', *The Indonesian Journal of Geography*, 7,33, 1-4

Chapman, M. and Prothero, R.M., 1977, 'Circulation between home places and towns: a village approach to urbanization', Unpublished paper, Working Session on Urbanization in the Pacific, Assoc. for Social Anthropology, California

Chisholm, M., 1982, *Modern World Development. A Geographical Perspective*, Hutchinson, London

Clammer, J., 1975, 'Economic anthropology and the sociology of development: "liberal" anthropology and its French critics' in I. Oxaal, T. Barnett and D. Booth (eds.), *Beyond the Sociology of Development*, Routledge and Kegan Paul, London, pp. 208-28

Clammer, J. (ed.), 1978, *The New Economic Anthropology*, Macmillan, London

Clark, C., 1940, *The Conditions of Economic Progress*, Macmillan, London

Clark, G.L., 1980, 'Capitalism and regional inequality', *Annals of the Association of American Geographers*, 70,2, 226-37

Clark, R.B., 1934, 'Geography in the schools of Europe' in I. Bowman, *Geography in Relation to the Social Sciences*, Report of the Commission on the Social Studies, Part V, Scribners', New York

Claval, P., 1975, 'Contemporary human geography in France', *Progress in Geography*, 7, 253-92

Claval, P., 1981, 'Epistemology and the history of geographical thought' in D.R. Stoddart (ed.), *Geography, Ideology and Social Concern*, Barnes and Noble, New Jersey, pp. 227-39

Cohen, R., 1980, 'Resistance and hidden forms of consciousness among African workers', *Review of African Political Economy*, 19, 8-22

Cohen, R., Copans, J. and Gutkind, P.C.W., 1978, 'Introduction' in P.C.W. Gutkind, R. Cohen and J. Copans (eds.), *African Labor History*, Sage Series on African Modernization and Development, Vol. 2, Sage, Beverly Hills, pp. 7-30

Cole, J.P., 1981, *The Development Gap. A Spatial Analysis of World Poverty and Inequality*, John Wiley, Chichester

Copans, J. and Seddon, D., 1978, 'Marxism and anthropology: a preliminary survey' in D. Seddon (ed.), *Relations of Production. Marxist Approaches to Economic Anthropology*, Trans. H. Lackner, Frank Cass, London, pp. 1-46

Coraggio, J.L., 1975, 'Polarization, development and integration' in A. Kuklinski (ed.), *Regional Development and Planning: International Perspectives,*

Sijthoff, Leydon, pp. 353-74

Critchfield, R., 1970, *Hello Mister Where Are You going: The Story of Hussen, a Javanese (Betjak) Driver*, The Alicia Patterson Fund, New York

Crystal, E., 1974, 'Cooking pot politics: a Toraja village study', *Indonesia, 18*, 119-52

Curtain, R., 1980, 'The structure of internal migration in Papua New Guinea', *Pacific Viewpoint, 21,1*, 42-61

Curtis, J.E. and Petras, J.W. (eds.), 1970, *The Sociology of Knowledge*, Duckworth, London

Darby, H.C. (ed.), 1943, *Indo-china*, B.R. 510 Geographical Handbook Series, Great Britain Naval Intelligence Division, Cambridge

De Souza, A.R. and Porter, P.W., 1974, *The Underdevelopment and Modernization of the Third World*, Commission on College Geography, AAG, Resource Paper No. 28, Washington

Dickinson, R.E., 1969, *The Makers of Modern Geography*, Routledge and Kegan Paul, London

Dickinson, R.E., 1976, *Regional Concept: The Anglo-American Leaders*, Routledge and Kegan Paul, London

Dietz, T., 1979, 'The redevelopment of Dutch imperialism with regard to Indonesia since 1965', *Research in Political Economy, 2*, 141-86

Dobby, E.H.G., 1950, *Southeast Asia*, 9th edn, 1966, University of London Press, London

Douglass, M., 1981, 'Thailand: territorial dissolution and alternative regional development for the Central Plains' in W.B. Stöhr and D.R.F. Taylor (eds.), *Development from Above or Below?* Wiley, Chichester, pp. 183-208

Dousset, R. and Taillemite, E., 1979, *The Great Book of the Pacific*, Trans. A. Mouravieff-Apostol, Books for Pleasure, Sydney

Drakakis-Smith, D. and Williams, S.W. (eds.), 1983, *Internal Colonialism: Essays Around a Theme*, Development Areas Study Group, IBG

Duncan, J. and Ley, D., 1982, 'Structural Marxism and human geography: a critical assessment', *Annals of the Association of American Geographers, 72,1*, 30-59

East, W.G., Spate, O.H.K. and Fisher, C.A. (eds.), 1950, *The Changing Map of Asia. A Political Geography*, 5th edn, 1971, Methuen, London

Ede, K.B., 1982, 'On two approaches to underdevelopment and regional inequality', *Area, 14,1*, 27-32

Edel, C.K. *et al.*, 1978, 'Uneven regional development: an introduction to this issue', *The Review of Radical Political Economics, 10,3*, 1-12

Ehrensaft, P. and Armstrong, W., 1978, 'Dominion capitalism: a first statement', *The Australian and New Zealand Journal of Sociology, 14*, 352-63

Elkan, W., 1976, *An Introduction to Development Economics*, Penguin, Harmondsworth

Elliott, D. and McCrone, D., 1982, *The City. Patterns of Domination and Conflict*, Macmillan, London

Eliot-Hurst, M.E., 1980, 'Geography, social science and society: towards a dedefinition', *Australian Geographical Studies, 18,1*, 3-21

Emmanuel, A., 1972, *Unequal Exchange: A Study in the Imperialism of Trade*, New Left Books, London

Evans, D., 1976, 'Unequal exchange and economic policies. Some implications of neo-Ricardian critique of the theory of comparative advantage', *Economic and Political Weekly, XI, 5,6,7,* 143-58

Fagan, R.H., 1980, 'The internationalisation of capital: a perspective on Stephen Hymer's work on transnational corporations' in R. Peet (ed.), *An Introduction to Marxist Theories of Underdevelopment*, Department of Human Geography Monograph 14, Australian National University, Canberra, pp. 175-80

Farmer, B.H., 1973, 'Geography, area studies and the study of area', *Transactions of the Institute of British Geographers, 60,* 1-15

Farmer, B.H., 1983, 'British geographers overseas, 1933-1983', *Transactions, of the Institute of British Geographers, 8,1,* 70-9

Fawcett, C.B., 1953, 'Geography and empire' in G. Taylor (ed.), *Geography in the Twentieth Century*, Methuen, London, 418-32

Fincher, R., 1983, 'The inconsistency of eclecticism', *Environment and Planning A, 15,* 607-22

Firth, R., 1975, 'The sceptical anthropologist? Social anthropology and Marxist views on society' in M. Bloch (ed.), *Marxist Analyses and Social Anthropology*, Malaby Press, London, pp. 29-60

Fisher, C.A., 1964, *South-East Asia*, 2nd edn, 1967, Methuen, London

Fisher, C.A., 1970, 'Whither regional geography?', *Geography, 55,4,* 373-89

Fitzgerald, F.T., 1981, 'Sociologies of development', *Journal of Contemporary Asia, 11,1,* 5-18

Forbes, D.K., 1979, 'Development and the "informal" sector: a study of pedlars and trishaw riders in Ujung Pandang' Indonesia', Unpublished PhD dissertation, Department of Geography, Monash University, Melbourne

Forbes, D.K., 1980, 'The articulation of modes of production: comments on Bradby' in R. Peet (ed.), *An Introduction to Marxist Theories of Underdevelopment*, Department of Human Geography Monograph 14, Australian National University, Canberra, pp. 201-9

Forbes, D.K., 1981a, 'Beyond the geography of development', *Singapore Journal of Tropical Geography, 2,2,* 68-80

Forbes, D.K., 1981b, 'Mobility and uneven development in Indonesia' in G. Jones and H. Richter (eds.), *Population Mobility and Development*, Development Studies Centre Monograph 27, Australian National University, Canberra, pp. 51-70

Forbes, D.K. 1981c, 'Population mobility in Indonesia revisited', *Prisma, The Indonesian Indicator, 20,* 69-77

Forbes, D.K., 1981d, 'Petty commodity production and underdevelopment', *Progress in Planning, 16, Part 2,* 104-78

Forbes, D.K., 1982, 'Energy imperialism and a new international division of resources: the case of Indonesia', *Tijdschrift voor Economische en Sociale Geografie, 73,2,* 94-108

Forbes, D.K. Kissling, C.C. Taylor, M.J. and Thrift, N.J., 1984, *Economic and Social Atlas of the Pacific Basin*, Far Eastern Economic Review, Hong Kong (forthcoming)

Forbes, D.K. and Rimmer, P.J., 1983, 'Vers une reinterpretation de l'integration de l'Asie du Sud-est dans l'economie mondiale', *L'espace Geographique* (forthcoming)

Forbes, D.K. and Thrift, N.J., 1981, 'Levels of abstraction, theories of articulation and the analysis of social formations', Unpublished paper, Department of Human Geography, Australian National University, Canberra

Forde, C.D., 1934, *Habitat, Economy and Society*, Methuen, London

Foster-Carter, A., 1976, 'From Rostow to Gunder Frank: conflicting paradigms in the analysis of underdevelopment', *World Development, 4,3*, 167-80

Foster-Carter, A., 1978, 'The modes of production controversy', *New Left Review, 107*, 47-77

Frank, A.G., 1967, *Capitalism and Underdevelopment in Latin America*, Pelican, London

Frank, A.G. 1969, *Latin America: Underdevelopment or Revolution*, Monthly Review Press, New York

Frank, A.G. 1978a, *World Accumulation 1492-1789*, Monthly Review Press, New York

Frank, A.G., 1978b, *Dependent Accumulation and Underdevelopment*, Macmillan, London

Freeman, D.B., 1979, 'The geography of development and modernization: a survey of present trends and future prospects', Discussion Paper No. 22, Department of Geography, York University, Toronto

Freeman, T.W., 1965, *A Hundred Years of Geography*, Duckworth, London

Freeman, T.W., 1980, 'The Royal Geographical Society and the development of geography' in E.H. Brown (ed.), *Geography Yesterday and Tomorrow*, Oxford University Press, Oxford, pp. 1-99

Friedman, J., 1974, 'Marxism, structuralism and vulgar materialism', *Man, 9*, 444-89

Friedman, J., 1976, 'Marxist theory and systems of total reproduction. Part I: negative', *Critique of Anthropology, 2,7*, 3-16

Friedmann, J., 1966, *Regional Development Policy: A Case Study of Venezuela*, MIT Press, Cambridge, Mass.

Friedmann, J., 1969, 'A general theory of polarized development', School of Architecture and Planning, UCLA, Los Angeles

Friedmann, J. and Weaver, C., 1979, *Territory and Function. The Evolution of Regional Planning*, Edward Arnold, London

Fröbel, F., Heinrichs, J. and Kreye, O., 1977, 'The tendency toward a new international division of labour', *Review, 1,1*, 73-88

Fröbel, F., Heinrichs, J. and Kreye, O., 1978, 'Export-oriented industrialisation of underdeveloped countries', *Monthly Review, 30*, 22-7

Fröbel, F., Heinrichs, J. and Kreye, O., 1980, *The New International Division of Labour*, Cambridge University Press, Cambridge

Fryer, D.W., 1965, *World Economic Development*, McGraw-Hill, New York

Fryer, D.W., 1970, *Emerging Southeast Asia. A Study in Growth and Stagnation*, Philip and Son, London

Furnivall, J.S., 1939, *Netherlands India: A Study of Plural Economy*, Cambridge University Press, Cambridge

Galbraith, J.K., 1977, *The Age of Uncertainty*, Andre Deutsch, London

Gastil, R.D. (ed.), *1981, Freedom in the World 1981, Political Rights and Civil Liberties*, Clio Press, Oxford

Geddes, A., 1937, 'The population of Bengal; its distribution and changes', *Geographical Journal, 89*, 344-68

Geddes, A., 1941, 'Half a century of population trends in India', *Geographical Journal, 98*, 228-53

Geertz, C.C. 1963, *Peddlers and Princes: Social Change and Economic Modern-*

ization in Two Indonesian Towns, University of Chicago Press, Chicago

George, C.H., 1980, 'The origins of capitalism: a Marxist epitome and a critique of Immanuel Wallerstein's modern world system', *Marxist Perspectives, 3,2,* 70-100

Gerry, C., 1978, 'Petty production and capitalist production in Dakar: the crisis of the self-employed', *World Development 6,9/10,* 1147-60

Gerry, C. and Birkbeck, C., 1981, 'The petty commodity producer in Third World cities: petit bourgeois or "disguised" proletarian?' in F. Bechhofer and B. Elliott (eds.), *The Petite Bourgeoisie. Comparative Studies of the Uneasy Stratum*, Macmillan, London, pp. 121-54

Gibson, K., 1980, 'The internationalisation of capital and uneven development within capitalist countries' in R. Peet (ed.), *An Introduction to Marxist Theories of Underdevelopment*, Department of Human Geography Monograph 14, Australian National University, Canberra, pp. 169-74

Gibson, K. and Horvath, R., 1981, 'Uneven development', Unpublished paper, ANZAAS, Brisbane

Gibson, K. and Horvath, R., 1983, 'Aspects of a theory of transition within the capitalist mode of production', *Society and Space, 1,2,* 121-38

Giddens, A., 1979, *Central Problems in Social Theory: Action, Structure and Contradiction in Social Analysis*, Macmillan, London

Giddens, A., 1981, *A Contemporary Critique of Historical Materialism. Vol. 1: Power, Property and the State*, Macmillan, London

Giddens, A., 1982a, *Profiles and Critiques in Social Theory*, Macmillan, London

Giddens, A., 1982b, *Sociology: A Brief but Critical Introduction*, Macmillan, London

Gilbert, A.G., 1974, *Latin American Development. A Geographical Perspective.* Penguin, Harmondsworth

Gilbert, A.G., 1976, 'Introduction' in A. Gilbert (ed.), *Development Planning and Spatial Structure*, Wiley, London, pp. 1-20

Gilbert, A.G. and Goodman, D.E., 1976, 'Regional income disparities and economic development: a critique' in A. Gilbert (ed.), *Development Planning and Spatial Structure*, Wiley, London, pp. 113-41

Gilbert, A. and Gugler, J., 1982, *Cities, Poverty and Development*, Oxford University Press, Oxford

Gilbert, E.W. and Steel, R.W., 1945, 'Social geography and its place in colonial studies', *Geographical Journal, 106,* 118-31

Ginsburg, N., 1961, *Atlas of Economic Development*, University of Chicago Press, Chicago

Ginsburg, N. (ed.), 1960, 'Essays on geography and economic development', *Department of Geography Research Paper No. 62*, University of Chicago, Chicago

Girvan, N., 1973, 'The development of dependency economics in the Caribbean and Latin America: review and comparison', *Social and Economic Studies, 22,* 1-33

Goldfrank, W.L. (ed.), 1979, *The World System of Capitalism: Past and Present*, Vol. 2, Political Economy of the World System Annuals, Sage, London

Goldstein, S., 1978, 'Circulation in the context of total mobility in Southeast Asia', *Papers of the East-West Population Institute No. 53*, Honolulu

Goldsworthy, D., 1977, 'Analysing theories of development', *Working Paper*

No. 12, Centre of Southeast Asian Studies, Monash University, Melbourne

Gordon, A., 1978, 'Some problems of analysing class relations in Indonesia', *Journal of Contemporary Asia, 8,* 210-18

Gordon, D.M., 1980, 'Stages of accumulation and long economic cycles' in T.K. Hopkins and I. Wallerstein (eds.), *Processes of the World-System*, Sage, Beverly Hills, pp. 9-45

Gough, K., 1968, 'New proposals for anthropologists', *Current Anthropology, 9,5,* 403-7

Gough, K., 1969, 'World revolution and the science of man' in T. Roszak (ed.), *The Dissenting Academy*, Penguin, Harmondsworth, pp. 125-44

Gould, P., 1970, 'Tanzania 1920-63: the spatial impress of the modernization process', *World Politics, 22,* 149-70

Gouldner, A., 1980, *The Two Marxisms*, Seabury, New York

Gourou, P., 1945, *Land Utilization in French Indochina*, Parts I-II, Institute of Pacific Relations, Washington

Gourou, P., 1955, *The Peasants of the Tonkin Delta: A Study of Human Geography*, Human Relations Area Files, New Haven (2 vols.)

Grano, O., 1981, 'External influence and internal change in the development of geography' in D.R. Stoddart (ed.), *Geography, Ideology and Social Concern*, Barnes and Noble, New Jersey, pp. 17-36

Gregory, D., 1978, *Ideology, Science and Human Geography*, Hutchinson, London

Gregory, D., 1981, 'Human agency and human geography', *Transactions, Institute of British Geographers, 6,1,* 1-18

Gregory, D., 1982, 'Solid geometry: notes on the recovery of spatial structure' in P. Gould and G. Olsson (eds.), *A Search for Common Ground*, Pion, London, pp. 187-219

Griffin, K., 1978, *International Inequality and National Poverty*, Macmillan, London

Griffin, K., 1981, 'Economic development in a changing world', *World Development, 9,3,* 221-6

Gülalp, H., 1981, 'Frank and Wallerstein revisited: a contribution to Brenner's critique', *Journal of Contemporary Asia, 11,2,* 169-88

Haddad, P.R., 1981, 'Brazil: economic efficiency and the disintegration of peripheral regions' in W.B. Stöhr and D.R.F. Taylor (eds.), *Development from Above or Below?*, Wiley, Chichester, pp. 379-400

Hamilton, F.E.I. and Linge, G.J.R. (eds.), 1979, *Spatial Analysis, Industry and the Industrial Environment. Vol. 1: Industrial Systems*, Wiley, Chichester

Hamilton, F.E.I. and Linge, G.J.R. (eds.), 1981, *Spatial Analysis, Industry and the Industrial Environment. Vol. 2: International Industrial Systems*, Wiley, Chichester

Hansen, A.H., 1938, *Full Recovery or Stagnation?*, A. and C. Black, London

Hansen, A.H., 1941, *Fiscal Policy and Business Cycles*, Norton, New York

Hansen, N.M., 1981, 'Development from above: the centre-down development paradigm' in W.B. Stöhr and D.R.F. Taylor (eds.), *Development from Above or Below?*, Wiley, Chichester, pp. 15-38

Harris, J.R. and Todaro, M., 1970, 'Migration, unemployment and development: a two sector analysis', *The American Economic Review, 60,* 126-42

Harriss, J. and B., 1979, 'Development studies', *Progress in Human Geography,*

3,4,, 576-84

Harriss, J. and B., 1981, 'Development studies', *Progress in Human Geography*, *5,4,* 572-81

Harrod, R.F., 1939, 'An essay in dynamic theory', *Economic Journal, 49,* 14-33

Harrod, R.F., 1948, *Towards a Dynamic Economics*, St Martins, New York

Hart, J.F., 1982, 'The highest form of the geographer's art', *Annals of the Association of American Geographers, 72,1,* 1-29

Hart, K., 1973, 'Informal income opportunities and urban employment in Ghana', *Journal of Modern African Studies, 11,1,* 61-89

Hartshorne, R., 1939, 'The nature of geography: a critical survey of current thought in the light of the past', *Annals of the Association of American Geographers, 29,* 171-658

Hartshorne, R., 1959, *Perspective on the Nature of Geography*, Rand McNally, Chicago

Hartshorne, R., 1968, 'The concept of geography as a science of space from Kant and Humboldt to Heffner', *Annals of the Association of American Geographers, 48,* 97-108

Harvey, D., 1982, *The Limits to Capital*, Blackwell, Oxford

Hebbert, M., 1983, 'The new decentralism – a critique of the territorial approach' in P. Healy *et al.*, (eds.), *Planning Theory in the 1980's*, Pergamon, Oxford (forthcoming)

Higgins, B., 1959, *Economic Development*, Constable, London

Higgott, R., 1983, *Political Development Theory*, Croom Helm, London

Higgott, R., 1984, 'Export oriented industrialisation, the new international division of labour and the corporate state in the third world: an exploratory essay in conceptual linkage', *Australian Geographical Studies, 22,1* (forthcoming)

Hilhorst, J.G.M., 1981, 'Peru: regional planning 1968-77; frustrated bottom-up aspirations in a technocratic military setting' in W.B. Stöhr and D.R.F. Taylor (eds.), *Development from Above or Below?*, Wiley, Chichester, pp. 427-50

Hindess, B. and Hirst, P.Q., 1975, *Pre-capitalist Modes of Production*, Routledge and Kegan Paul, London

Hindess, B. and Hirst, P., 1977, *Modes of Production and Social Formation*, Macmillan, London

Hirschman, A.O., 1958, *The Strategy of Economic Development*, Yale University Press, New Haven

Hobsbawm, E.J., 1969, *Industry and Empire*, Penguin, Harmondsworth

Hobsbawm, E.J., 1974, *The Age of Revolution, 1789-1848*, Abacus, London

Hodder, B.W., 1968, *Economic Development in the Tropics*, Methuen, London

Hoogvelt, A.M.M., 1976, *The Sociology of Developing Societies*, Macmillan, London

Hopkins, T.K. and Wallerstein, I. (eds.), 1980, *Processes of the World System*, Vol. 3, Political Economy of the World System Annuals, Sage, London

Hoselitz, B., 1960, *Sociological Aspects of Economic Growth*, The Free Press, Illinois

Hudson, B., 1977, 'The new geography and the new imperialism: 1870-1918', *Antipode, 9,2,* 12-19

Hugo, G.J., 1977, 'Circular migration', *Bulletin of Indonesian Economic Studies, XIII,3,* 57-66

Hugo, G.J., 1978a, *Population Mobility in West Java*, Gadjah Mada University

Press, Yogyakarta

Hugo, G.J., 1978b, 'New conceptual approaches to migration in the context of urbanization: a discussion based on Indonesian experience', Seminar paper for 'New Conceptual Approaches to Migration in the Context of Urbanization', Bellagio, Italy, June 30-July 3, 1978

Hugo, G.J., 1979, 'Patterns of population movement to 1971'; 'Migration to and from Jakarta'; 'The impact of migration on villages in Java' in R.J. Pryor (ed.), *Migration and Development in South-East Asia. A Demographic Perspective*, Oxford University Press, Kuala Lumpur

Hugo, G.J., 1982, 'Circular migration in Indonesia', *Population and Development Review, 8,1*, 59-83

Hymer, S., 1975, 'The multinational corporation and the law of uneven development' in H. Radice (ed.), *International Firms and Modern Imperialism*, Penguin, Harmondsworth, pp. 37-62

IDRC (International Development Research Centre) 1975, *Hawkers and Vendors in Asian Cities*, Ottawa, Canada

ILO (International Labour Office) 1972, *Employment, Incomes and Equality: A Strategy for Increasing Productive Employment in Kenya*, ILO, Geneva

ILO (International Labour Office), 1977, *Poverty and Landlessness in Rural Asia*, ILO, Geneva

Jalée, P., 1968, *The Pillage of the Third World*, Monthly Review Press, New York

Jalée, P., 1969, *The Third World in World Economy*, Monthly Review Press, New York

James, P.E. and Martin, G.J. (eds.), 1954, *American Geography: Inventory and Prospect*, Syracuse University Press, Syracuse

James, P.E. and Martin, G.J., 1979, *The Association of American Geographers: The First Seventy-Five Years*, Association of American Geographers, Washington DC

Jaycox, E., 1978, 'The Bank and urban poverty', *Finance and Development, 15,3*, 10-13

Jellinek, L., 1975, 'The life of a Jakarta street trader', *Working Paper No. 9*, Centre of Southeast Asian Studies, Monash University Melbourne

Jellinek, L., 1977, 'The life of a Jakarta street trader – two years later', *Working Paper No. 13*, Centre of southeast Asian Studies, Monash University, Melbourne

Jellinek, L., 1978a, 'The pondok system and circular migration' in *The Life of the Poor in Indonesian Cities*, Public lectures on Indonesia, Centre of Southeast Asian Studies, Monash University, Melbourne

Jellinek, L., 1978b, 'Circular migration and the *Pondok* dwelling system: a case study of ice-cream traders in Jakarta' in P.J. Rimmer, D.W. Drakakis-Smith and T.G. McGee (eds.), *Food, Shelter and Transport in Southeast Asia and the Pacific*, Department of Human Geography Monograph 12, Australian National University, Canberra, pp. 135-54

Jensen-Butler, C., 1982, 'Capital accumulation and regional development: the case of Denmark', *Environment and Planning A, 14,10*, 1307-40

Johnston, R.J., 1979, *Geography and Geographers. Anglo-American Human Geography Since 1945*, Edward Arnold, London

Johnstone, M.A., 1980, 'Unequal exchange and the flow of surplus in the world capitalist system' in R. Peet (ed.), *An Introduction to Marxist Theories of*

Underdevelopment, Department of Human Geography Monograph 14, Australian National University, Canberra, pp. 145-60

Jonas, W.J., 1980, 'Samir Amin: accumulation on a world scale' in R. Peet (ed.), *An Introduction to Marxist Theories of Underdevelopment*, Department of Human Geography Monograph 14, Australian National University, Canberra, pp. 161-8

Kahn, J.S., 1974, 'Imperialism and the reproduction of capitalism: towards a definition of the Indonesian social formation', *Critique of Anthropology, 2*, 1-35

Kahn, J.S., 1975, 'Economic scale and the cycle of petty commodity production in West Sumatra' in M. Bloch (ed.), *Marxist Analyses and Social Anthropology*, Malaby Press, London, pp. 137-58

Kahn, J.S., 1976, ' "Tradition", matriliny and change among the Minangkabau of Indonesia', *Bijdragen Tot de Taal-, Land- En Volkenkunds, 132*, 64-95

Kahn, J.S., 1978, 'Marxist anthropology and peasant economics: a study of the social structures of underdevelopment' in J. Clammer (ed.), *The New Economic Anthropology*, Macmillan, London, pp. 110-37

Kahn, J.S. and Llobera, J. (eds.), 1980, *The Anthropology of Pre-capitalist Societies*, Macmillan, London

Kaplan, B.H. (ed.), 1978, *Social Change in the Capitalist World Economy*, Vol. 1, Political Economy of the World System Annuals, Sage, London

Kay, G., 1975, *Development and Underdevelopment: A Marxist Analysis*, St Martins Press, New York

Keltie, J.S., 1885, 'Geographical education', *The Scottish Geographical Magazine, 1,10*, 497-505

Keltie, J.S., 1886, 'Geographical education. Report to the Council of the Royal Geographical Society', *Supplementary Papers of the Royal Geographical Society, 1,4*, 439-595

Keynes, J.M., 1936, *The General Theory of Employment, Interest and Money*, Macmillan, London

Kiernan, V.G., 1974, *Marxism and Imperialism*, Edward Arnold, London

Kiernan, V.G., 1978, *America: The New Imperialism – From White Settlement to World Hegemony*, Zed Press, London

Kindleberger, C.P., 1965, *Economic Development*, 2nd edn, McGraw-Hill, New York

Kirby, A., 1980, 'An approach to ideology', *Journal of Geography in Higher Education, 4,2*, 16-26

Kitching, G., 1982, *Development and Underdevelopment in Historical Perspective. Populism, Nationalism and Industrialization*, Methuen, New York

Kobori, I., 1966, 'Regional studies in foreign countries by Japanese geographers – Part II' in A. Bekki *et al.* (eds.), *Japanese Geography 1966. Its Recent Trends*, Association of Japanese Geographers, Tokyo, pp. 161-4

Kon, I.S., 1975, 'The crisis of western sociology and the second discovery of Marxism' in T.B. Bottomore (ed.), *Crisis and Contention in Sociology*, Sage, London, pp. 55-70

Laclau, E., 1971, 'Feudalism and capitalism in Latin America', *New Left Review, 67*, 19-38

Lacoste, Y., 1976, *La géographie, ça sert, d'abord, à faire la guerre*, Maspero, Paris

Lall, S., 1975, 'Is "dependence" a useful concept in analysing underdevelopment?', *World Development, 3,11-12*, 799-810

Layder, D., 1981, *Structure, Interaction and Social Theory*, Routledge and Kegan Paul, London

Leaver, R., 1979, 'Samir Amin on underdevelopment', *Journal of Contemporary Asia, 9,3*, 325-36

Le Brun, D. and Gerry, C., 1975, 'Petty producers and capitalism', *Review of African Political Economy 3*, 20-32

Le Clair, E.E. and Schneider, H.K., 1968, 'The development of economic anthropology' in E.E. Le Clair and H.K. Schneider (eds.), *Economic Anthropology. Readings in Theory and Analysis*, Holt, Reinhart and Winston, New York pp. 3-13

Lefebvre, H., 1974, *La Production de l'Espace*, Maspero, Paris

Lefebvre, H., 1976, *The Survival of Capitalism*, Allison and Busby, London

Lehmann, D. (ed.), 1979, *Development Theory: Four Critical Studies*, Cass, London

Lenglet du Fresnoy, N., 1737, *The Geography of Children or a Short and Easy Method of Teaching or Learning Geography*, S.R. Publishers/Johnson Reprint Corporation, New York (1969 reprint)

Lenin, V.I., 1956, *The Development of Capitalism in Russia*, Foreign Languages Publishing House, Moscow

Lenin, V.I., 1965, *Imperialism, The Highest Stage of Capitalism*, Foreign Language Press, Peking

Lewis, J.R. and Williams, A.M., 1981, 'Regional uneven development on the European periphery: the case of Portugal, 1970-78', *Tijdschrift voor Economische en Sociale Geografie, 72,2*, 81-98

Ley, D. and Samuels, M.S. (eds.), 1978, *Humanistic Geography*, Croom Helm, London

Leys, C., 1977, 'Underdevelopment and dependency: critical notes', *Journal of Contemporary Asia, 7,1*, 92-107

Leys, C., 1978, 'Capital accumulation, class formation and dependency – the significance of the Kenyan case', *The Socialist Register*, pp. 241-66

Lichtheim, G., 1964, *Marxism. An Historical and Critical Study*, 2nd edn, Routledge, London

Lichtheim, G., 1967, *The Concept of Ideology and Other Essays*, Random House, New York

Lincoln, D., 1979, 'Ideology and South African development geography', *The South African Geographical Journal, 61,2*, 99-110

Lipietz, A., 1977, *Le Capital et Son Espace*, Economie et Socialisme, No. 34, Maspero, Paris

Livingstone, I., 1981, 'The development of development economics', *Overseas Development Institute Review, 2*, 1-19

Lo, F.-C. and Salih, K., 1981, 'Structural change and urbanization in Asia, 1960-1980: implications for urban policy and development', Conference on Urbanization and National Development, Honolulu

Luxemburg, R., 1963, *The Accumulation of Capital*, Routledge and Kegan Paul, London

McGee, T.G., 1967, *The Southeast Asian City*, Bell, London

McGee, T.G., 1971, *The Urbanization Process in the Third World*, Bell, London

McGee, T.G., 1973, *Hawkers in Hong Kong: A Study of Planning and Policy in a Third World City*, Centre of Asian Studies Occasional Paper No. 17, University of Hong Kong, Hong Kong

McGee, T.G., 1974, 'In praise of tradition: towards a geography of anti-development', *Antipode, 6,3,* 30-50

McGee, T.G., 1976, 'The persistence of the proto-proletariat', *Progress in Geography, 9,* 1-38

McGee, T.G., 1978a, 'An invitation to the "ball". Dress – "formal" or "informal"?' in P.J. Rimmer, D.W. Drakakis-Smith and T.G. McGee (eds.), *Food, Shelter and Transport in Southeast Asia and the Pacific*, Department of Human Geography Mongraph 12, Australian National University, Canberra, pp. 3-28

McGee, T.G., 1978b, 'Rural-urban mobility in South and Southeast Asia: different formulations and different answers' in W. McNeill and R.S. Adams (eds.), *Human Migration. Patterns and Policies*, University of Indiana Press, Bloomington, pp. 199-224

McGee, T.G., 1981, 'Labour mobility in fragmented labour markets, rural-urban linkages, and regional development in Asia' in F.C. Lo, (ed.), *Rural-Urban Relations and Regional Development*, Maruzen Asia, Singapore, pp. 245-64

McGee, T.G., 1982a, 'Labour mobility in fragmented labour markets, the role of circulatory migration in rural-urban relations in Asia' in H.I. Safa (ed.), *Towards a Political Economy of Urbanization in Third World Countries*, Oxford University Press, Delhi, pp. 47-66

McGee, T.G., 1982b, 'Urban systems, labour markets and the urbanization process in Southeast Asia: research priorities for government policy' in R.P. Misra (ed.), *Regional Development,* Maruzen Asia, Singapore, pp. 115-38

McGee, T.G. and Yeung, Y.M., 1977, *Hawkers in Southeast Asian Cities: Planning for the Bazaar Economy*, IDRC, Ottawa

McKay, D.U., 1943, 'Colonialism in the French geographical movement 1871-1881', *Geographical Review, 33,2,* 214-32

McLellan, D., 1979, *Marxism after Marx. An Introduction.* Macmillan, London

Mabogunje, A.L., 1980, *The Development Process: a Spatial Perspective*, Hutchinson, London

Mack, A., Plant, D. and Doyle, U. (eds.), 1979, *Imperialism, Intervention and Development*, Croom Helm, London

Mackinder, H.J., 1895, 'Modern geography, German and English', *Geographical Journal, 6,4,* 367-79

Magdoff, H., 1969, *The Age of Imperialism*, Monthly Review Press, New York

Magdoff, H., 1978, *Imperialism: From the Colonial Age to the Present*, Monthly Review Press, New York

Magubane, B. *et al.*, 1971, 'A critical look at indices used in the study of social change in colonial Africa', *Current Anthropology, 12,4-5,* 419-45

Mamak, A. and Ali, A., 1979, *Race Class and Rebellion in the South Pacific*, Allen and Unwin, Sydney

Mandel, E., 1968, *Marxist Economic Theory*, Trans. B. Pearce, Merlin Press, London

Mandel, E., 1976, 'Capitalism and regional disparities', *Southwest Economy and Society, 1,* 41-7

Mandel, E., 1980, *Long Waves in Capitalist Development*, Cambridge University Press, Cambridge

Mannheim, K., 1936, *Ideology and Utopia. An Introduction to the Sociology of Knowledge,* Trans. L. Wirth and E. Shils, Routledge and Kegan Paul, London

Marsden, W.E. (ed.), 1980, *Historical Perspectives on Geographical Education,* University of London Institute of Education, London

Martin, G.J., 1973, *Ellsworth Huntington. His Life and Thought,* Archon Books, Connecticut

Marx, K., 1959, *Capital. Vol. III,* Progress Publishers, Moscow

Marx, K. (Intro. by E.J. Hobsbawm), 1964, *Pre-capitalist Economic Formations,* Lawrence and Wishart, London

Marx, K., 1973, *Grundrisse,* Trans. with a Foreword by M. Nicolaus, Penguin, Harmondsworth

Marx, K. and Engels, F., 1979, *Pre-capitalist Socio-Economic Formations. A Collection,* Progress Publishers, Moscow

Massey, D., 1978, 'Regionalism: some current issues', *Capital and Class, 10,* 106-25

Massey, D., 1979, 'In what sense a regional problem?', *Regional Studies, 13,2,* 233-43

Massey, D., and Meegan, R.A., 1979, 'The geography of industrial reorganization', *Progress in Planning, 10,* 155-237

Mazumdar, D., 1976, 'The urban informal sector', *World Development, 4,8,* 655-79

Mead, W.R. 1980, 'Regional geography' in E.H. Brown (ed.), *Geography Yesterday and Tomorrow,* Oxford University Press, Oxford, 292-302

Medawar, P.B., 1969, *The Art of the Soluble,* Penguin, Harmondsworth

Meier, G.M. (ed.), 1964, *Leading Issues in Development Economics,* Oxford University Press, New York

Meier, G.M. and Baldwin, R.E., 1957, *Economic Development. Theory, History, Policy,* Wiley, New York

Meillassoux, C., 1972, 'From reproduction to production', *Economy and Society, 1,1,* 93-105

Mercer, D. 1977, 'Conflict and consensus in human geography', *Monash Publications in Geography No 17,* Monash University, Melbourne

Merrington, J., 1975, 'Town and country in the transition to capitalism', *New Left Review, 93,* 71-92

Mingione, E., 1981, *Social Conflict and the City,* Basil Blackwell, Oxford

Minshull, R., 1967, *Regional Geography: Theory and Practice,* Hutchinson, London

Missen, G.J., 1972, *Viewpoint on Indonesia: A Geographical Study,* Nelson, Melbourne

Missen, G.J. and Logan, M.I., 1977, 'National and local distribution systems and regional development: the case of Kelantan in West Malaysia', *Antipode, 9,3,* 60-73

Mitchell, J.C., 1978, 'Wage-labour mobility as circulation: a sociological perspective', Unpublished paper, International Seminar in the Cross-cultural Study of Circulation, East-West Centre, Honolulu

Mommsen, W.J., 1981, *Theories of Imperialism,* Weidenfeld and Nicolson, London

Mortimer, R., 1972, 'The Indonesian Communist Party and land reform 1959-

1965', *Monash Papers on Southeast Asia No. 1*, Monash University, Melbourne

Mortimer, R., 1979, 'Wallerstein's world-system theory and the problems of class analysis', Seminar on Contemporary Indonesia, Monash University, Melbourne

Moser, C.O.N., 1978, 'Informal sector or petty commodity production: dualism or dependence in urban development', *World Development, 6*, 1041-64

Mouzelis, N., 1980, 'Modernization, underdevelopment, uneven development: prospects for a theory of Third World formations', *The Journal of Peasant Studies, 7*, 353-74

Myrdal, G., 1957, *Rich Lands and Poor*, Harper and Row, New York

Nafziger, E.W., 1979, 'A critique of development economics in the U.S.' in D. Lehmann (ed.), *Development Theory: Four Critical Studies*, Cass, London, pp. 32-48

Naim, M., 1973, 'Merantau: Minangkabau voluntary migration', Unpublished PhD thesis, University of Singapore, Singapore

Naim, M., 1976, 'Voluntary migration in Indonesia' in A.H. Richmond and D. Kubat (eds.), *Internal Migration: The New World and the Third World*, Sage, Beverly Hills

Nelson, J.M., 1979, *Access to Power. Politics and the Urban Poor in Developing Nations*, Princeton University Press, New Jersey

Newbigin, M.I., 1924, *Commercial Geography*, 2nd edn (1928), Thornton Butterworth, London

Newfarmer, R.S. and Topik, S., 1982, 'Testing dependency theory: a case study of Brazil's electrical industry' in M.J. Taylor and N.J. Thrift (eds.), *The Geography of Multinationals*, Croom Helm, London, pp. 33-60

Nichols, V., 1969, 'Growth poles: an evaluation of their propulsive effect', *Environment and Planning A, 1*, 193-208

Nurkse, R., 1953, *Problems of Capital Formation in Underdeveloped Countries*, Oxford University Press, Oxford

Obregon, A.Q., 1974, 'The marginal pole of the economy and the marginalised labour force', *Economy and Society, 3,4*, 393-428

O'Connor, J., 1970, 'The meaning of economic imperialism' in R.I. Rhodes (ed.), *Imperialism and Underdevelopment: A Reader*, Monthly Review Press, New York, pp. 101-51

Odell, P.R. and Preston, D.A., 1973, *Economies and Societies in Latin America*, Wiley, Chichester

Ollman, B., 1968, 'Marx's use of "class" ', *The American Journal of Sociology, 73,5*, 573-580

Olsson, G., 1975, 'Birds in egg', *Michigan Geographical Publication No. 15*, Department of Geography, University of Michigan, Michigan

Oxaal, I., Barnett, T. and Booth, D. (eds.), 1975, *Beyond the Sociology of Development*, Routledge and Kegan Paul, London

Palloix, C., 1975, 'The internationalisation of capital and the circuit of social capital' in H. Radice (ed.), *International Firms and Modern Imperialism*, Penguin, Harmondsworth, pp. 63-88

Palloix, C., 1977, 'The self-expansion of capital on a world scale', *Review of Radical Political Economics, 9*, 3-27

Palma, G. 1978, 'Dependency: a formal theory of underdevelopment or a methodology for the analysis of concrete situations of underdevelopment?', *World Development, 6*, 881-924

Papanek, G., 1975, 'The poor of Jakarta', *Economic Development and Cultural Change, 24,1,* 1-28

Parkes, D.N. and Thrift, N.J., 1980, *Times, Spaces, and Places. A Chronogeographic Perspective*, John Wiley, Chichester

Pearson, H.W., 1968, 'Parsons and Smelser on the economy' in E.E. Le Clair and H.K. Schneider (eds.), *Economic Anthropology. Readings in Theory and Analysis*, Holt, Reinhart and Winston, New York, pp. 234-43

Peet, R., 1977, 'The development of radical geography in the United States', *Progress in Human Geography, 1,3,* 64-87

Peet, R., 1979, 'On comradely criticism and Marxist geography', *Newsletter, Union of Socialist Geographers, 4,3,* 20-6

Peet, R. (ed.), 1980, *An Introduction to Marxist Theories of Underdevelopment*, Research School of Pacific Studies, Department of Human Geography Monograph 14, The Australian National University, Canberra

Pelzer, K.J., 1948, *Pioneer Settlement in the Asiatic Tropics*, American Geographical Society, New York

Pelzer, K.J., 1953, 'Geography and the tropics' in G. Taylor (ed.), *Geography in the Twentieth Century. A Study of Growth, Fields, Techniques, Aims and Trends*, Methuen, London, pp. 311-44

Perrons, D.C., 1981, 'The role of Ireland in the new international division of labour', *Regional Studies, 15,* 81-100

Perroux, F., 1950, 'Economic space; theory and applications', *Quarterly Journal of Economics, 64,* 89-104

Perroux, F., 1971, 'Note on the concept of growth poles' in I. Livingstone (ed.), *Economic Policy for Development: Selected Readings*, Penguin, Harmondsworth, pp. 278-89

Petras, J., 1978, *Critical Perspectives on Imperialism and Social Class in the Third World*, Monthly Review Press, New York

Petras, J. and Trachte, K., 1979, 'Liberal, structural and radical approaches to political economy: an assessment and an alternative', *Contemporary Crises, 3,* 109-47

Porter, P.W., 1970, 'The concept of environmental potential as exemplified by tropical African research' in W. Zelinski, L.A. Kosinski and R.M. Prothero (eds.), *Geography and a Crowding World*, Oxford University Press, Oxford, pp. 187-217

Porter, D., 1983, 'Development practice: a question of authority', PhD thesis in preparation, Department of Human Geography, Australian National University, Canberra

Portes, A., and Walton, J., 1981, *Labor, Class, and the International System*, Academic Press, New York

Poulantzas, N., 1973, *Political Power and Social Classes*, New Left Books, London

Poulantzas, N., 1975, *Classes in Contemporary Capitalism*, Trans. D. Fernbach, New Left Books, London

Pred, A., 1981a, 'Everyday practice and the discipline of human geography' in A. Pred (ed.), *Space and Time in Geography: Essays Dedicated to Torsten Hägerstrand*, Lund Studies in Geography, Ser. B., Human Geography No. 48, Lund, pp. 30-55

Pred, A., 1981b, 'Social reproduction and the time-geography of everyday life', *Geografiska Annaler, 63B,* 5-22

Pred, A., 1982, 'Social reproduction and the time-geography of everyday life' in P. Gould and G. Olsson (eds.), *A Search for Common Ground*, Pion, London, pp. 157-86

Preston, P.W., 1982, *Theories of Development*, Routledge and Kegan Paul, London

Przeworski, A., 1977, 'Proletariat into a class: the process of class formation from Karl Kautsky's *The Class Struggle* to recent controversies', *Politics and Society, 7,4*, 340-3

Rees, J., Hewings, G. and Stafford, H. (eds.), 1981, *Industrial Location and Regional Systems*, Bergin, New York

Regan, C.A. and Eliot-Hurst, M.E., 1976, 'A geography of the development of underdevelopment' in D.A.M. Lea (ed.), *Geographical Research: Application and Relevance*, University of New England, Armidale

Rendra, W.S., 1980, *State of Emergency*, Trans. Swami Anand Haridas, Wild and Woolley, Sydney

Research Working Group on Cyclical Rhythms and Secular Trends, 1979, 'Cyclical rhythms and secular trends of the capitalist world-economy: some premises, hypotheses, and questions', *Review, 11,4*, 483-500

Rey, P.-P, 1973, *Les Alliances de classes*, Maspero, Paris

Rey, P.-P., 1975, 'The lineage mode of production', *Critique of Anthropology, 3*, 27-79

Rey, P.-P., 1979, 'Class contradiction in lineage societies', *Critique of Anthropology, 4, 13/14*, 41-60

Rhodes, R.I. (ed.), 1970, *Imperialism and Underdevelopment: A Reader*, Monthly Review Press, New York

Riddell, J.B., 1970, *The Spatial Dynamics of Modernization in Sierra Leone: Structure, Diffusion and Response*, Northwestern University Press, Evanston

Riddell, R., 1981, *Ecodevelopment: Economics, Ecology and Development, an Alternative Growth to Imperative Models*, Gower, Farnborough

Rimmer, D., 1979, 'Some origins of development economics', *Institute of Development Studies Bulletin, 10,4*, 33-7

Rimmer, D., 1981, ' "Basic needs" and the origins of the development ethos', *The Journal of Developing Areas, 15,2*, 215-38

Rimmer, P.J. (ed.), 1984, *Southeast Asia: Geographical Perspectives*, Methuen, London (forthcoming)

Rimmer, P.J. and Forbes, D.K., 1982, 'Underdevelopment theory: a geographical review', *Australian Geographer, 15,4*, 197-211

Robequain, C., 1944, *The Economic Development of French Indo-China*, Oxford University Press, London

Robequain, C., 1958, *Malaya, Indonesia, Borneo, and the Philippines*, 2nd edn, Trans. E.D. Laborde, Longmans, London

Roberts, B., 1978, *Cities of Peasants: The Political Economy of Urbanization in the Third World*, Edward Arnold, London

Roberts, B., 1982, 'Cities in developing societies' in H. Alavi and T. Shanin (eds.), *Introduction to the Sociology of 'Developing Societies'*, Macmillan, London, pp. 366-86

Robinson, J., 1971, *Freedom and Necessity. An Introduction to the Study of Society*, Vintage Books, New York

Rogerson, C.M., 1981, 'Industrialization in the shadows of apartheid: a world-systems analysis' in F.E.I. Hamilton and G.J.R. Linge (eds.), *Spatial Analysis, Industry and the Industrial Environment, Vol. 2: International Industrial Systems*, John Wiley, London, pp. 395-421

Rogerson, C.M., 1982, 'Multinational corporations in Southern Africa: a spatial perspective' in M.J. Taylor and N.J. Thrift (eds.), *The Geography of Multinationals*, Croom Helm, London, pp. 178-220

Rogerson, C.M. and K.S.O. Beavon, 1982, 'Getting by in the "informal sector" of Soweto', *Tijdschrift voor Economische en Sociale Geografie, 73,4*, 250-65

Rose, S., and Rose, H., 1979, 'Radical Science and its enemies', Seminar, Monash University, Melbourne

Rostow, W.W., 1958, 'The take-off into self-sustained growth' in A.N. Agarwala and S.P. Singh (eds.), *The Economics of Underdevelopment*, Oxford University Press, Delhi, pp. 154-88

Roxborough, I., 1976, 'Dependency theory in the sociology of development: some theoretical problems', *West African Journal of Sociology and Political Science, 1,2*, 116-33

Ryan, A., 1970, *The Philosophy of the Social Sciences*, Macmillan, London

Said, E.M., 1978, *Orientalism*, Pantheon, New York

Salinas, P.W., 1977, 'Le developpement regional et les limites d'une reforme: l'experience au Perou du gouvernement militaire', *Revue Tiers-Monde, 18*, 723-36

Salinas, P.W., 1983, 'Mode of production and spatial organization in Peru' in F. Moulaert and P.W. Salinas (eds.), *Regional Analysis and the New International Division of Labour*, Kluwer-Nijhoff, The Hague, pp. 79-95

Salinas, P.W. and Moulaert, F., 1983, 'Regional political economy: an introduction and overview' in F. Moulaert and P.W. Salinas (eds.), *Regional Analysis and the New International Division of Labour*, Kluwer-Nijhoff, The Hague, pp. 3-12

Samuel, R., 1980, 'British Marxist historians, 1880-1980: Part One', *New Left Review, 120*, 21-96

Samuel, R. and Stedman-Jones, G., 1976, 'Sociology and history', *History Workshop, 1*, 6-8

Sandbrook, R., 1982, *The Politics of 'Basic Needs': Urban Aspects of Assaulting Poverty in Africa'*, University of Toronto Press, Toronto

Santos, M., 1979, *The Shared Space*, Methuen, London

Sau, R., 1978, *Unequal Exchange, Imperialism, and Underdevelopment*, Oxford University Press, Calcutta

Saunders, P., 1981, *Social Theory and the Urban Question*, Hutchinson, London

Sayer, A., 1981, 'Abstraction: a realist interpretation', *Radical Philosophy, 28*, 6-16

Sayer, A., 1982, 'Explanation in economic geography', *Progress in Human Geography, 6,1*, 68-88

Sayer, A., 1983, 'Review of *A Contemporary Critique of Historical Materialism*', *Society and Space, 1,1*, 109-14

Schiffer, J., 1981, 'The changing post-war pattern of development: the accumulated wisdom of Samir Amin', *World Development, 96*, 515-37

Schumpeter, J.A., 1934, *The Theory of Economic Development*, Harvard University Press, Cambridge, Mass.

Seddon, D. (ed.), 1978, *Relations of Production: Marxist Approaches to Economic Anthropology*, Frank Cass, London

Seers, D., 1979, 'The birth, life and death of development economics (revisiting a Manchester conference)', *Development and Change, 10,4*, 707-19

Seers, D., 1980, 'Introduction: the congruence of Marxism and other neo-classical doctrines' in A.O. Hirschman *et al., Toward a New Strategy for Development*, Pergamon, Oxford, pp. 1-18

Seidman, A. and O'Keefe, P. 1980, 'The United States and South Africa in the changing international division of labour', *Antipode, 12,2*, 1-16

Sethuraman, S.V., 1975, 'Urbanisation and employment: a case study of Djakarta', *International Labour Review, 112*, 191-205

Sethuraman, S.V., 1976a, *Jakarta, Urban Development and Employment*, Press Centales Lausanne SA, Geneva

Sethuraman, S.V., 1976b, 'The urban informal sector: concept, measurement and policy', *International Labour Review, 114*, 69-81

Shaikh, A., 1978, 'An introduction to the history of crisis theories' in *Union for Radical Political Economics (ed.) U.S. Capitalism in Crisis*, URPE, New York, pp. 219-41

Shivji, I., 1975, 'Peasants and class alliances', *Review of African Political Economy, 3*, 10-20

Simon, R.M., 1980, 'The labour process and uneven development: the Appalachian coalfields, 1880-1930', *International Journal of Urban and Regional Research, 4,1*, 46-71

Simpson, J.R., 1976, 'The origin of United States academic interest in foreign economic development', *Economic Development and Cultural Change, 24,3*, 633-44

Singer, H., 1983, 'Dudley Seers 1920-1983', *Annual Report 1982*. The Institute of Development Studies, University of Sussex, Brighton

Singer, M., 1964, 'The social sciences in non-Western studies', *Annals of the American Academy of Political Science, 356*, 30-44

Skocpol, T., 1977, 'Wallerstein's world capitalist system: a theoretical and historical critique', *American Journal of Sociology, 82,5*, 1075-90

Slater, D., 1973, 'Geography and underdevelopment — Part I', *Antipode, 5,3*, 21-32

Slater, D., 1975a, 'The poverty of modern geographical enquiry', *Pacific Viewpoint, 16,2*, 159-76

Slater, D., 1975b, 'Underdevelopment and spatial inequality', *Progress in Planning, 4,2*, 97-167

Slater, D., 1977, 'Geography and underdevelopment — Part II', *Antipode, 9,3*, 1-31

Smith, A., 1950, *Wealth of Nations*, Methuen, London

Smith, N., 1979, 'Geography, science and post-positivist modes of explanation', *Progress in Human Geography, 3*, 356-83

Smith, S., 1980, 'The ideas of Samir Amin: theory or tautology', *The Journal of Development Studies, 17,1*, 5-21

Soja, E.W., 1968, *The Geography of Modernization in Kenya: A Spatial Analysis of Social, Economic and Political Change*, Syracuse University Press, New York

Soja, E.W., 1980, 'The socio-spatial dialectic', *Annals, Association of American Geographers, 70,2,* 207-25

Soja, E.W., 1981, 'A materialist interpretation of spatiality', Seminar on the Geographical Transfer of Value, Department of Human Geography, Australian National University, Canberra

Soja, E.W. and Hadjimichalis, C., 1979, 'Between geographical materialism and spatial fetishism: some observations on the development of Marxist spatial analysis', *Antipode, 11,3,* 3-11

Spate, O.H.K., 1954, *India and Pakistan: A General and Regional Geography,* 2nd edn (1957), Methuen, London

Spate, O.H.K., 1979, *The Spanish Lake. The Pacific Since Magellan,* Vol. I, Australian National University Press, Canberra

Spate, O.H.K., 1983, *Monopolists and Freebooters. The Pacific Since Magellan,* vol. II, Australian National University Press, Canberra

Spencer, J.E., 1954, *Asia East by South. A Cultural Geography,* Wiley, New York

Stamp, L.D., 1929, *Asia. A Regional and Economic Geography,* 9th edn (1957), Methuen, London

Stamp. L.D., 1960, *Our Developing World,* Faber and Faber, London

Steel, R.W., 1956, 'Geography and the tropics:the geographer's contribution to tropical studies' in R.W. Steel and C.A. Fisher (eds.), *Geographical Essays on British Tropical Lands,* Philip, London, pp. 1-16

Stilwell, F.J.B., 1978, 'Competing analyses of the spatial aspects of capitalist development', *The Review of Radical Political Economics, 10,* 18-27

Stilwell, F.J.B., 1982, 'Capital accumulation and regional economic performance: the Australian experience', *Australian Geographical Studies, 20,2,* 131-43

Stoddart, D.R., 1966, 'Darwin's impact on geography', *Annals, Association of American Geographers, 56,4,* 683-98

Stoddart, D.R., 1975, 'The RGS and the foundations of geography at Cambridge', *The Geographical Journal, 141,* 1-24

Stoddart, D.R., 1980, 'The RGS and the "new geography": changing aims and changing roles in nineteenth century science', *The Geographical Journal, 146,2,* 190-202

Stoddart, D.R., 1981, 'Ideas and interpretation in the history of geography' in D.R. Stoddart (ed.), *Geography, Ideology and Social Concern,* Barnes and Noble, New Jersey, pp. 1-7

Stoddart, D.R. (ed.), 1981, *Geography, Ideology and Social Concern,* Blackwell, Oxford

Stöhr, W.B., 1981, 'Development from below: the bottom-up and periphery-inward development paradigm' in W.B.Stöhr and D.R.F. Taylor (eds.), *Development from Above or Below?,* Wiley, Chichester, pp. 39-72

Stöhr, W.B. and Taylor, D.R.F., 1981, 'Introduction' in W.B. Stöhr and D.R.F. Taylor (eds.), *Development from Above or Below?,* Wiley, Chichester, pp. 1-12

Stöhr, W.B. and Todtling, F., 1978, 'Spatial equity – some antitheses to current regional development strategy', *Papers of the Regional Science Association, 38,* 33-53

Storper, M. and Walker, R., 1983, 'The theory of labour and the theory of location', *International Journal of Urban and Regional Research, 7,1,* 1-43

Streeten, P., 1980, 'Development ideas in historical perspective' in A.D. Hirschman *et al., Toward a New Strategy for Development*, Pergamon, Oxford, pp. 21-52

Sunkel, O., 1977, 'The development of development thinking', *IDS Bulletin, 8,3*, 6-11

Swift, M.G., 1971, 'Minangkabau and modernization' in L.R. Hiatt and C. Jayawardena (eds.), *Anthropology in Oceania*, Angus and Robertson, Sydney, pp. 225-67

Swindell, K., 1979, 'Labour migration in underdeveloped countries: the case of SubSaharan Africa', *Progress in Human Geography, 32*, 239-60

Szentes, T., 1971, *The Political Economy of Underdevelopment*, Akamediai Kiado, Budapest

Taaffe, E.J. Morrill, R.J. and Gould, P.R., 1963, 'Transport expansion in underdeveloped countries: a comparative analysis', *Geographical Review, 53*, 503-29

Tatham, G., 1953, 'Geography in the nineteenth century' in G. Taylor (ed.), *Geography in the Twentieth Century. A Study of Growth, Fields, Techniques, Aims and Trends*, 2nd edn, Methuen, London, pp. 28-69

Tawney, R.H., 1932, *Land and Labour in China*. Allen and Unwin, London

Taylor, G., 1953, 'Geopolitics and geopacifics' in G. Taylor (ed.), *Geography in the Twentieth Century. A Study of Growth, Fields, Techniques, Aims and Trends*, 2nd edn, Methuen, London, pp. 587-608

Taylor, G. (ed.), 1953, *Geography in the Twentieth Century*, Methuen, London

Taylor, J., 1972, 'Marxism and anthropology', *Economy and Society, 1,3*, 339-50

Taylor, J., 1974, 'Neo-marxism and underdevelopment: a sociological phantasy', *Journal of Contemporary Asia, 4,1*, 5-23

Taylor, J., 1975, 'Pre-capitalist modes of production', *Critique of Anthropology, 4/5*, 127-55

Taylor, J., 1976, 'Pre-capitalist modes of production (Part 2)', *Critique of Anthropology, 6,2*, 56-69

Taylor, J., 1979, *From Modernization to Modes of Production*, Macmillan, London

Taylor, M. and Thrift, N., 1981, 'The place of the semiperipheral country in the modern world system: some geographical implications of foreign investment in Australia', *Tijdschrift voor Economische en Sociale Geografie, 72,4*, 194-213

Taylor, M.J. and Thrift, N.J., 1982, 'Introduction' in M.J. Taylor and N.J. Thrift (eds.), *The Geography of Multinationals*, Croom Helm, London, pp. 1-13

Taylor, M.J. and Thrift, N.J., 1984, 'The regional consequences of a dualistic industrial structure: the case of Australia', *Australian Geographical Studies, 22,1* (forthcoming)

Taylor, P.J. 1976, 'An interpretation of the quantification debate in British geography', *Transactions, Institute of British Geographers, 1,2*, 129-42

Temple, G., 1974, 'Migration to Jakarta: empirical search for a theory', Unpublished PhD thesis, University of Wisconsin, Madison

Temple, G., 1975, 'Migration to Jakarta', *Bulletin of Indonesian Economic Studies, XI,1*, 76-81

Terray, E., 1972, *Marxism and 'Primitive' Societies*, Monthly Review Press, New York

Thompson, E.P., 1978, *The Poverty of Theory and Other Essays*, Merlin Press, London

Thrift, N., 1979, 'Limits to knowledge in social theory: towards a theory of practice', Seminar, Department of Human Geography, Australian National University, Canberra

Thrift, N., 1980, 'Frobel and the new international division of labour' in R. Peet (ed.), *An Introduction to Marxist Theories of Underdevelopment*, Department of Human Geography Monograph 14, Australian National University, Canberra, pp, 181-90

Thrift, N., 1981, 'Owner's time and own time: the making of a capitalist time consciousness, 1300-1830' in A. Pred (ed.), *Space and Time in Geography*, Lund Studies in Geography, Series B, Human Geography, No. 48, pp. 56-84

Thrift, N.J., 1982, 'Editorial: towards a human geography', *Environment and Planning A, 14,* 1280-2

Thrift, N.J., 1983, 'On the determination of social action in space and time', *Society and Space, 1,1,* 23-58

Thrift, N.J., 1983, 'Flies and germs: a geography of knowledge' in D. Gregory and J. Urry (eds.), *Social Relations and Spatial Structures*, Macmillan, London (forthcoming)

Thrift, N.J. and Forbes, D.K., 1983, 'A landscape with figures: political geography as human conflict', *Political Geography Quarterly, 2,3,* 247-63

Tichelman, F., 1980, *The Social Evolution of Indonesia: The Asiatic Mode of Production and its Legacy*, Studies in Social History, 5, Martinus Nijhoff, The Hague

Titus, M.J., 1978, 'Interregional migration in Indonesia as a reflection of social and regional inequalities', *Tijdschrift voor Economische en Sociale Geografie, 69,4,* 194-204

Todaro, M., 1977, *Economic Development in the Third World*, Longman, London

Touraine, A., 1977, *The Self-Production of Society*, Chicago University Press, Chicago

Turner, B.S., 1978, *Marx and the End of Orientalism*, Allen and Unwin, London

Ullman, E.L., 1953, 'Human geography and area research', *Annals of the Association of American Geographers, 43,* 54-66

United Nations, 1981, *World Economic Survey 1980/81*, United Nations, New York

United Nations, 1981, *1978 Report on the World Social Situation*, United Nations, New York

Uno, K., 1980, *Principles of Political Economy*, Harvester Press, Sussex

Van Binsbergen, W.M.J. and Meilink, H.A., 1978, 'Migration and transformation of modern African society: Introduction', *African Perspectives, 1,* 7-20

Van der Kroeff, J.M., 1981, *Communism in South-east Asia*, Macmillan, London

Van Nieuwenhuijze, C.A.O., 1982, *Development Begins at Home. Problems and Prospects of the Sociology of Development*, Pergamon, Oxford

Varma, B.N., 1980, *The Sociology and Politics of Development: A Theoretical Study*, Routledge and Kegan Paul, London

Vidal de la Blache, P., 1926, *Principles of Human Geography*, Edited by E. de Martonne, Trans. by E.T. Binham, Constable, London

Vogeler, I. and de Souza, A.R. (eds.), 1980, *Dialectics of Third World Development*, Alanheld, Osmun and Co., Montclair, NJ

Walker, R. and Storper, M., 1981, 'Capital and industrial location', *Progress in Human Geography, 5,4,* 473-509

Wallerstein, I., 1974a, *The Modern World-System: Capitalist Agriculture and the Origins of the European World-Economy in the Sixteenth Century*, Academic Press, New York

Wallerstein, I., 1974b, 'The rise and future demise of the world capitalist system: concepts for comparative analysis', *Comparative Studies in Society and History, XVI,* 387-415

Wallerstein, I., 1976, 'Semi-peripheral countries and the contemporary world crisis', *Theory and Society, 3,* 461-83

Wallerstein, I., 1979, *The Capitalist World-Economy*, Cambridge University Press, London

Wallerstein, I., 1980, *The Modern World-System II. Mercantilism and the Consolidation of the European World-Economy, 1600-1750*, Academic Press, New York

Ward, R.G., 1980, 'Migration, myth and magic in Papua New Guinea', *Australian Geographical Studies, 18,2,* 119-34

Warren, B., 1973, 'Imperialism and capitalist industrialization', *New left Review, 81,* 3-44

Warren, B., 1980, *Imperialism: Pioneer of Capitalism*, Verso, London

Watson, J.B., 1970, 'Society as organized flow: the Tairora case', *Southwestern Journal of Anthropology', 26,* 107-24

Weaver, C., 1981, 'Development theory and the regional question: a critique of spatial planning and its detractors' in W.B. Stöhr and D.R.F. Taylor (eds.), *Development from Above or Below?*, Wiley, Chichester, pp. 73-105

Williams, W.A., 1969, *The Roots of the Modern American Empire*, Random House, New York

Willis, P.E., 1977, *Learning to Labour: How Working Class Kids Get Working Class Jobs*, Saxon House, Farnborough

Wilmoth, D., 1978, 'Book Review. *Capital versus the Regions by Stuart Holland'*, *The Review of Radical Political Economics,* 10,3, *145-7*

Wirth, L., 1936, 'Preface' in K. Mannheim (ed.), *Ideology and Utopia. An Introduction to the Sociology of Knowledge*, Routledge and Kegan Paul, London, pp. xiii-xxi

Wolfe, T., 1982, *From Bauhaus to Our House*, Cape, London

Wolpe, H., 1980, 'Introduction' in H. Wolpe (ed.), *The Articulation of Modes of Production*, Routledge and Kegan Paul, London, pp. 1-43

Wong, S.T. and Saigol, K.M., 1984, 'Comparison of the economic impacts of six growth centres on their surrounding rural areas in Asia', *Environment and Planning, 16,1,* 81-4

World Bank, 1978, *Employment and Development of Small Enterprises*, Sector Policy Paper, Washington DC

World Bank, 1979, *World Development Report, 1979*, Oxford University Press, New York

World Bank, 1980, *World Development Report, 1980*, The World Bank, Washington, DC

World Bank, 1981, 'World Development Report 1981 – principal themes', *Finance and Development, 18,3,* 6-10

Wright, E.O., 1976, 'Class boundaries in advanced capitalist societies', *New Left*

Review, 98, 3-41

Wright, E.O., 1980, 'Varieties of Marxist conceptions of class structure', *Politics and Society, 9,3,* 323-70

Wright, J.K., 1952, *Geography in the Making – the American Geographical Society 1851-1951,* AGS, New York

Wright, J.K. 1953, 'The field of the geographical society' in G. Taylor (ed.), *Geography in the Twentieth Century. A Study of Growth, Fields, Techniques, Aims and Trends,* 2nd edn Methuen, London, pp. 543-65

Wright, J.K., 1966, *Human Nature in Geography,* Harvard University Press, Cambridge, Mass.

Zelinsky, W., 1971, 'The hypothesis of the mobility transition', *Geographical Review, 42,2,* 219-49

INDEX

For Product Safety Concerns and Information please contact our EU
representative GPSR@taylorandfrancis.com
Taylor & Francis Verlag GmbH, Kaufingerstraße 24, 80331 München, Germany

www.ingramcontent.com/pod-product-compliance
Ingram Content Group UK Ltd.
Pitfield, Milton Keynes, MK11 3LW, UK
UKHW021829240425
457818UK00006B/133